ADVANCED GOLF

ADVANCED GOLF

OR, HINTS AND INSTRUCTION
FOR PROGRESSIVE PLAYERS

BY

JAMES BRAID
OPEN CHAMPION, 1901, 1905, AND 1906

WITH EIGHTY-EIGHT PHOTOGRAPHS AND DIAGRAMS

PHILADELPHIA
GEORGE W. JACOBS & CO.
PUBLISHERS

Printing Statement:

Due to the very old age and scarcity of this book,
many of the pages may be hard to read due to the
blurring of the original text, possible missing pages,
missing text and other issues beyond our control.

Because this is such an important and rare work, we
believe it is best to reproduce this book regardless of
its original condition.

Thank you for your understanding.

James Braid

CONTENTS

CHAPTER XVII

CHAPTER XVIII

CHAPTER XIX

CHAPTER XX

LIST OF ILLUSTRATIONS

ix

ADVANCED GOLF

CHAPTER I

INTRODUCTORY

TO begin with, let me say exactly what I mean by the title that I have chosen for this book, which contains all the advice that I can think of for the improvement of the game of any kind of golfer who has fairly grappled with the early difficulties of swinging his driver on the tee and playing his mashie for a pitching stroke, even if he has not surmounted them. I do not wish to frighten away any young players who are coming on, but who have yet some way to go before they will be at all proficient, by speaking of "advanced golf" as if meaning to suggest something of an exceedingly intricate and difficult character far beyond their understanding. Little boys at school very soon get to advanced arithmetic, and they do not find when they reach it that it is so terrible as they had imagined it to be while making their sums in simple addition and subtraction. But before they could do anything at all with their advanced arithmetic it was necessary that they should know all about the little sums to begin with, and the way in which to work them out, even if they sometimes made mistakes in them ; and much time was occupied in learning the way to do them, and obtaining a thorough grasp of the principle that one and one make two, and that one from two results in only one being left. It is very easy to see that this is the case ; but it is not quite so easy for the beginner at school to work it out on paper. It is just in this way that I have come to call this book "Advanced Golf," and for many reasons I think it is the best title that I could have given to it, because no other would have so exactly represented the scheme of the book. But none of my readers, however long their handicaps may be, must be frightened by it, just as I think however short their handicaps may be they will find in it nothing at all that is unworthy of their serious attention. At least I hope that that may prove to be the case.

The fact of the matter is this, that when a man of considerable experience in golf, and one who, judging by the results of various competitions, seems to have got into a little better and surer way of playing it than most other people, sets about the task of writing a book for the benefit of the others who want to improve their game, he is faced by a serious and unpleasant difficulty to begin with. This is, that he must devote the best part of his book to an attempt to teach the most elementary principles of the game to his readers, well knowing that, however thoroughly he may perform his task, it cannot be a complete success, for the simple reason that it is next to impossible to teach golf right from the very beginning by means of written words only. At the best they can only be a help to the practical teaching that is necessary, and that nearly every beginner wisely seeks from a professional player or from some amateur friend in whose skill he has some confidence. That fact again makes the task of attempting to teach, by writing, the most rudimentary principles of the golfing swings a most disappointing one, because the teacher suspects that his time is being wasted, for the reason that his reader will already have gained that knowledge in a more direct way by practical tuition. Yet at the same time he feels that if he is going to write a book on golf he must begin at the beginning, and ought not to assume any knowledge or experience whatever on the part of his reader; and then, when he enters upon this task, he finds out that it is such a difficult thing to explain the simplest thing about any stroke in golf to a man who knows absolutely nothing whatever about the game, that the space he has set at his disposal for the book is almost entirely exhausted in this attempt to teach the simplest rudiments, and he has none left in which to talk about all the many matters which would do so much more to improve the game of almost any man. Besides, if one is able to assume that the reader knows a little about the game, no matter how very little it may be, it makes such a lot of difference to the way in which the writing can be done. One has not to stop every minute to explain the simple matters that almost every player knows, and such explanations must often be very irritating to them. Also, one can speak in just the same way to the golfer of a little experience as to him who has had a great deal. I have had all this impressed upon me very much in the course of my practical teaching on the links. When I have to begin teaching a man who knows nothing at all about the game, and who holds a club in his hand for about the first time in his life, I have, like all other teachers, to spend hours in driving into him the very simplest things, at least those that are simplest to everybody who has a slight knowledge of the game. On the other hand, when one is engaged in coaching a man who does know something about it, but realises that he has much more to learn, one can tell him more in half an hour than you could tell the other man in a week, and improve his game more if he has the capacity to benefit by what he is told. All this that I have said will explain the title, the idea, and the system of this book. I assume at the beginning that the player who reads it knows something about the game, even if it is not very much. I take it for granted that he has played many games with a full set of clubs, and that he has been taught by a competent teacher what he must do if he wishes to get a satisfactory result from his various shots. After that I do not care whether he is on the scratch mark or whether he has a long handicap. What I have to say will do very well for him in either case, and when I am able to assume the preliminary knowledge I am left free to talk about other things in a much more thorough and pointed manner than would otherwise have been the case. No matter how good a man's game may be, he knows that there is a great deal left for him to learn, and I want to teach him a lot of those things—as many as I can think of— and suggest to him why many of his shots are not so good as they ought to be, and may be if he goes about mending his faults in the right way.

While I have said that the best way in which to teach an absolute beginner, and indeed the only way, is by practical instruction on the links, when there is a ball there to hit and the pupil and the teacher both have clubs in their hands, I am also of opinion that a golfer will get on far better afterwards if he thinks and reflects upon his game, and has at the same time some reliable authority at his side to help him. I have often heard of golfers finding out their very worst faults, and not only that but the right way in which to cure them, simply by thinking earnestly over their game when they have been sitting down in the evening after the day's play was over. Very likely many of my readers now will remember that they themselves decided to shorten their swings a little, having come to the conclusion that they were overswinging and losing control of their clubs, as the result of an exchange of remarks in a railway carriage, and some reflection upon them after they had got home; and in the same way a golfer may have decided at night that next day he would putt in an entirely different way from that in which he had been accustomed to putting, and was never afterwards sorry for the fact. It is in the spare time like this, when there is no match hanging in the balance and much opportunity for thought, that one's game should be considered and decisions as to future methods made, and not in the few moments while one is waiting for the other man to play his shot. I have now explained the scheme of this book, and I do not remember that anyone else has started with the advantage that I have thus taken, in assuming that little preliminary knowledge which takes so many words and pages to impart even to the most intelligent reader.

Now there are some other things to say. The first is about the personal element in the teaching that I offer in these pages. Most players are agreed upon main principles; but after that there are con‑ siderable differences. One man prefers a certain kind of club; another likes something quite different. Then one player always uses what is called the open stance in driving, and thinks that it is not only the easiest but that it is the best for getting long and straight balls. On the other hand, another man swears by the square stance, and thinks there is nothing like it. It would not be a very wise thing for me to advocate methods which I do not employ myself, even though I knew that quite a majority of good players employed those methods. Even if I did I could not hope to convince my readers or to set them so surely on the right road as when I told them to do things in just the same way that I do them myself. (As a matter of fact, I do not know any important detail of the game in regard to which I am at variance with the general body of golfers, and there is nothing that to my knowledge is at all singular in my methods, so readers may have no fears upon this subject, or feel that they are commit‑ ting themselves to anything at all rash or dangerous, which may suit me, but which is not at all likely to suit anyone else.) Therefore I state just how I do the things myself, and how I would go about curing the faults that I suppose to exist in others. At the same time, whenever there is a generally recognised alterna‑ tive method, I explain it impartially and to the best of my ability, so that those who are already convinced in its favour may not be neglected.

It is sometimes said that there are two kinds of golfers, those who are born golfers and those who are made golfers, and no doubt there is some truth in the remark, for some people seem to fall into a game quite naturally at the very beginning, and adopt systems and ways from which they get brilliant results, and which never seem to cause them any trouble, but with which many other people would find serious difficulty. They seem to play more or less by instinct, and there is no doubt that in many cases these men are very great golfers indeed, and are much to be envied. Any man who is a born and cultivated golfer of this sort will have comparatively little need for this book or for instruction of any kind. But the majority of people are anything but born golfers, and they have very little instinct to guide them in making any of their strokes or to help them out of any of the faults which from time to time cause them so much trouble and often seem to destroy their pleasure in the game, since it begins to seem that they never will get any better at it, but if anything rather worse. These men have to improve by a very slow process. They get a little better one day, and then something else goes wrong for a time and they slip back. A little while afterwards they correct the faults from which they have been suffering, and they are playing better than ever once more, and seem on the high road to complete success. Then they have another spell of failure, and so it is all the way through, always learning a little and losing a little, but generally leaving a small balance on the right side, so that after some years their game is improved to a very large extent. That is the way in which most golfers progress, and it is the way in which golfers who are not born golfers become made ones. There is plenty of satisfaction in struggling through with the game in this way after all; in fact, those who at last succeed, and find themselves scratch or better, have the greatest pleasure in looking back through their long time of perseverance, which in the end was well rewarded, as it deserved to be. A game that is laid on foundations of this kind is generally very steady at the finish, and the player rarely goes off to any considerable extent for a long period. It is a very dogged, persistent sort of game, and some of those who have learned their golf in this way have done great things with it, although to some eyes it may not be quite so easy and pretty to look at as is the game of the purely natural golfers. This is how I learned the game myself, and it seems to me that I had more than an ordinary share of difficulties and troubles to encounter, and at one time it hardly looked that I should ever do much good in the golfing world, for whatever points there may be about the rest of a man's game, its position is rather serious when he is both a short driver and a bad putter, as was the case with me. My only way out of these difficulties was to watch others, and think about and study all that I saw, with the greatest care, and at the same time to practise and practise for all that I was worth. In this way I made my game a better one, and it is because I think the majority of players have pretty much the same task set them, that I think the advice I have to give and the methods I teach will be of service to them, and they may have an advantage over what was my own experience, in that I have thus endeavoured to cut short their troubles and to help them on with their improvement a little faster. I need only add this, at the end of the consideration of this personal side of the thing, that I have thought not once but several times over every sentence that I have written in this book, and have no word of excuse to make for anything that I say. I take complete responsibility.

In what I have already said there has been suggested the spirit and intention with which this book should be read. The idea on the part of the reader should be that with serious thought, study, and practice he can make himself a considerably better golfer than he is at present, and that he intends to persevere until he is so. I have no doubt that nearly every man can improve his game if he really tries; but the trouble is that so many either do not try or they do not try properly; and a very large proportion of players, after acquiring some kind of a game which is satisfactory enough as far as it goes, do not trouble any more to improve, being either contented with the skill that they have, or quite satisfied that they can never make it any greater. Of course in the former case there is very little to say, and if a golfer gets all the pleasure that he wants out of his play, and has no desire whatever to play better, preferring not to be worried by the trouble of learning any more, he is from his own point of view quite justified. But these players are very few indeed; while the majority of those who do not progress but stick at the same handicap for years, when they would very gladly be better, are generally wrong in thinking that they cannot be. There is this also to be said, that however much pleasure a man may get from playing what may be described as a middling sort of game, the general experience is to the effect that most pleasure is obtained from playing a better one, and I am quite certain that there is no delight in golf equal to thinking out what sort of a shot is wanted in certain circumstances, and then being reasonably sure that one can make it or one very much like it, so that if anything goes wrong it is the reckoning and the judgment that are chiefly at fault. It is this reckoning up of the situation presented that is denied to the golfer who is not by any means a master of his strokes, at least reckoning it up with any earnestness, because he has always the fear of complete failure before him, not on account of error of judgment, but simply because his shot is foozled. Therefore a man gets more enjoyment out of the game when he knows that he can really do certain things that he wishes to do. Then he can begin to think of making variations in his game. Of course everybody makes a bad shot now and then, and nobody can tell exactly what is going to happen when he strikes at the ball, but occasional mistakes and missed shots are very different from the constant unreliability of many players.

There is a stage in the progress of most golfers which is a very critical one for the future of their game. They learn the rudiments of the game to start with, and then they generally go on improving very slowly for some time. Their handicaps come down stroke by stroke, and all seems to be going fairly well, but then the improvement stops, and no more strokes are taken off for perhaps years, or it may be for ever. Instead, they often have difficulty afterwards in playing up to the handicap to which they had arrived. Sometimes this stop comes when they are only eighteen-handicap men ; sometimes it is at fourteen ; other times at twelve or ten ; and again, it is often when they are about six, and then it is generally the most vexing of all, for they had begun to think they would be down to scratch before long.

But at whatever stage the stop comes this is the most critical period, for the golfer must then make an unusually determined effort to go forward. The stoppage in the progress is often due to some serious fault in style or method, but, on the other hand, it is frequently because after a certain point is reached—particularly when the long game has been cultivated to a very excellent state—progress naturally becomes slower and more difficult than before, and it is often the case that laborious practice, for which the reward is very slow, is needed in two matters, the short game and the powers of recovery. It is in these two points that the very good player is oftenest distinguished from him who is just good. The possibilities of improvement are there for nearly everybody if they will acknowledge them, and in saying this I wish particularly to emphasise that players need never be afraid of not being able to make good golfers of themselves because they do not start early enough in life. Naturally it is an enormous advantage to begin the game as a boy, for the player then acquires without much difficulty a certainty in making his strokes that is very hard to acquire afterwards. But it can be acquired, as has been proved over and over again ; and even the man who begins the game at middle age may make a good golfer of himself, even if not one of the best. Why so many of those who do not begin the game until they are grown up fail to get on at it, is because they do not try hard enough, do not think enough, and cannot give sufficient time to practice. They may have lost much of the power of trying, and they must recover some of it if they are to do any good. Nobody can teach a man to play a good game of golf, either by showing him on the links or by writing a book for him, if the man himself does not try very hard. Golf is not at all that sort of game, and neither I nor anyone else would pretend that a man has simply to read a book on the game and then go out on to a course and find himself at once able to do all the things that he has been reading about. He must first of all make sure that he is on the right line, and then he must think and practise as much as he is able to do.

In other parts of this book I have much to say about particular methods to be adopted by the player who is wanting to improve his golf, and there is no occasion to make mention of them here; but it may just be said that one of the very best ways of effecting such an improvement is to watch very closely at every opportunity the play of the best players. Study of this kind is not much use unless the watcher has himself a very good idea of the fine points of the game, such as I shall endeavour in some measure to explain to him, because for the most part what he saw would not convey much meaning to him, and he would probably overlook some of the most important matters. Besides, he would run the risk of admiring and trying to copy from a model that was not at all a good one, despite the generally satisfactory results obtained. Some good players do things in a particular way, and do them well nearly every time, when they are the only ones who could do them in that way.

It is necessary to make such explanations and warnings, and extend such encouragements, at the beginning of a book like this, as I have done. Now we all know exactly where we are, and what we are going to try to do.

CHAPTER II

THE SELECTION AND EFFECT OF WOODEN CLUBS

IT is of the utmost importance that the player
should be on terms of the most complete confidence and intimacy with all the clubs in his
bag, and particularly the wooden clubs, from which he
gets his length. Such confidence is not generally
established during the first few seasons of his experience. It needs a long time and much thought
to understand what are the essential features of a
wooden club that make it exactly suited to the
peculiarities of a particular player.

Points for chief consideration are those concerning
the all-important questions of the length of the shaft
and the weight of the club, which have a close relation
to each other. It is very likely that during the early
training and difficulties of the player there are no
matters upon which he is so constantly doubtful of
his judgment and upon which he is so frequently
inclined to change his mind as these. It may often
happen that, as the eventual result of so much
hesitation and doubt, the player settles down at last
to the regular use of a club which is not by any
means the best adapted to his style and his system
of play. It is not until this style and system are
properly developed, and their peculiarities thoroughly
understood, that a club can be selected with perfect

satisfaction and with something approaching certainty that it will enable its owner to get the most possible out of his game. Therefore it may often be a mistake to cling too faithfully to the clubs of one's golfing youth. The question as to what is best is often complicated and made more difficult by the crazes that in these days seem to pass periodically over the golf world. One season there is a rage for shafts of extraordinary length; the next, extreme shortness may have a run of popularity. Then everybody must have the head spliced on to the shaft instead of socketed, and at another time the superior qualities of very short faces are being praised on every links. There is only one good thing about these crazes, and that is that they generally die off very soon, and then we get back to the normal state of things.

Now, generally speaking, I prefer the medium in both length and weight of wooden clubs to anything else. Except for very strong and quite extraordinary reasons, I do not think that medium length of shaft should be departed from; in the matter of weight there is more excuse for appreciable differences. These questions should be settled not so much according to the fancy of the player, based on a mere handling of a club in a shop, but by the nature and the peculiarities of his swing; and he is not always the best judge as to how the club should be adapted to these circumstances.

The features of the swing which must to a large extent determine the choice of the wooden club, are its length and its speed. Then let me say that I think the only type of swing to suit the very long-shafted driver which usually goes by the name of the

"fishing-rod," and upon which there was a great run
a season or two ago, is the rather slow and very
smooth swing—a swing in which there is very little
suggestion of strength or application of physical
power.   If the swing is anything other than this, the
timing of the shot will become a most difficult matter,
and one that is practically outside the regulation of
the ordinary player.   In the consideration of all these
questions it should be borne in mind that it is the
club that must be adapted to the style, and not the
style to the club.   The system that may have been
built up by years of practice cannot be altered at
short notice, and in very few cases would it be
advisable to do so if it could.   On the other hand,
the great objection to the very short-shafted clubs
with which some players profess to get better results,
particularly in the matter of direction, than with any
others, is that a quite excessive amount of power
has to be put into the strokes that are played with
them in order to get the distance required.   Many
users of short drivers profess that it is easy to put
this power in when they have so much command over
the club, and so much confidence that they will keep
straight and hit the ball cleanly.   But I do not think
that this is a satisfactory view of the situation.   They
are giving something away that they ought not to
do—making, that is, an allowance for their own
uncertainty.   Ought it not rather to be their object
so to cultivate their game that they have the same
command over and confidence with a driver of
medium length, when almost on their own showing
they would be the gainers?   They would have the
full power of the club, and the full power of the man
at the same time.   It can be done.   If he would only

persuade himself of the fact, nearly every man who uses a shorter club than his stature would suggest for him, can train himself to using one of full length just as well. An important principle is involved in this matter. It is a bad thing for the future of a man's game when he begins to make all kinds of allowances for his own difficulties without having made a thorough and determined attempt to master them. He begins to give away bit by bit the best possible game of which he is capable, and there may be regrets when it is too late. Also, while it may be true that many players get a straighter ball with a short club than with a long one, it is equally true and is constantly in evidence, that if a man does begin to pull and slice with such a club he does it very much worse than other men, and he finds it far more difficult to stop doing so, simply because he is hitting so furiously all the time.

Now the whole art of driving, or the greater portion of it, anyhow, consists in the proper timing of the stroke, the proper adjustment of the various movements of the body and limbs to the changing positions of the club in its upward and downward swings and follow through ; and a factor of enormous importance in this timing is the relation of the weight of the club to the swing. I would lay it down as a rule that the faster and longer a player swings, the lighter should be the club which he employs ; and, conversely, that for a short and deliberate style of swing, a heavy club may be employed to advantage.

These recommendations are made solely with a view to facilitating the accurate timing of the stroke. If a man makes a very long swing with all his power put into it, he must inevitably find it a matter of difficulty to steady himself properly when about the top of the swing if his club is a very heavy one, so strong will be its pull on him and so great its tendency to take him off his balance. You will nearly always find that the best players with full swings prefer comparatively light clubs, and yet there is an idea about that the man who swings long and strong should have a heavy club to swing with. Perhaps this arises from the supposition that the big swinger is the stronger man, which is not by any means always the case. It is well worth weeks or even months of experiment in adjusting the weight of a driver or brassey in order to find out that which most exactly suits the player's swing; for when he has found it he will have confidence and satisfaction in his play, and also very likely a length in his stroke that he never had before. I am quite certain that if the weight of my own driver were altered one ounce either way it would entirely upset my swing. I might mention that, having a strong, quick swing, I myself use what I consider to be a fairly light club.

But before coming to a determination to interfere with the lead in the head of the club, make sure that everything practicable or advisable has been done in the way of adjusting the grip of the club. The relation of the thickness of the grip to the balance and general effect of the club is not realised nearly so fully as it ought to be. A very small difference at the top of the club makes a very large one at the bottom; and it will often be found that a driver that seems too light and ineffectual for its owner when it has a grip of full thickness on it, is made to feel heavier and much more powerful and easier to follow through with when that grip is reduced by

2

putting thinner stuffing under the leather; and, conversely, that if a club seems too heavy in the head it may be given a lighter feel by a slight thickening of the grip, always assuming that such changes are suited to the hands of the player. Alteration in the grip has an enormous effect in changing the balance of a club; and while thickening of it is not so often to be recommended, I do certainly think that a large proportion of players who feel that they want more weight in the head of the club, and take it to the shop to have lead put in, would be better advised to see first if a reduction in the thickness of the grip would not meet the case. As golfers go in these days, I think that what might be called the standard grip, or that which you usually find on new clubs, is too thick, and it is impossible to feel complete mastery over a club when this is the case. My own hands are not small; but every player would describe my grips as quite thin. A thing to be remembered, however, is that a really thin grip demands considerable strength in the fingers—not in the hand and wrist generally, but in the fingers. In such a case the grip is chiefly with the fingers, and the work is done by them. If the player is weak in the fingers, particularly those of the left hand (the right hand is generally stronger than the left one), then he must have a thicker grip, which he will take hold of more in the palm of the hand. In such a case I advise a very pronounced tapering of the grip—thick at the top of the handle and thin at the bottom, for it is the left hand that has to grip hard and tight, and the right which has to hold the club delicately to guide it. The grips on all new clubs are tapered a little in this way; but in the case I am suggesting I want them to be more so.

For powerful play with wooden clubs I favour shafts of medium stiffness, with just a little pleasant spring in them. It must always be borne in mind that the real and permanent spring in a shaft is not discovered until the club has been played with for some little time. First appearances in this matter are usually deceptive, and it is necessary to make some allowance in a new club for the relaxation in the shaft which always comes with use. Players generally seem to like the spring in the shaft to be low down in it, not much above the binding or the socket; but while this may be all a matter of fancy, I must confess that for my own part I like to feel the spring pretty well up the shaft, not near the grip, but say halfway up. It seems to make the club feel easier. There is really considerable difference in clubs in the places where the spring comes from, as anyone may discover who puts a number of old drivers to the test. I do not believe in very whippy shafts, and particularly do I think they are bad for a player with a long, fast swing, for it must be obvious that their variations in the course of the swing, particularly when they are complicated by wind, make the accurate hitting of the ball more difficult than it would otherwise be.

Two drivers in the bag are always to be re-commended, not merely for the sake of having a reserve in case of accidents, but for the difference in the stiffness of the shaft which should exist between the two. A driver should be carried which has a shaft appreciably stiffer than the one which is employed on ordinary occasions, and the time for its employ-ment is when there is a big wind blowing. This is not so much because a stiff shaft is really necessary when playing with a storm in your teeth if the stroke is made as it ought to be made, but because in such circumstances the player, no matter who he is or how much he may have satisfied himself in private reflection that such a proceeding is a mistake, finds the tendency to hit harder than usual quite irresistible. It is a mistake, and in the proper place I shall advise slow swings when wind is blowing, but it is part of the human nature of the golfer, and one of those things for which allowance has to be made. Therefore with this harder hitting there is more spring backwards and forwards in the shaft than when the ordinary stroke is played, and the ball is not hit in the same way. So it is best to have a club with a stiffer shaft, in order that the give shall be the same when the hit is harder as it is with the other club when the stroke is of the usual strength. In other respects the two clubs should be quite identical.

This question of the selection of the shaft is really one of enormous importance, for it is infinitely easier to get a head to suit you exactly, and to be to all intents and purposes perfect, than it is to get a perfect shaft. The latter, indeed, is a comparatively rare thing. Much care and experience and discretion are needed in its selection, and when one is found to suit exactly, the greatest care should be taken of it, for it is the shaft that makes the club, and once spoiled it may never be satisfactorily replaced. When a player has found at last what is for him the perfect driver with the perfect shaft, he will be well advised to do his utmost to find a capable understudy to it without delay, instead of waiting until the old one gives out, when he would be left in a bad state of helplessness, which might upset his game for a very long time. It

is easier and better to find this reserve and to experiment with different shafts in it, and to have slight
alterations continually made in it until it is right, than
it is to do so when the new club is wanted for all the
work at once.   In going about the making of a first-
class reserve in this manner, first of all get the head
of the favourite accurately copied.   This is a comparatively simple matter.   After that experiment with
the shafts, and nothing but experiment will do, for
two shafts that look exactly similar to the eye may
be altogether different in their playing peculiarities.

I am inclined to think that the relative merits of
the scared or socketed adjustments of the head to
the shaft are somewhat exaggerated.   For my part I
do not think that there is any real difference between
them, and that a club is no better or worse for being
of one sort or the other.   In only one case do I
think that any preference may be shown, except as a
pure matter of fancy, and that is in the case of the
hard hitter who plays in all kinds of weather, and
generally puts his club to rougher usage than others
might do.   For him I think the scared club is the
better ; but only because his hard hitting provokes a
tendency for the socket in a socketed club to give
out.   It becomes weakened there, and then the club
is not quite the same as it was, while it may give out
altogether when least expected.   I have a fancy
myself that I can get just a few yards farther with a
socketed driver than with one of the other kind ;
but other men think the opposite.   I ought to say
that I am strongly of opinion that in the case of all
socketed drivers the shaft ought to go clean through
to the sole of the club.   This is generally done in
these days, though it was not when socketed drivers

first came in, and most of the faults of those clubs could be traced directly to bad fitting and to weakness at the joint.

The lie of a club is a point upon which players are constantly liable to go wrong, and nothing is more fatal to their game. One frequently sees old golfers making their tee shots with drivers the toes of which are cocked up when the ball is being addressed; and some of them go so far as to defend such a proceeding, for which there can be no justification. The elementary principle of the lie is, of course, very simple: when the player stands in his natural position for addressing the ball, the sole of the club should lie quite flat upon the turf, and it follows then that a tall player will generally need a more upright lie than a short one. But at the same time it must be understood, as is too seldom done, that different lies involve radical differences in the style of play. A moment's reflection will show that the swings are different, that is, that with a flat lie a round, sweeping swing is generally made, and with an upright lie the swing is of itself upright in character. At all events, the natural tendencies are in these directions. From this point we are led to infer, what is the fact, that while the flat swing with the flat lie may be a little more powerful than the other one, it is more uncertain, particularly in regard to direction. Therefore, within the very small margin of choice that is left to the player, I would recommend him to lean towards the more upright lie. He must particularly remember that there is a great danger in having his lie too flat, because in that case there is an obvious tendency to dig the toe of the club in the turf, which means the certain ruin of the shot. If he

cannot have the right one it is better that he should
have a too upright lie, and that the heel of the club
should be lowest to the turf, because then there may
be some chance of a respectable shot being made.   If
you need, and are accustomed to, a very flat lie, make
certain that your style of play is well adapted to it,
taking the precaution at all times, for instance, to see
that you reach well out in order to keep the toe of the
club free.   Don't think that I am advocating the use
of clubs with upright lies, irrespective of circumstances.
Each is right for the right man, and I only point out
the need for the most careful discrimination.

The size and shape of the face of the driver are
matters of more importance than they are often given
credit for being.   Perhaps it is not sufficiently realised
to what a large extent the characteristics of the flight
of the ball are governed by the particular kind of face
that is on the driver, and this remark has special
reference to its depth.   The golfer of experience should
be careful that he knows something of the theory of
different faces—a very simple theory, but one to
which there is not often given a moment's consideration.   As a preliminary observation, let me say
that I am no believer in the very short, stunted faces
for which there was such a great fancy some little
time since, and which even yet are favoured by many
players in the belief that they give you a better ball.
I cannot see that there is any sound basis for such
a belief, and in my own practice I have found that the
better ball comes from a longer face, one of full
medium length.   It is certainly much easier to play
with a club having this type of face, if only for the
reason that, however accurate one may be, one has
more confidence in playing with it.

Now there are shallow, medium, and deep faces, and I would put the range of depth from the first to the last at from $1\frac{1}{4}$ in. to $1\frac{7}{16}$ in. Anything beyond the latter is certainly too deep for ordinary practical purposes. The medium face, and that which is most generally useful and reliable, and which may be taken as the standard from which there should be no deviation without very sound reason, is $1\frac{5}{16}$ in. to $1\frac{3}{8}$ in. It is not straining the case to emphasise the difference of sixteenths. A sixteenth of an inch, as stated on paper in this way, may seem an insignificant matter, and one which could not have any important bearing on the practical effect of a club ; but a sixteenth extra, or under, on the face of a club looks an enormous difference, and it would surprise many people if they put the measure on two clubs which seemed to have a wide difference in this respect, to notice then how little it actually was. But what it *seems* to be it is in practical effect ; that is, the mere sixteenth makes a great difference in the play of the club. The difference in depth makes a corresponding difference in the flight and run of the ball. The shallow face, by increasing the underspin of the ball, gives you a long carry and comparatively little run, and the deep face affords short carry and long run. In the former case the club takes more effect proportionately on the lower part of the ball at the moment of impact, and in the other an increased proportion of the upper part is acted upon.

At the moment of impact the ball is severely compressed on to the face of the club, and not merely the middle of the ball but a large portion of its surface is for a moment in actual contact with the face and under its influence ; and, as I seem to see the theory of the matter, the nature of the drive varies in some degree according to the extent to which face and ball are in contact. The golfer will be satisfied instantly as to the large proportion of the ball that does actually come into contact with the club, when he remembers how much of it is represented in pimples on the chalked face of a driver or on an iron club after a hard shot has been made. Now, if one always drove off the very centre of the face it might not make much difference, except in the case of extremes, whether the face were shallow or deep; but in the average case it generally happens that the centre of the impact is a little above the centre of the face, when the stroke is made quite sweetly from the tee. That leaves you with a full covering power of the face for the lower part of the ball, but an incomplete one for the upper part, and this incompleteness varies according to the depth of the face. At the moment of impact, with a hard full shot, the lower part of the ball will be called upon for its resiliency more than the upper, which circumstance one may fairly assume will tend towards imparting underspin to the ball, and cause it to rise. We may believe that it is the resiliency taking effect in this manner that makes the rubber-cored ball rise so much more quickly than the old gutta, which flattened much less on the club under concussion. It will now appear that the shallower the face of the club, and accordingly the less the upper part of the ball is covered, so much greater will be the resilient effect on the lower part, and so much more the spin and the rise, and *vice versâ*. Of course the angle at which the face of the club is laid back and the character of the swing are chief factors in the making of underspin, and it might help the reader it at this stage he glances forward to Chapter XV., on "The Science of the Stroke," which deals with these matters in another way.

I have recommended a medium face for ordinary purposes, and indicated what I consider to be such a satisfactory medium ; but if a golfer were set to play constantly, or on very important occasions, where and when a particular character of drive might be required, he would certainly be well advised to adapt the face of his drivers slightly to the end in view. For example, if he were playing at Sandwich he might do well to play with a club with a somewhat shallow face, because here he would have specially long carries to negotiate constantly. It is of less importance to get a lot of run on the ball on these courses than that there should be no doubt about the carries being effected, and this is not always a simple matter. On the other hand, when playing at St. Andrews or Hoylake, where there is comparatively little carrying of any kind to be done, it is of the utmost importance to gain all the length possible by run on the ball, and to do this it is clear that it will be advantageous to play with a club with a deeper face than the average. I do not say that I should change my own driver, if playing occasional matches on such courses, because I should lose more by playing with a club to which I should not be accustomed than I could possibly gain in any other way ; but if I were to be regularly playing on these courses, I should see to it that I made a favourite of a driver that was best adapted to them on the lines that I have indicated.

And now there are the upward and the outward angles of the face to consider very briefly. As for the former, it is a mistake to imagine that a shade of loft

MODEL HEAD OF DRIVER

MODEL HEAD OF BRASSEY OR SPOON WITH ROUND SOLE

on the driver will to any extent diminish its driving capacity. It is quite as easy to get a low ball with a little loft as it is without, and the play is much easier. When the face is quite vertical the player is very apt to dig at the ball, fearing that he may not get it up unless he does so. But care must be taken that the loft is not too much. There should be just so much of it, and only so much, as will enable the player to see the face when the club is laid before him in the position to drive. It will be found that the most satisfactory angle of loft for a driver is 85 degrees. Concerning what I have referred to above as the outward angle, I am one of those who are strong advocates of having a little hook on the faces of all drivers. It can hardly do harm, and it will constantly do good, for there is a tendency among the great majority of even the best players to slice, and the hook does something to counteract it. This tendency is greater with socketed clubs than with those of the scared variety, the socket giving a little more when the ball is struck. Therefore the need for hook on socketed clubs is greater. What I personally regard as the best model for the head of a driver is shown in the full-sized illustration on another page, which is a photograph of my own favourite club.

So much of what has been said about the driver applies directly to the brassey, and the remainder is so obvious that there is little advice that I can give to players of some experience. Briefly, I advocate the brassey being exactly the same as the driver, except that there should be a shade more loft on the face— say, an angle of 80 degrees—and that the shaft should be a little stiffer. I don't believe in a smaller face, and I think the length of the shaft and the weight of the club should be the same. There is one hint I may give, and that is that when it is necessary, the player may do a little towards adapting his brassey to the peculiar needs of his course. If the lies he gets through the green are frequently of the cuppy order, or if, even when they are not, the ball constantly lies very close down, it is a good thing to have the sole of the club slightly curved from toe to heel, and at its deepest at the hitting point, as shown in the second of the photographic illustrations of wooden clubs that are submitted to the reader. This ensures the club nipping under the ball properly. For such play, also, it is well that the face of the brassey should not be too deep. The difficulty when dealing with such lies is to make the ball rise as it should do, and, as we have already seen, a shallow face helps it to do so.

As to the spoon (about the use of which there is, in these days of cleeks and driving mashies, which have largely superseded it, so much conflicting testimony), there is just this to be said, that it is not generally a difficult club to play with, and that those who like it play very well with it. There is one particular shot for which it excels, and it is this one for which I would recommend it, and for which I would have it specially adapted, namely, the shot where a long carry is wanted and very little run afterwards. You would have this shot presented when there is a far bunker to carry and the green is close up to the bunker on the other side, so that run on the ball after pitching is to be avoided as far as possible. Some players can do this shot beautifully with a cleek, but it is far from easy. With a brassey it is very difficult, too much run being given to the ball. The spoon is better than either, and in order to give the spoon the fullest advantage in playing it, I would have it made with plenty of loft, a shallow face, and a curved sole. This will give the maximum of carry and the minimum of run to the ball. I like plenty of weight in a spoon, and the shaft of the club may be a couple of inches shorter than that of the driver or brassey.

CHAPTER III

THE SELECTION AND EFFECT OF IRON CLUBS

I T does not generally happen that the iron clubs
with which a player is educated in the game are
of much service to him after he has attained pro-
ficiency in it. Now and again you find a favourite
club in the golfer's bag which has survived the severe
test of experience; but generally this experience and
the fixing of style bring with them a firm conviction as
to what particular class of iron is best suited to the
game of each individual player, and it would have
been a more than usually lucky chance if such irons
had been alighted on when the mere beginner at
the game was making his first collection of clubs,
whatever excellent advice he may have had while
doing so.

Sometimes a golfer never gets on terms of absolute
confidence with his iron clubs. This is generally
because he has not given sufficient amount of thought
and study to his own particular requirements in irons,
and the sure result is that his game is weaker and
less certain than it ought to be. The exact irons
that are wanted, and all of them, are not to be found
in a week or in a month, or even in a year, and there
are many good and wise golfers who will tell you
that those which they possess and play with are
the survivors of hundreds which have been bought

from time to time, at a total cost of very many pounds. As a general rule, when a man has once come by the irons that he really wants and needs, he is safe from much further trouble, because the best forgers will be able to copy his set very faithfully whenever that is needed, and very slight alterations may be made in them to suit a possible slow change in the player's fancy. It has always to be borne in mind, however, that two irons which are identical in dimensions, weight, appearance, and everything else, and which would defy the efforts of anyone to find a difference between them, are sometimes very different in playing quality. One of them is good and the other is not good, and the player may be able to exercise his fullest power and control in the one case and not at all in the other. Plainly, there is no rule for separating the good from the bad ; and indeed it generally happens that they are only good and bad according to the player who uses them, and what may be good for one style of game is bad for the other, and *vice versâ*. It may also be suggested in this place that the shaft affects an iron in the same way as a driver, but not nearly to the same extent, since the shafts of irons are shorter and are always stiffer. Still, they do very considerably affect the balance of the club, and an iron that may be perfect for a particular player may seem like a strange club to him when it has been reshafted, although a new shaft as much like the old one as possible was put in. I might say here that with the heavy work it is put to, and the constant jerks it gets, the shaft of every iron club is bound to go in time. It need not, however, be replaced unless it is found that the balance of the club has been so much affected as to make it difficult to play with. Because the shaft is bent a little is not enough reason for having it replaced. When a shaft is new there is a tendency for it to warp, and this may be counteracted by occasionally bending it back gently.

The supreme test of a particular iron for a particular player is that when he has made a shot which is exactly according to his regular style, and which, so far as he is concerned, is perfect, there should be a complete absence of that semi-vibratory, dead kind of feeling at the grip at the moment of impact. It is difficult to describe this feeling in words, but every golfer of any experience knows what I mean. It is as if the ball had found the wrong place on the club, and a hollow place at that. Even though the ball may go away quite well, there is nothing sweet about the feeling of the shot, and, whatever the result may be, the player is left with a sense of dissatisfaction. Such an experience constantly repeated is a plain indication that something is wrong with the balance of the club, and it is next to useless to persevere with it when once this opinion has been definitely arrived at. There is no mistaking an iron shot properly played with a club that suits and is well balanced. The player is just conscious of the impact of the ball upon the blade as a kind of soft, easy, delicate touch, the sensation of which is distinctly pleasurable, and it is almost as if there were no extension of the feeling along the shaft to the hands, and not a suspicion of vibration anywhere. If a golfer of experience has a club in constant use with which he never gets this pleasurable sensation, and to which consequently he is not much attached, he may depend upon it that it does not suit him or there is something wrong with it ; and if it is the same when it is tried with a new shaft (this often effects a cure), the best thing that he can do is to put it on the retired list and make a new purchase.

Now, considering the iron clubs collectively, as one may do in regard to several of their principal features, let me say, to begin with, that the shafts of them all, from the cleek to the putter, should be absolutely dead stiff, without any more trace of give in them than it is impossible to avoid in such a length of wood. If you always took the ball cleanly and with an easy swing it might not be so necessary to insist upon this point; but so many of your iron shots have to be jerked that give is out of place. Whip in the shaft is apt to make the club run away with you. It is generally the case that you overswing, and then you mistime the shot.

Next in these generalities, I would say that it is advisable that all iron clubs should be fairly heavy. I do not want the player to go to any extreme in the matter, but if he is a man who has a strong leaning towards light clubs, he may very well be advised, when hesitating between which of two irons to choose, to give his preference to the heavier one. I like irons with weight in them, because it is never advisable in iron play to swing too freely and fully. A short swing with irons is always better and generally more effectual than a long one, and for a short swing a heavy club is certainly the best, whether it is wood or iron. Feeling the weight in the head, the player is more likely to carry straight through. And from this point one is led naturally to suggest as thin grips as the player can use with safety and comfort for all iron clubs except the niblick, because with the thin grip you feel the full weight of the head and have the full command of the club. In the case of the

3

niblick you generally grip rather more tightly and more in the palm of the hand, and just a little extra thickness is advisable.

Now it is a matter of extreme importance that the lie of all iron clubs should be exactly suited to the player and the shots that he plays, and yet it is one to which far too many players give little or no attention, even when they are most careful in getting themselves properly suited with the lie of their wooden clubs.   They will select an iron which they may be of opinion suits them well, and yet they may have taken no notice of its lie, and even when the club has been in use some time, they may be similarly unconcerned, and even ignorant of the fact that if the lie is not what it ought to be from their point of view it is a very small matter to have an alteration made in it. The lie must suit the man, and, making due allowance for the varying lengths of shafts, all the iron clubs in the set should be of the same degree of lie.   So far as the player's style will permit him to have a choice in the matter, he may be most strongly advised to let it lean in the direction of upright lies.   Very flat lies in iron clubs are to be strongly condemned.   Those of the opposite character are the better and safer, for two principal reasons.

The first of these reasons is that, as I have occasion to explain in fuller detail in another chapter, it is best to play a fairly upright swing with all iron shots, and in order to do so the player will stand well over his ball.   In such circumstances the upright lie will become a necessity.   The chief point to remember in considering the effect and the object of all play with irons is that accuracy of direction and not length is what is chiefly aimed at.   If length were chiefly what

is wanted, as when driving, we should play with wood
and not iron ; but as it is accuracy, and we can choose
our iron so that we can get the distance well within
the full value of the club—thus enabling us to play
what kind of shot we like, and not necessarily the
longest one with that club—we do so choose it and
play with an upright swing, since, with the head of
the club all through the swing kept nearer to the
intended line of flight of the ball, one has the maximum of control over direction.   A half to three-
quarter swing with an iron club is, or ought to be, the
most certain of all shots in the matter of direction.

The second reason for favouring the upright lie,
or rather, as one might almost venture to put it, for
the player adopting a lie which is just the very
smallest fraction more upright than his natural address
to the ball with that club would seem to require, is
because, even though it may be no advantage to him
for the heel of his club to be lower to the turf than the
toe of it, it is absolutely fatal when the reverse is the
case, and the toe of the club either takes the turf when
the heel does not, or takes more of it.   In the case of
mashie play I am not at all against employing a club
of so upright a lie that the heel is always well down
and the toe almost clear ; in fact, I like such a club
and such a method of play.   With the more powerful
irons the best shot undoubtedly is that where the sole
of the club is quite level with the turf, but the very
smallest trace of heel may not be a bad thing, while
the least suspicion of toe will very likely be fatal.
When the heel comes first to the turf the player's
control over the club is not sensibly affected ; what
goes wrong chiefly is the way in which the ball is
taken by the face of the club.   But when the toe takes

the turf and leaves the remainder of the blade free, all control is immediately lost, and the club twirls in the hand, with the result that the ball is taken with the face at a sharp angle, the toe pointing to the back of the player.   Now then, inasmuch as it is not humanly possibly to play the club so that the sole sweeps exactly level upon the turf every time without fail, it will be realised that the player is effecting a very good kind of insurance against fatally bad shots by allowing the lies of his clubs to lean the smallest trifle to the upright side.

A wrong lie is more easily detected in a wooden club than an iron one, and a smaller inaccuracy in the case of the latter counts for more.   It is a good thing, therefore, to test the lies of your clubs, and for this purpose a very hard, smooth surface which will indicate a very trifling inaccuracy is much better than the smooth boards of the floor of the professional's shop, while the smoothest turf is of very little use.   Let the golfer fall into the natural position for playing his shot, and sole his club on, say, a marble floor, and if it does not lie quite flat, the error, whichever way it is, will readily be discovered.   If the lie is too flat the club will turn upon the toe when the shaft is twisted, while a turn upon the heel indicates that the lie is on the upright side.

As I have said, it is too often not realised that small corrections in the lie of most iron clubs can be made by almost any professional at very short notice, for the club is simply put in a vice and the blade hammered up or down according to requirements, a better job being made of it when the iron has been heated.   Long and fairly narrow blades, such as those of cleeks and mid-irons, yield very easily to such

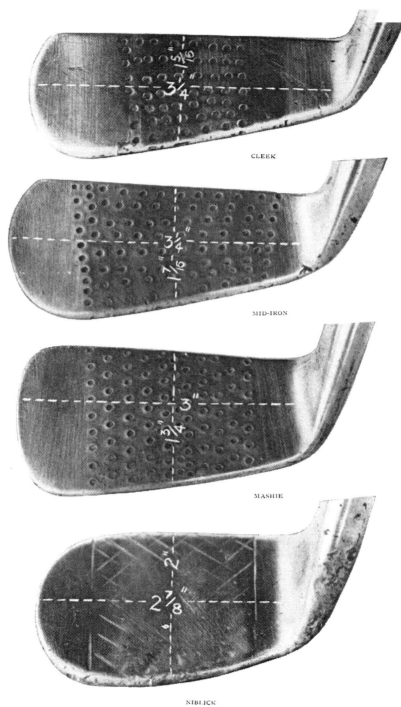

CLEEK

MID-IRON

MASHIE

NIBLICK

MODEL HEADS OF IRON CLUBS

treatment; but it is obvious that the process is not quite so easy, or even always practicable, in the case of clubs with deep faces such as those that are on most modern mashies. In choosing a new club from a stock, in place of having one forged to match a particular pattern, it is well to remember the fact that the lie may be slightly changed in this manner, so that the preference need not be given to a club which has the right lie, but which is otherwise not completely to the golfer's taste, while there is another one that he likes immensely, but which seems to him to have the great drawback of being a little too upright or too flat in the lie.

Two other points in the general features of irons call for mention. First, there is the question as to the depth of the face, since it will be found that there is considerable variation in this respect in the irons designed by leading players which they have forged for them, apart from the fact that most irons are now being made deeper in the face than in the days of the gutta ball, to check the tendency of the rubber core to rise too much. Personally, I cannot see that such variations as exist, length being no object, make any appreciable difference to the play, though in the case of courses which have what we call soft bottoms, which means a more or less permanent softness of the turf, into which the club cleaves its way with very little resistance, I am prepared to admit that there may be an advantage in employing irons with rather deeper faces than usual, so that there may be no fear of the club cutting too much underneath the ball and not leaving enough of the face to do the proper work of the shot. As many players regard the taking of plenty of turf as essential to many of their mashie shots this may be an argument for the constant use of deep-faced mashies, and I always use one myself, though I am not convinced of any striking superiority on their part in general circumstances.   So far as the standard patterns are concerned, there is very little choice in the length of faces in these days, the very long faces having almost completely gone out.

The second general feature that I have in mind concerns the often discussed marking of the face either with cross lines or dots punched in, so as to present a rough instead of a smooth surface to the ball.   Some people protest that there is no advantage in the scored face, but the experience of a very large majority of the best players is entirely against them, and I for one should never think of playing regularly with an iron club that had a perfectly smooth face.   In dry weather there may be little advantage of the one variety over the other, but when the turf is wet as the result of rain or of a heavy dew, there is always a tendency for the ball to skid, and this tendency is very much greater than many people imagine.   Many a time when the ball shoots away to the right it is the result of skid and not of slice, or it may be a very little slice converted into a very big skid.   A rough face helps to keep the ball firmly on it while the club is going through, and thus reduces the danger of skid to a minimum.   Besides, the rough face certainly helps the player to get the underspin of the ball that is wanted.   If a golfer's old and favourite irons have smooth surfaces, he might do very much worse for himself than to get a quantity of dots punched upon the surface.

Having thus arrived at some determination as to what good irons in general ought to be, one may proceed very briefly to consider the points of particular clubs. At the top of the list of irons there is, of course, the cleek, which becomes more and more useful and indispensable according to the increasing skill of the player. Some people say that it is a difficult club to employ with success, and such difficulty as exists is generally most pronounced in a golfer's early days. When he gets a little farther on in the game there is sometimes a tendency to discard the cleek altogether, and the excuse is made that its employment is not necessary to a good game. This is wrong. For anything approaching to a perfect game of golf the cleek is quite one of the most necessary clubs, for there are shots to be done with it that are not within the capability of any other, and the sooner an ambitious player makes up his mind that he has got to master the cleek, the better for his game. Moreover, it is a club the command of which gives the greatest pleasure to the player, and for my own part I must confess to a great liking for my cleek. Boy golfers commonly begin with cleeks, and can never do without them afterwards, and it is no use for their elders to be frightened of this club, as they so often are. The pattern of cleek that I like best is that with a round back, and with what is commonly termed the centre balance. The weight of this club seems to be concentrated immediately behind the ball, which seems to give it extra power and sweetness of impact when playing with it. I don't believe in straight-faced cleeks ; there should be a fairly pronounced loft on the face. A common mistake is that golfers who have difficulty with their cleeks will play with too heavy ones. The cleek should never be too heavy. Get accustomed to one of medium weight.

As for the driving mashie, which is generally regarded as the alternative to the cleek, the popularity which this club has enjoyed in recent seasons seems to be on the wane, and in the interests of golfers generally I cannot say that I am sorry. As everybody knows, it is deeper in the face than the cleek, and it is usually decidedly deeper at the toe than at the heel. It is supposed to be easier to use than the cleek, and to get the ball away better from an indifferent lie. As a matter of fact I am convinced that it is much more difficult to use, that it is not so powerful, that a cleek properly played will get the ball away just as well from a poor lie, and that, owing to its design, it is a very hard thing to get a driving mashie that is properly balanced. However, some players get better results from it than from the cleek, and that settles the matter so far as they are concerned. I would only add that the driving mashie really must have loft on the face ; most of those that are made have not got enough of it.

Next you have irons and mid-irons of varying weights and patterns, from a heavy driving iron down to the light iron. There is danger in carrying too many, and, as a likely result, being complete master of too few. Personally, I think that one good mid-iron ought to be enough for anybody, and it is very seldom indeed that I use anything else for shots that come between the mashie and the cleek. A driving iron is useful for playing up to the hole against a wind, and some players find it the best club for running up ; but it is not often that I include it in my bag. The driving irons that are made are generally too heavy at the heel. More weight is wanted at the toe ; but weight without any extra width. The effect of this lightness

MODEL HEAD OF APPROACHING
CLEEK

MODEL HEAD OF
ALUMINIUM PUTTER

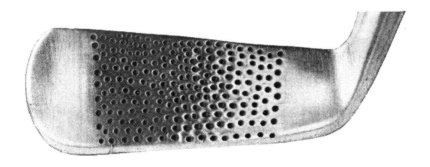

MODEL HEAD OF PUTTING CLEEK

at the toe in most driving irons that one sees is to give them a strong tendency to slice. The driving iron has become popular with some people since the rubber-cored ball came in. They believe it keeps the ball down better. However, I don't care very much for it. You can get practically every iron shot from a mid-iron, and you get them all the better through having only the one club. Its resources are wonderful, and it constantly becomes the club to use when the player is in a state of perplexity. It is good for getting a fair distance out of the rough ; and when you have a bunker shot to play which leaves you just a chance of getting a long way down the course, such length being urgently needed, it is in nine cases out of ten the club that is indicated for the task when it has been decided that the niblick could not possibly get you far enough. I think this club should be fairly heavy, and *very* stiff in the shaft, and since its work is so varied and of such extreme importance, I consider that the very utmost care should be taken to see that it is well balanced, and that the lie is quite exact.

As to the mashie, I have already said that I see no particular merit in the deep face except when the club is employed chiefly on courses with soft bottoms. A more important matter is, that it should be heavy in the sole, as weight at the bottom helps it to cut easily through the turf and to stop the ball fairly dead after it has pitched. I think it is just as well to carry a second mashie, having not quite so much loft on it as the one that is generally used, this reserve coming in very useful when playing against the wind, and for those shots to which a little extra run is wanted after pitching. It would hardly be justifiable to lay down any hard-and-fast rule as to what should be the exact amount of loft on this and other iron clubs, since much depends on the style and skill of the player and his personal preferences. In the diagram on this page I indicate what might be regarded as standard lofts for the different clubs, but allowances have to be made for different styles and different tastes.

For short running-up approaches—one of the most valuable shots in which a golfer can excel—for which different players use all kinds of clubs, from cleek to putter, I have become very much attached to

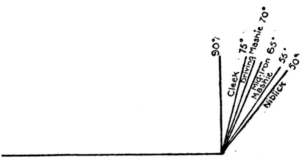

ANGLES OF LOFT ON DIFFERENT IRON CLUBS

a particular kind of approaching cleek, as it is called, which has slightly more loft than an ordinary cleek, and is heavily weighed with a substantial piece of projecting metal just at the back of the hitting part of the blade, as shown in the photograph of my own, which is reproduced on another page. The extra solid touch which this seems to give in the case of those shots which have to be most gently played, and which helps to gauge strength and distance to the utmost nicety, is of the greatest advantage.

The niblick should be large and heavy, and the shaft strong. The face must be deep, and the club should have plenty of weight at the sole. Many good players have a preference for the Fairlie pattern. With its face always in front, as it were, it has many merits. In playing from the rough it gets at the ball before the shaft is interfered with as much as it is with other clubs. A Fairlie niblick should be rather large in the face, and I think that when playing with it one ought to have the ball more towards the left foot than when using an ordinary club. Later on I hope to say something about the value of the niblick for playing lofted approaches; its duties should never be considered to be restricted to bunker play.

Concerning putters, it is well known I have a strong preference for the aluminium variety, and except for the man who is a genius on the green, I think they are the best and safest, chiefly because I consider that the broad sole helps to steady the body, and because nine men out of ten swing easily with an aluminium, while they are inclined to hit and nip their putts when playing with a putting cleek. The latter is the better on a rough green, as the ball does not run so close down as when played with the aluminium club. I have a preference for what is called the Braid-Mills type of aluminium pattern, which is deeper in the face, the result being that there is less tendency to make the ball jump.

As to mashie irons, mashie niblicks, jiggers, and other clubs of their class, there is no harm in them when they are strongly fancied. Belief in a club counts for everything. Generally speaking, the feature of such as these is that they are easier to play with, but correspondingly less exact and effectual in the result. For example, some men, when they fail with the mashie, are put on to a lofted jigger, and do excellently with it.   But there is not the same crispness about an approach with the jigger as with the mashie.   It would almost seem that, like so many other clubs that have become very fashionable at particular periods, the jigger has had its day and is going out.   It seems to me that we have got nearly to the end of the evolution of the iron club, although there may be a little to be done in determining whether the weight should be massed at particular points or not.   There is a good deal more to be said for the mashie iron, for it often happens that it becomes the most useful club in the bag when playing on an inland course where there is a lot of long grass.   It is really a deep-faced mashie with less loft than an ordinary mashie—about the same as a mid-iron.   This depth of face reduces the danger of going clean under the ball when playing from long grass.   The club is also very useful as a mashie against the wind.

If a man is called upon to play in a match which he wants to win quite as much as any he has ever played in, he might do well, in the case of some courses, to take a left-handed club in his bag.   A course with sheds or railings, or anything of that kind on the left-hand side going out or coming in, is, for instance, that on which a left-handed shot may often be called for, and nothing is more exasperating than to be without the means of making the shot when it is urgently demanded.   Generally, if a left-handed club is to be carried it should be a lofted one. The advisability of carrying such a club was impressed on me in the 1900 championship at St. Andrews, when at the last hole I overran the green and was tucked up against the rails.

CHAPTER IV

LONG DRIVING

THIS question of long driving is a difficult one. "Why drive so far?" some people ask, and according to the way in which they frame their arguments they are very hard to answer. They say it is not good to drive a long way if you cannot drive straight. I agree. They also say that, taking some sort of average, the farther you drive the more liable you are to drive off the course into the rough, or into some bunker, or to pull and slice all over the place. There is a certain amount of truth in this suggestion. Then they say that the man who makes a speciality of short but very straight and reliable driving "gets there" every time, and is the man who will usually come out on top. That may possibly be, or it may not.

Now I am quite in agreement with those who favour the shorter driving (I prefer that term to "short driving," for really short driving is not much use to anyone when first-class golf is being considered), so long as it is always accurate; and I strongly believe in a man driving well within himself, and not feeling that he has put the very last ounce into his shot, and that in the effort most other considerations have been removed from his mind for the time being. It is usually fatal to try to get the very long ball from strength alone. But it has to be remembered that even the short driver is not always accurate—not by any means so much so as those who talk of the advantages of short driving would make him out to be. There is no reason whatever why he should be any more accurate than the long driver, who still drives, as I have said, well within himself. Then, if accuracy is equal, it is absurd to pretend that short driving is so good as long, or so effectual. The long driver has an advantage at every hole which is more than a full shot in length, and in the course of a round this advantage is likely to work out to something considerable in holes gained. The advantage tells most in the second shot at fairly long holes. The long driver reaches the green in comfort; the other man is short. The long driver is dead with his third, and the shorter one has either a pitch or a run-up to play as the like, and is then left to make a desperate struggle for the half. This is the natural course of events. Even when neither is on the green, and the shorter driver is playing the odd, it is not correct to say that it does not make much difference what kind of an approach shot has to be played. There is nothing more true than that the shorter the approach shot the more one can, and does, concentrate oneself on accuracy; and while the man with a full or even half iron is quite satisfied to get on the green within 6 or 8 yards of the pin, he who is only from 30 to 50 yards from the hole is now aiming at the hole and not merely at the green, and, being relieved of all anxiety as to getting the ball away properly, is straining every nerve to get it dead. In such a situation there is a great advantage to the long driver. Moreover, as the tendency is to stretch all courses to 6000 yards or more, the short driver is becoming more and more at a discount, and if his ambition is to play the very best golf he is in a serious difficulty. Therefore, to the limit of his ability, every player may be well advised to cultivate the art of long driving. Besides, whether it pays or not, there is no getting away from the fact that driving a very long ball, sweetly and cleanly, is one of the most delightful sensations in the whole range of sport, and golfers are quite willing to sacrifice many other advantages for the sake of experiencing it. If there were some power that could confer golfing qualities on a man, and it gave him the choice of always being able to drive 220 yards or of never again missing a 2 yards putt, there is no doubt as to which of the alternatives would be selected in nine cases out of ten—that is, among comparatively moderate players. They would hold their hands up for the long drives; although the man who chose the putts would probably win more matches. So we must have long driving.

How exactly the very long driver gets his long balls he is generally at some loss to explain. A man may become a good driver, and he knows how he has done so. Then in turn he may become an exceedingly powerful driver; and though he is conscious perhaps of certain changes in his system, he is unable to give any satisfactory explanation of the improvement. In my own case the transformation was amazingly sudden and quite inexplicable to me. However, that is not the point. To-day we have thousands of golfers who have carefully studied the game, and have with great perseverance and with the help of capable instructors brought themselves to a certain point of skill in it. They know all the main principles of driving, and practise them; but they do not get the long ball, and they realise that until they do they bear a handicap which will prevent them from going forward so far as they can wish. Now, without any question of making these men very long drivers, the longest drivers of their club, they can certainly be transformed into such long drivers that they never need fear that their driving will let them down in the best of company. It is a question of paying very particular attention to certain points, of a very strong determination to uproot certain defects that have got into the system of the swing—even though generally speaking that swing does not appear to be a bad one—and, of course, incessant practice. We know how to get the medium ball; now let us see how we can get the really long one that is going to enable us to reach the green at the fairly long holes with the second shot.

The club we have already considered. Now, in the first place, there is the question of stance, about which there is obviously not much to be said, but concerning which there are just a couple of points taken from my own experience upon which I feel obliged to make some sort of emphasis. There is the question of the square stance or the open one. In the former the toes, when the stance has been taken up for the address, are nearly in a straight line with each other, parallel to the intended line of flight of the ball. The left may be just an inch or so behind. With the open stance the left foot is very appreciably behind—sometimes it is as much as twelve inches or more. Thus the whole attitude of the player towards his ball and towards the stroke is different. It is not yet settled, and perhaps never will be, as to which of these stances is really the better and the more effectual. You see what Harry Vardon can do with the open stance; but then consider what a great control he has over his club. For my part I believe that the square stance is the easier of the two to play with; and when it comes to striving for the long ball I am most inclined to favour it. I think the player can keep straighter while he is putting his power into the stroke, and will generally feel rather more comfortable and free. What I consider to be the chief danger of the open stance is the tendency which undoubtedly exists to put the body into the stroke too soon. The body seems to want to get in almost as soon as the club begins the down-swing, and when the player is a little off his game it is constantly getting there before the club. Therefore, unless the player is a strong man physically, and has a very safe and sure style of play, I think he will find that timing is a more difficult matter with the open stance than with the square, and also that the tendency to slice is increased. I have heard some people say that timing is easier with the open stance, but not many, and I do not think there can be much doubt that the square stance is the better one for a player who is not very strong physically. You often find men who have played for a long time with the open stance change over to the square and do better with it; but it very seldom happens the other way about. However, on this matter I do not wish to dictate very firmly, since it is highly probable that the reader will have settled for himself which is the best stance for him. I would only say that if he is one of the many men who change and change about, he may be recommended to give longer trials to the square stance.

4

The other point about the stance is of more importance. I do not believe you can ever become a long driver if you stand close to the ball, and the great fault of many players is that they stand far too close to it. It is clear that the closer they get to the ball the more cramped and restricted are their movements; their swing will have a strong tendency to be both short and upright, and anything in the nature of a long ball becomes impossible. For length there must be a round free swing; anything else is fatal to distance. I do not want the player to go in for any exaggerations in the reach that he is setting himself; but assuming that he is a short driver, and that he is capable of improvement, I want him to try to accustom himself gradually to standing farther from the ball until he feels that he is at the limit that is compatible with being easy and getting fairly hold of it, and with complete freedom of body. The change may be made so gradually as to be almost imperceptible. When he has fallen into his ordinary stance, let him just wriggle his feet an inch farther back without raising them from the tee, and try the drive from that position. If he does this every time, he will soon find that he is standing appreciably farther away; and he may stop at that for a while. In accustoming himself to this new state of things, it is quite likely that for a time he will feel uncomfortable in his swing, and that many shots will go entirely wrong in consequence; but satisfaction will come in due course, and he will find that unconsciously the swing itself has been undergoing a change all the time as the result of the changing stance, and that it is now made on a style quite different from the old one, much freer and fuller, and

THE DRIVE. STANCE AND ADDRESS

THE DRIVE. TOP OF SWING

A VIEW OF THE LEG AND BODY POSITIONS AT THE TOP OF THE SWING
WHEN DRIVING

THE DRIVE. FINISH

with vastly more power in it. Of course it must always be remembered that it is in the highest degree necessary that the stance on both feet should be thoroughly firm, and that the weight should be kept well back on the heels, particularly the right one ; but it will be found from experience that there is nothing incompatible between keeping the weight thus well back on the heels and cultivating the long reach. A little thing that might be mentioned is the direction in which the feet are placed. The photographs show what position I adopt, and I think this should be taken as the standard, but it often happens that a man feels much securer and better balanced, and his weight falls more naturally on to his heels by moving the toes—generally of the right foot—just an inch or two one way or the other. He might experiment in this way if he generally feels some insecurity in his stance. It is a point that depends to some extent on the physical peculiarities of the player.

Now there is another important matter in which it is generally found that the short driver is at fault, and that is in regard to the twisting of his body, or its pivoting upon the hips as it is sometimes called, both in the upward swing and the follow through, but particularly in the former. When you are first taught to drive you are told that the body must turn in its middle and upper parts while the upward swing is being made ; but nine players out of ten settle down to a system of driving without cultivating this twist ; and as for some time they drive what are for the time being regarded as satisfactory balls, they grow up in golf with this very serious fault in their system. Their bodies do not twist, and the result is that their swings are too upright, and their movements alto-

gether too cramped.   One of the chief objects of the
twisting is the same as that indicated as the object of
standing as far away from the ball as possible, that is,
to allow of the free sweep when making the swing.   The
long ball with the stiff body is impossible, and the player
must realise that fact and act accordingly.   The man
who has been driving for years with the stiff body
may quite likely find it a difficult matter to turn as
he ought to do, that is, to twist well round upon a
definite axis whilst keeping his head in the same
place and guarding against anything in the nature of
sway, and his first efforts at driving on the revised
system may be quite ineffectual.   But ease, confidence,
and accuracy will come as the result of determined
practice ; and, apart altogether from the extra length
that will accrue, the pleasure of getting in this body-
work will be found to be a most exhilarating thing.
The stiff body men do not know all of the pleasures
of driving a golf ball, even though they may hit
some fairly good ones at times.   Another good result
of proper body-twist is that the tendency to sway is
almost entirely removed.

One factor of importance in this consideration is
the part played by the left leg while the upward swing
is being made.   All the men who play with the stiff
body, and many others besides, get into the way of
pivoting on the left toe and bending the leg more
outwards than in any other direction.   But you ought
not to pivot on the toe at all, and the bend in the knee
ought not to be outwards.   You should pivot on the
fore and inner part of the shoe, that part which is
occupied by the ball of the foot and the big toe, and
when the bend in the leg is made in response to the
upward swing it should be inwards and towards the

right toe. A purely outward bend is of no more use than if not made at all; while, on the other hand, the inward bend not only greatly facilitates the upward swing, but might almost be said to encourage the body to do the necessary twist.

I would draw the reader's very careful attention to the sectional photographs that are given on a separate page, and which in this form show the various workings of the different parts of the body while the swing is in process as they could not be shown in any other way. They have all been prepared from photographs of myself, taken for the special purpose of this book. In some cases, in order to show more completely the progress of the different movements from the top of the swing to the finish, the position at the moment of striking is included. Theoretically, that ought to be exactly the same as the position at the address; and even in practice it will be found to be as nearly identical as possible, in the case of good driving, that is. Therefore, for the sake of precision, the third photograph in each series of four is a simple repetition of the first, and is not a special photograph. It might be as well to point out the extreme importance of seeing that at the top of the swing the line of sight is directed over a point a few inches to the right of the middle of the left shoulder (see one of the photographs), as showing that the body has got well round. Ask the average player of some experience where that line of sight should be when his club is at its topmost point, and he will promptly say, "Nearly over the middle of the left shoulder," having probably been told hundreds of times that this is the place, and having seen it written in many text-books on the game; but if he will make a close examination of his own position at the top of his swing, he will often find that his line of sight is far away from that point. When the shoulder is in its proper place, it is as if the spring of the body has been wound up, and now at the top of the swing there is a sense of keen tension, so that when the club comes back again it does so with a snap that would be quite impossible if the body had not been turned. The whole difference between swinging and driving with the twisted body and the straight, stiff body, is that in the one case you have all the elasticity that is comprised in the entire human framework stretched out and employed in the making of the drive, while in the other case you dispense with it altogether and content yourself with a mere pendulum swing and such momentum as you can convey to your club in a simple downward passage from the top to the ball.

There is very little to say about the upward swing to the player of experience, who is now setting about the improvement of his drive with a view to getting greater length, except that he had better see to it that the increase of confidence which he has gained in his years of play, and the certainty that he possesses of always getting the ball well away in some fashion or other, has not resulted in his increasing the pace of that upward swing to an improper extent, and completely forgetting that there is for experienced players as well as beginners very much good in that old maxim, " Slow back, but quick on the ball," although I always warn those who ask my advice that there is danger in going too slowly back. It generally follows that the quicker the backward swing the slower is the club in returning to the ball, as if

an appreciable portion of the available energy had
been expended in this backward swing. Also, while
I like to see a suspicion of bend in the right knee
when the player is addressing the ball—giving a
position of complete comfort, suppleness, and power,
which is just what is wanted when the club gets back
to the ball, everything, as we have just said, then
being naturally in just the same position as when the
ball was being addressed—that leg must gradually
stiffen while the upward swing is being made, and at
the top should be quite stiff and rigid. This is all
part and parcel of that preparation of momentary high
tension at the top, in anticipation of a quick reaction.

Again, it is impossible to exaggerate the importance of seeing that the wrists work properly in going
back. Unless they do so they cannot get in their
proper action when they are on the downward swing,
and I fear that in too many cases the bearing of the
preliminary wrist action in the upward swing on the
reverse action in coming back is not at all appreciated.
It is laid down as a rule, and it is an excellent one,
that in going back the left wrist should gradually turn
so that at the top of the swing it is right underneath
the shaft, the toe of the club having thus been
brought to point to the turf.

The whole object of this is that the wrists also
shall be brought to a state of tension at the top, and
that they shall be in the best possible position for a
quick spring back. When the wrists are in their
proper place at the extreme point of the up-swing this
tension is plainly felt, and there is a very perceptible
feeling of power in the wrists alone, such as is impossible when they are in any other position. Unless
they are in the correct one there is absolutely no oppor-

tunity for any work on their part in coming down, and by the time they reach the ball they are almost lifeless. The best way in which to regard this wrist action is that the wrists are doing a little swing of their own—a swing on their own account inside the big swing of the arms and the club—and this supplementary swing will add enormously to the effect of the drive. They have a little up-swing of their own, a down-swing, and in due course they follow through. That is the wrist action about which I shall have another word to say a little farther on. It is sufficient for the present to lay final and extreme emphasis on the importance of getting the left wrist underneath the shaft, and so ready for work. Another point— see that, in going up, the left arm is held loosely from the body; this will promote power and encourage follow through when coming back; and look to it, also, that the right elbow is kept well in control and fairly close to the side, in order to promote tension at the top. Left elbow up and out, right down and in, that is the rule. At the top of the swing, although nearly all the weight will be on the right foot, the player must feel a distinct pressure on the left one, that is to say it must still be doing a small share in the work of supporting the body. If it is merely touching the turf, it is a sign that the weight has been thrown too far backwards and the proper balance of the body been disturbed. This is a very common mistake, and the frequent result is that the shot is mistimed.

When the ball is being addressed the shoulders should be in such a relative position that the left one is about four or five inches higher than the right. It will be found that this is quite a natural and easy position if the right knee is bent slightly, and the

reason for adopting it is that as the body is twisted
in the upward swing the right shoulder rises gradually,
so that even in this case it will be a shade higher
than the left when the top of the swing is reached.
The general result is that the swing is flatter and of
a more sweeping character than it would have been
if the shoulders were level when the ball was being
addressed. In the latter case the left knee would dip
much more, so too would the left shoulder, and the
swing would be very upright, so that a strong tendency
to dig into the ground when coming down would be
induced. Finally, so far as going up with the club
is concerned, keep the body as upright as is consistent
with a fair degree of comfort; guard severely against
any tendency to stoop. This is a common failing.

Now for the return journey. Here at the top,
arms, wrists, body—all are in their highest state of
tension. Every muscle and joint in the human golfing
machinery is wound up to the highest point, and there
is the feeling that something must be let go at once.
Let the man regard himself as a dangerous explosive
that will kill something when it goes off, and therefore
to be handled very carefully and kept severely in check
until the moment arrives for the damage to be done,
which is when the club comes on to the ball. Therefore at the top of the swing encourage this feeling
of restraint upon the tension to the fullest extent.
Nevertheless, when commencing the downward swing,
do so in no gentle, half-hearted manner, such as is
often associated with the idea of gaining speed
gradually, which is what we are told the club must
do when coming down from the top on to the ball.
It is obvious that speed will be gained gradually,
since the club could not possibly be started off at its

quickest rate. The longer the force applied to the down swing, the greater do the speed and the momentum become. But this gradual increase is independent of the golfer, and he should, as far as possible, be unconscious of it. What he has to concern himself with is not increasing his speed gradually, but getting as much of it as he possibly can right from the top. No gentle starts, but hard at it from the very top, and the harder you start the greater will be the momentum of the club when the ball is reached. All this may sound very much like advice to press, and we are told not to press. But this term "press" must be rightly understood. A man is pressing in the wrong and dangerous sense only when his swing and timing are not perfect, when he knows that they are not, when he has no confidence, and when he is merely trying to make up in strength what he knows is wanting in technique and skill. But when he has got all his movements right, when his timing is correct, and when he has absolute confidence that all is well, the harder he hits the better. Therefore, while as a general rule the advice not to press is the very best that can be given to the beginner and the moderate player, it is out of place when applied to the more accomplished player when well on his game. In what I have just written I am quite plainly advocating pressing in the downward swing.

When the club is coming down there is the great question of the timing of the stroke involved. What exactly the timing of the swing is would be very hard, and perhaps impossible, to explain. Everybody knows when he has timed his stroke correctly and when he has not. In the one case there is the sensation of

supreme power at the time of impact, and the ability
at the critical moment to put every ounce of available
strength into the blow which is given to the ball, while
the follow through proceeds perfectly smoothly and
almost of its own accord. There is no feeling of
restraint or uneasiness from start to finish. On the
other hand, when something has gone amiss with the
timing there is a feeling of something wrong somewhere, usually just as the club is coming on to the ball.
The player is conscious of a restraint somewhere
which he cannot overcome, and at the moment of
impact he experiences something in the nature of a
sense of helplessness and feebleness, the hit is half-
hearted, and the follow through is short and limp. The
impact feels like an uncomfortable jerk. In broad
principle, timing, of course, is the maintenance of perfect and scientific harmony between the movements of
the head of the club and the shaft on the one hand, and
those of the arms and the body on the other; but what
precisely the relations between these movements must
be it is next to impossible to state in words or to illus-
trate in pictures, and I doubt if they could be scientific-
ally demonstrated by anybody, since the arrangement
is so extremely complex, and is so largely dependent
on a peculiar instinct, properly trained as it is in
the case of the experienced player. Given strict
attention to all the main essentials, the instinct will
come, and the player who has perfected himself in
all the chief technical principles of his drive, as he
knows them, will never have any difficulty in timing
his shot properly when he is on his game. The
chief object of the timing, stated simply, is to make
the moment of impact and the attainment of the
supreme force of the swing simultaneous, and the

great danger is lest the swing, wound up under such high tension as we have seen, should go off too soon, so to speak. The passage of the club from the top of the swing down to the ball and clean through is but the work of an instant; and with the whole attention concentrated on the forthcoming impact, from the moment when the club begins to come back from its topmost point, it is clearly evident that there must be a risk of the whole thing happening too quickly. It is such a speedy business that ordinary calculation is almost out of the question, and therefore it has to be left to that educated instinct which I have mentioned, while so far as he is able the player must give it the fullest practical assistance in the execution of its extremely delicate duty. If the player has got to the top of his swing all right, and is then in absolute control over his body and club, his timing of the shot afterwards will generally be satisfactory.

The early part of the downward swing should be from the arms. Keep the body and wrists under tension a little longer. Another most important point in the timing—there is a strong inclination on the part of the head and body to sway forward as soon as the club gets well under weigh in the downward swing, in too eager anticipation of the finish. When this happens it is fatal. When body and head get in front of the club the latter is rendered almost useless, and at the moment of impact it is being merely dragged through. Be determined to hold the body well back, and the head well back too, but don't go to extremes. Keep them behind the club; never let them get in front. In this way the sense of tension and available spring is still further increased, and much is done towards the proper timing of the ball.

ADDRESS   TOP OF SWING

ARM AND SHOULDER ACTION IN DRIVING

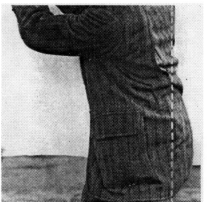

ADDRESS   TOP OF SWING

ARM AND WAIST ACTION IN DRIVING

IMPACT   FINISH

ARM AND SHOULDER ACTION IN DRIVING

IMPACT   FINISH

ARM AND WAIST ACTION IN DRIVING

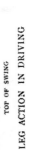

TOP OF SWING

LEG ACTION IN DRIVING

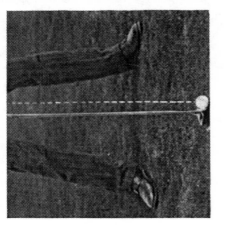

STANCE

Then comes the moment of impact. Crack! Everything is let loose, and round comes the body immediately the ball is struck, and goes slightly forward until the player is facing the line of flight. The right shoulder must not come round too soon in the downward swing, but must go fairly well forward after the ball is hit.

If the tension has been properly held, all this will come quite easily and naturally. The time for the tension is over, and now it is allowed its sudden and complete expansion and quick collapse. That is the whole secret of the thing—the bursting of the tension at the proper moment—and really there is very little to be said in enlargement of the idea. At this moment the action of the wrists is all-important, but it cannot be described. Where exactly the wrists begin to do their proper work, I have never been able to determine exactly, for the work is almost instantaneously brief. Neither can one say precisely how they work, except for the suggestion that has already been made. It seems, however, that they start when the club-head is a matter of some 18 inches from the ball, and that for a distance of a yard in the arc that it is describing they have it almost to themselves, and impart a whip-like snap to the movement, not only giving a great extra force to the stroke, but, by keeping the club-head for a moment in the straight line of the intended flight of the ball, doing much towards the ensuring of the proper direction. It seems to be a sort of flick—in some respects very much the same kind of action as when a man is boring a corkscrew into the cork of a bottle. He turns his wrist right back ; for a moment it is under high tension, and then he lets it loose with a short, sudden snap. Unless the wrists are in their proper place, as described, at the top of the swing, it is impossible to get them to do this work when the time comes. There is nowhere for them to spring back from. It may be worth stating that proper wrist action generally comes very much more easily with clubs with fairly thin grips than with thick ones; and while strong, powerful wrists are obviously an advantage in long driving, the idea of the weakness of small and slender ones is often very much exaggerated; in fact, a man of generally delicate physique must often depend very largely upon getting his long ball from the wrists, if he is to get it at all.

As for the follow through, there is very little that can be said here which is not already perfectly understood, if it is not always practised. After impact, and the release of all tension, body and arms are allowed to swing forward in the direction of the flight of the ball, and I would allow the right knee to give a little in order to remove all restraint. But the weight must not be entirely taken off the right foot. That foot must still be felt to be pressing firmly on the turf, showing that though the weight has been changed from one place to another the proper balance has not been lost.

Many men who get a fair length with their drive set the right arm and wrist to do nearly all the work from the top of the swing to the finish; but, besides being an irregular proceeding, this is a very dangerous one. It is true that the right arm in command will often give a longer ball from a defective swing and body movement than when the work of the two hands and wrists is properly apportioned, but it is almost a case of counteracting the effects of one mistake by making another, and there is reduced con-

trol over the flight of the ball in such circumstances.
Nobody is less likely to keep on the line than the man
who addresses the ball with his right hand turned
round so much that the palm is facing upwards. He
cannot be so certain of his direction, and will be more
liable to pull and slice. There are, however, exceptions to most rules in golf, and I may mention here
that both Mr. John Ball and Mr. Robert Maxwell
seem to grip their clubs in this way, and very possibly
they would not drive such fine balls if they did not do
so. But they have been doing it all their lives ; it is
natural to them ; and the best way to regard it is that
they are exceptions that prove the rule, and that it
would be dangerous for the majority of players to try
to copy their grip.

In these days of the rubber-cored ball the same
strict attention is not paid to the follow through as it
used to be in the time of the gutta, for the simple
reason that in the latter period nobody could drive
any length at all who did not follow through fairly
well, while the rubber core is so different that quite a
good length is often obtained when the follow through
is comparatively short, and thus there is a strong
tendency in these times to reduce it. This is bad, and
the man who wants great length in his drive may well
be advised to cultivate following through with the
utmost care, for three main reasons. The first of
these is that, even if he can get a fair length without
it, he can certainly get very much farther with it. It
gives extra length as much as it did with the gutta,
though it may not act for the same extent of the swing.
In the second place, a proper follow through is the
almost natural and inevitable result of accuracy in the
earlier parts of the swing ; and when once a player

begins to neglect it he is preparing future trouble for himself in all other departments of his drive. Thirdly, when there is only a very short follow through, there is not so much control over the flight of the ball nor as much run on it. The follow through, short as is the duration of impact, seems to guide the ball along and gives it a very fair start on a straight journey; and the very fact of following through makes a better insurance against pulling and slicing, while the players who finish their strokes with their hands no more than waist high are more liable to this pulling and slicing. Mind that, in following through, the body gets well round, and the breast faces the line of flight of the ball.

Everybody knows what trajectory of the ball is the best for long driving. The high ball is useless except in a following wind. Too much of the length that comes from it is in the direction of the sky instead of towards the hole, and there is no run on the ball when it comes down. On the other hand, the very low ball comes down too soon, and all the run it gets cannot make up for the lost flight. A sliced ball, be the slice ever so little, is fatal to length. A pulled ball is better than a sliced one, but a bad pull is very nearly as bad as anything. The perfectly straight ball, rising gently for a while and then seeming to get a new lease of life and rising again to its topmost point when its flight has been three-parts completed, is the ball to travel far and sure. Look forward to the chapter on " The Science of the Stroke."

I hardly feel it to be necessary to say more than a passing word about pulling and slicing—that is, when they are faults, and not wanted; there is a chapter to follow about making them when they are necessary.

If the trouble is only for a day it is perhaps the best thing to let it alone, in the belief that it will right itself, rather than begin to tamper with the stance and swing, which may have the effect of disturbing the golfer's system for quite a long time. But if the fault continues, and something has to be done, a little attention may be given to the manner of gripping the club. In the case of slicing, hold the right hand a little more tightly and more under the club, and if this does not cure, the stance may be very slightly altered, the right foot being brought farther back. Slicing, however, is most frequently caused by drawing in the arms at the moment of impact, and there is only one cure for it then, which is not to draw in the arms—a habit that is often difficult to get out of if it is allowed to continue for any length of time. As to pulling—not such a common fault, and one that comes oftenest when the man has got too well on to his drive instead of too much off it—let it alone unless it becomes very bad and persistent, in which case try the remedy of gripping with the right hand a little more over and more loosely, and make the stance just a trifle more open.

During the last few years two new styles of driving seem to have come in—the result of the rubber-cored ball again! One must call them styles now, because so many people adopt them, or perhaps one should say fall into them. One is the hit, or "cricket stroke," as it is most generally called, since men who have played much cricket most frequently use it, finding it difficult after all their cricket experiences to swing as golfers ought to do; and the other is the very short swing. Taking these in order, there can be no doubt that some of the men who use

5

the cricket stroke, and particularly those who have been good cricketers, do get very long balls with it. All the same it is not what one would call a proper golfing stroke, and it is certainly one to be avoided by all who do not feel themselves forced into it by reason of the long time they have spent at cricket. You often see young players who are very strong in the body and limbs getting into it chiefly because they have that exceptional muscular power and use it in the simplest way possible, instead of taking the trouble to cultivate the true swing. The cricket stroke is a hit pure and simple. The club is taken up on no particular system, but generally in an upright direction, and it is brought back on to the ball with terrific force, and there the stroke ends, there being practically no follow through. I have watched the stroke being made by many prominent cricketers, including Dr. W. G. Grace, who plays a fair amount of golf now, and from what I have seen I am convinced that the length that he gets is the result of muscular force pure and simple, together with very pronounced and strong wrist action, which amounts to much the same thing. The amount of wrist work that Dr. Grace gets into his tee shots is quite remarkable. But it is difficult to become a really first-class golfer when the driving is done in this way, for the player has next to no control over the ball. The margin for error is very much less than it is in the case of the proper swing, though it is small enough even then, and the liability to pull and slice and get into all sorts of trouble is very much greater, while when these players are really off their drive they are generally almost helpless. In every way their shots are most difficult to regulate, especially in a wind. Of course the flight of their ball is quite different from that of one driven in the proper way, and what that flight is, and how it is got, is indicated in remarks made by Professor Tait, which are quoted in Chapter XV. It seems to be certain that in the case of the cricket stroke there is far less underspin given to the ball, and so it is simply slogged through the air with considerably more "initial elevation" than is given to a ball that is properly driven. The old cricketer, who does not take up golf until he has almost finished his cricket, may find it difficult to get out of the stroke, but those who do not, and others who have fallen into the habit without the same good excuse that the cricketers have, will do very well to take the greatest pains to change their style of driving to something more orthodox.

Now, as to the second of the two new styles to which I have referred, that of short swinging. In the days of the gutta ball you very seldom saw it, because a full swing was then almost necessary in order to get any length at all. Other things being equal, the longer the swing—up to a certain point—the greater is the momentum of the club-head at the time that it reaches the ball, and therefore the greater is its driving power. But it certainly does not need quite so much power to propel the rubber-cored ball as in the case of the gutta, and it happens in this way that many men have got into a system of shortening their swings—particularly, I should say, their backward swings, because they find the result is that they gain something in the accuracy and certainty of the stroke. Some of the short swings that one sees are very short indeed, and it is surprising what length is obtained from them. Nevertheless I am quite sure that a certain amount of length is lost, and on the whole I cannot think that the short swing is by any means so good as a full one, at all events for those who have the capacity to make the full one.   But one thing I ought to say here is, that I think many men of comparatively small physical power make swings that are too long for them, and indeed it seems to be characteristic of the weak man that he swings too much.   When a man makes a swing that is really too long for him, the usual result is that he does not turn his body as he ought to do, and then the club goes straight up, and at the top almost drops down his back. The club must always be brought round the body, and not drawn back in the line that the ball has to take, and if the player finds that he really cannot get the club round in the proper way, making the full swing that he does, he might perhaps with advantage try a shorter swing and see if he can get more body work in by that means.

Mention of this matter leads me to make a remark upon the question of gripping the club low down on the handle.   You often see players doing this for a time, and sometimes they get into a habit of it. Well, it is excusable when a man is rather off his game with his wooden clubs, because the effect is to give him more control over them, and also practically to put a club in his hands with a different balance. Among them these changes are likely to make a difference, and in the circumstances it naturally most usually happens to be one for the better.   Therefore, as a temporary measure, and as a remedy for constant foozling, it may be permitted ; but the player must never think of continuing to grip in this way, for two reasons, the first being that he is certain to get into greater trouble than ever with his driving if he does, and the second, that he cannot possibly get the length in this way that he can in the other. After a day or so of short gripping he will often find that he is all right again when driving in the old and proper way, and there the matter usually ends.

As my last word on this subject, I would just like to say that when a man is driving really well and at his very best, it is not merely a case of arms or wrists or body, but everything that he has got in him is put into his stroke, and he can feel it being put there. That is where the satisfaction and the delight of long driving are. The whole man is thrown into the shot. At the end of this chapter, therefore, I would like to quote some remarks made by that most famous of long drivers, Mr. Edward Blackwell, which were made with direct reference to what I have written. Mr. Blackwell said : " My opinion is that the secret of long driving is the correct timing of the stroke. By this I mean the appliance of the power that is at the command of the player at the time of hitting the ball. The more muscles one can bring into force the better, provided that they are all working together. There is no doubt there is a great diversity of opinion among expert golfers as to which muscles are brought into use. I am sure in my own case the feet play not the least important part, in the way they grip the ground. Everyone knows that as soon as the feet slip or shift from the position they are meant to be in, power is lost, even if the player hits the ball truly. It is the same in boxing ; if the right foot is off the ground when hitting with the right hand the blow has not the weight it would have had if the foot had been firm on

the ground.   Therefore I say that the feet must have a
firm hold of the ground.   The calf of the right leg will
be hard, and the muscles at the back of the thigh also.
The more I can get out of my back the better.   The
club is firmly gripped when in contact with the ball,
which means that the forearm is at work.   If I do all
this at the right time I am surprised if I do not get
a good drive.   I am asked what part I think the
wrists play in the stroke.   In my drive I don't think
they do very much, because I know the weak part of
my anatomy.   If I could use my wrists as Arnaud
Massy uses his, I have no doubt I could drive a
longer ball.   It would only mean bringing more
muscles into play, and the more the better.   Many
men who are not physically strong get what is called
a long ball.   That shows they have the secret of timing
the stroke correctly.   But if one could pick out the
four longest drivers, I think they would be found to be
men above the average size and physically strong,
and these men have the time right and the extra
strength."

CHAPTER V

INTENTIONAL PULLING AND SLICING

IF a golf ball when struck always travelled in a straight line—taking the definition of the straight line as that which lies evenly between two given points, no matter where these points may be—golf would be very much easier to play, and it would be played generally to much better effect, that is to say, rounds would be played in fewer strokes than they are at present. Pulling and slicing are among the most disturbing complications of the game that tend constantly to the player's undoing. In his early days on the links they are entirely his faults, and he tries to avoid them as he would the most dangerous hazards; for, indeed, as he knows to his cost, there is a close connection between them and the hazards. They remain more or less his faults, though they happen less frequently, for most of his golfing life; but if in time his skill becomes great, he may at last have them almost under his control, and then he begins to think of turning these old enemies to his service. But, unless his skill is great indeed, they are likely to prove treacherous servants, and the player who employs them may sometimes be tempted to the reflection that they were better in their capacity of open enemies.

Let me say at once that the idea with which
many people grow up in golf, that they must make it
their ambition to cultivate skill in intentional pulling
and slicing, and that they cannot play really first-
class golf until they possess such skill, is a greatly
exaggerated one.   Nine times out of ten the simplest
shot is the best shot ; and the player who always
wonders what kind of variation he can make on the
ordinary full drive, or the ordinary shot with his
brassey, to suit some special circumstances which he
thinks exist at the time, and which are often largely
imaginary, is laying in for himself a very big stock of
doubt, confusion, and trouble.   Not for a moment do
I wish to under-estimate the value of the capability to
play for a pull and slice when the occasion really
requires one or the other, as undoubtedly it does
sometimes.   There are, it must be fairly stated, times
when these shots — properly played — result in
substantial gain to the player ; and his ability to play
them at such times is a quality of which he may well
be proud, stamping him, indeed, as a very fine golfer.
A pull or slice perfectly played is a splendid thing to
do and to see done.   My point, however, is that these
occasions are rare, and are, in fact, much rarer than
the ambitious golfer who has, so to speak, got the
fancy shots "on the brain," will allow that they are,
so that he is often worrying about them, to the
detriment of the plain, straightforward stroke which is
so very dependable and so regularly serviceable.
Therefore it is as if we need a large red label with
the warning word "Poison" to be placed on these
shots, and the strict injunction that they are to be
used only very sparingly, and according to directions.
Players of the very best class use them far less

frequently than others who are their inferiors do—or try to do.

Having thus come to some general understanding with my readers as to the limitations of the proper employment of the pull and the slice, I would state simply the occasions on which I consider it to be necessary to do either. Both are occasionally useful in order to circumvent some formidable obstacle which lies in the direct line between the ball and the place to which it is desired to play it; as, for example, a shed or building, a patch of ground which is out of bounds, a clump of trees, or anything of that kind, which it might not be wise or proper to attempt to carry. In such cases it sometimes pays better and is less risky to attempt to pull or slice round the obstacle, but such obstacles do not usually come in one's way except in the case of the second shot, when the first one has been off the line; or at least they ought not to do so, for they do not represent a good class of hazard.

Then there are some holes of the dog-leg variety which are constantly puzzling, particularly in certain winds. Generally it is a question of whether to attempt a dangerous long straight shot, or to play round with the necessary pull or slice. In this connection one calls to mind the seventeenth at St. Andrews, the first at Hoylake, the Cardinal at Prestwick, and the seventeenth on my home course at Walton Heath. Thirdly, a little pull or slice is frequently expedient for the purpose of helping the ball to fight against a sideways slope of the course through the green, or in other circumstances to act with such a slope for an advantage to be gained. A little slice is also good to get the ball up from a bad or a hanging lie.   But the time when they are of greater value than in any of these cases, and when they might be said to be more clearly marked as the shots to play — shots for which there is no other proper equivalent—is when a ball of very full length is wanted right up to the green, and when there is a difficult wind blowing from the right or the left.   In such cases we are often enabled by a combination of wind and slice, or wind and pull, to get an even better result than could be obtained from a straight, simple drive in the absence of wind ; we make the wind favourable to us instead of being apparently to a very large extent unfavourable.   Such circumstances are, to my mind, the big justification for the deliberate pull and slice as recognised shots in golf.   Anything that will help us to gain length and preserve a safe line, when both are urgently needed, is obviously a valuable acquisition.   It is no exaggeration to say that the pull or slice judiciously applied in the proper circumstances should result in a gain of a good many yards.   In themselves, unaided by wind, they necessarily give a shorter ball than would be forthcoming from a good straight drive, apart from the loss of distance through being off the line, and this is particularly the case with the slice, as, by the very circumstances in which it is made, there is less power put into the stroke, and it is exerted in a less effective manner.   I must describe the most effective manner of combination of wind with these strokes a little farther on ; but in the meantime we must have some understanding of the exact mechanical way of playing them.

Let us take the slice first.   The chief object in the variations of stance and swing that are made for

STANCE AND ADDRESS TOP OF SWING

PLAYING FOR A SLICE

PLAYING FOR A SLICE

the purpose of this stroke is to effect a very slight drawing of the face of the club across the ball at the moment of impact. Of course, it would be very easy to concentrate one's whole attention on this drawing or slicing the club across the ball and making quite sure of it ; but it would be very difficult, by doing it so deliberately, to do the very little that is ample for the purpose and to avoid an exaggeration that would be hopeless ; and at the same time it would be next to impossible to get the ball away properly. To produce a pronounced result, all that is wanted is the very least suspicion of actual slicing of the ball by the club, so little as almost to be better described as a tendency ra(' er than an actual fact, and not enough for the player to be conscious of it at the time of impact any more than he is conscious of it at that time when he makes it accidentally. Therefore this extreme trifle is brought about safely and surely by an adaptation of the stance and the swing. In the matter of the grip there is little to be said, except that the player may discover for himself some slight variation of the usual grip which may help him in the other parts of the process of slicing. For my own part I grip just as I would if I were trying to drive straight, though possibly now and again I may have my right hand turned a little over the handle of the club. I hesitate, however, to recommend this or any other as the "proper" way, since I am fully aware that there is no universal practice. While Harry Vardon makes no change whatever in his grip, there are some authorities of great importance who suggest a trifling change of the position of the right hand in the opposite direction to that at which I hinted, and so it seems to be more a matter of fancy, or rather

natural tendency, than scientific principle. Concerning the stance and the up-swing, however, one may
be more certain. In principle and in practice the
stance that is clearly indicated for the slice is an
exaggerated open stance, that is, one in which the
right foot is well advanced, and I would arrange
matters so that the ball is as nearly as possible in a
line with the left heel. By such a stance you give a
plain invitation to the slice. The up-swing has to be
of a more vertical type than for an ordinary drive,
and at the top of it the shaft of the club is, as it were,
nearer to one's neck. It is a straight swing, with as
little as possible of the round-the-body business ; and
it follows that the body is not twisted for power in
the same way as in the straightforward drive. But
while this up-swing is, in a manner, simpler than in
normal circumstances, it needs to be very carefully
regulated ; and I am inclined to recommend that it
should be taken a little more easily than usual, for
when you are slicing a ball it is of the utmost importance that the ball should be hit dead in the centre
of the face of the club. If you do not make this a
point of the first importance in the task upon which
you are engaged, the probability is that you will take
the ball some way from the centre of the face, and
quite likely off the very toe, with the result that you
will not merely obtain a slice but a very bad shot
clean away to your immediate right. Your up-swing
having been straighter, or more vertical, it follows
that the finish will be along the same line, and what
it amounts to is that the sliced shot needs more of an
arm and less of a body movement than is the case
when a long straight drive is made. This is as much
as can be said for the methods of making the slice,

which, simple as they are, will need much patience in cultivation to obtain any sort of reliability with them.

Now for the pull. Just as it is in the result, it is also in the most important details of its method very much the reverse of what the slice is. The stance is reversed, for now we not only bring the ball farther back towards the right, but we place the right foot back and make the stance an exaggerated square. Allow the body to twist freely, bring the club round more in the up-swing, so that it is carried over the point of the right shoulder, and all the way through the swing keep the right shoulder high. With all this, and the right hand turned round a little towards the under side of the handle, you will get a flat swing, and it will come to a finish with the club over the point of the left shoulder. That is the way to pull or hook the ball, and the ball which is only pulled or hooked just a little is generally a very good traveller indeed. There are many players of the first rank who hook regularly as part of their fixed golfing systems, making allowance for it in the direction imparted to the ball in the early period of its flight, and very fine drivers such players often are.

At the beginning of a further consideration of the manner of employing to the best advantage the pulling and slicing shots, which the golfer will in due course have provided himself with, it is well to point out two other distinctive features which these shots possess beyond the swerve in different directions which they give to the ball. These features are occasionally of value in themselves, so that one may sometimes play either shot when direction or wind has got nothing at all to do with the matter. Again, they are opposite in their results, opening up a further variety of resource to the player who occasionally feels himself in want of such variety. What I have to point out is that in the case of the sliced shot the ball rises very quickly and its flight is high, while its run when it pitches is comparatively limited. On the other hand, the pulled ball always flies low, and for this reason, if for no other, gets a comparatively good length, while it has very great running power when it comes down.

Now for getting over obstacles, or fighting against side slopes of the course through the green, the method of procedure in pulling and slicing is quite plain, and is so simple that no words need be spent upon it. Neither is it necessary, after what has been said, to do more than mention that when the ball has obtained a hanging lie, or an indifferent lie that is not one of the hanging variety, and the circumstances demand that length shall be obtained, while there is the difficulty presented of getting the ball to rise properly if the brassey is employed, a slicing stroke, for which due allowance is make in direction, is calculated to meet the demands of the situation. The only alternative is the iron, and the length-power of the iron may not be enough for the case. Furthermore, it sometimes happens that when a long second shot is wanted the ball is found lying behind a more or less formidable hillock, or something more than a hillock, at such a distance as to make it very doubtful if in the ordinary course of procedure with a brassey it will rise quickly enough to clear it. In such a case the sliced shot is clearly the one that should be played. It might be well to mention here, as the converse of the hanging lie, that when the ball is found lying on a slope facing the player there is neither of

PLAYING FOR A PULL

IMPACT   FINISH

PLAYING FOR A PULL

these fancy shots to be deliberately played, but only
an allowance made for the natural and inevitable tendency that there is to pull in such circumstances.
However, this question of "abnormal stances" is
fully dealt with in another chapter.

In very exceptional circumstances it is sometimes
a good thing to put a little slice on the ball, with the
one and only object of keeping its length short, again,
of course, making due allowance for direction. It may
be that the length wanted is just under that which
would be given by a full, straight shot with a wooden
club, and yet it might be straining the capabilities of
the most powerful iron to attempt to get to the desired
point with it. You have, therefore, the alternatives of
playing an "easy" shot with the wooden club—always
a difficult and very frequently a dangerous thing to
attempt—or of forcing it with the iron club. Such a
situation may be a dilemma to the player, and it is at
such times that he thinks he is a club short. Of course,
there is the spoon, but he may not have a spoon, or
he may not like it. In such a case the full brassey,
with a little slice, may very often do exactly what is
necessary ; but it goes without saying that the player
who tries it will need to have the fullest confidence in
his slicing capabilities, for he is avoiding the risks of
the straight shots for what will often be a greater risk
in the employment of the slice.

Let us now take into consideration the generally
most satisfactory of all situations for using pulls and
slices, namely, those in which there is a wind blowing
sideways, which, with the aid of this extra skill, we
shall press into our service and make it an advantage and of very substantial assistance, instead of
being an annoyance and hindrance, as it is to the

golfer who has only one shot with his wooden clubs
at his disposal, the simple straight one—even though
it is the best—so that he is reduced to the weak mode
of procedure of "making allowances" and suffering an
inevitable loss of distance.   The perfect, or the nearly
perfect, golfer can use all kinds of winds, like the
skipper of a sailing boat on the sea.   The circumstances when the wind is straight with him or straight
against him I shall take into consideration when
dealing with other matters of simple windage in
another chapter.   The winds that we can use and
benefit by when pulling and slicing are those which
blow across from right to left and from left to right,
and more particularly those cross-slanting winds which
blow more forward to the hole than back from it.

I need not tell experienced readers that the golfing
novice would have an entirely erroneous idea of how
to use his pull and slice—if he had them—in a cross
wind.   He would think his duty well done by slicing
into a wind coming from the right, and thereby, as he
would explain, setting the tendency of the ball to swerve
to the right to fight the tendency of the wind to blow
it away to the left, with the result that these two forces
would neutralise each other, and the ball would be
kept straight.   And so in the same way by pulling
into a wind coming from the left.   Certainly the ball
would be kept straight, but that would be the solitary
advantage of its flight, for all its length would be
sacrificed in this fight between wind and ball.   The
wind would be the constant and serious enemy of the
player.   This will not do; the sideways wind must
be taken in alliance as a friend, and instead of fighting
the wind from the right with a slice, the ball must join
it with a pull.   Therefore, when the wind does thus

come from the right, and all the better if it is a little behind as well (let us call it a south-easterly wind when the hole is due north of the golfer), let the golfer face round about somewhat and play his ball, so far as preliminary direction goes, rather across that wind, but with a pull. The facing into the wind and playing into it is simply by way of making direction allowance for what is to follow. Before that ball has gone very far it will have surrendered itself completely to the wind, and the pull that is in it will, if the direction was reckoned aright, be driving the ball straight down the wind and in the line for the hole. Wind-power and man-power are now evidently both entirely favourable to the flight, and while there is some advantage during the time the ball is in the air, there is a greater one when it pitches, for it will then be full of life and have an enormous amount of run. A longer ball can be got in this way than by a straight shot where there is no wind. A very little reflection will show that everything depends on the accurate calculation of the forces at work and their proper adjustment to each other; and thought, experience, and practice can alone ensure success.

The converse case in which the wind comes from the left (west or south-west when the hole is to the north), is by the same principle dealt with by playing well to the left with a slice. In due course, at a point away out to the west, slice and wind join forces and drive the ball at full speed in the direction of the flag.

Critical players who have not yet experienced the satisfaction of these things, may ask whether the advantage gained by getting wind and pull, or wind and slice, as the case may be, to work together during

6

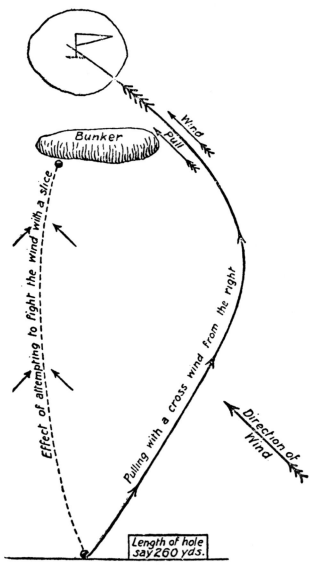

SHOWING THE GAIN OF LENGTH BY PULLING *WITH* A CROSS WIND
FROM THE RIGHT, AND THE INFERIOR RESULT WHICH WOULD
FOLLOW FROM SLICING *AGAINST* SUCH A WIND.   *See page* 80.

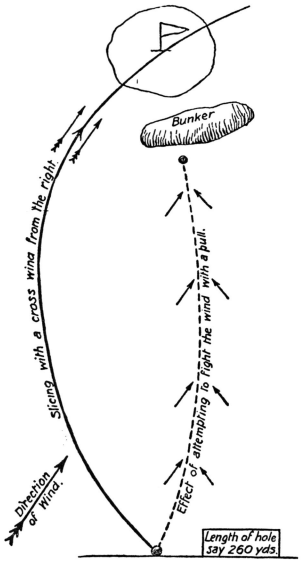

Bunker

Slicing with a cross wind from the right.

Effect of attempting to fight the wind with a pull.

Direction of Wind.

Length of hole
say 260 yds.

THE SITUATION REVERSED. LENGTH GAINED BY SLICING *WITH* A
CROSS WIND FROM THE LEFT. *See page* 81.

the second and most important stage of the journey, is not largely, or even entirely, discounted in advance by the loss of driving power that the ball must sustain while engaged in the preliminary process of boring its way across the wind to that point where it will turn round and receive its assistance. What is over-looked when such a point is raised is that during this first section of the flight the ball is low and is escaping the adverse wind effect as much as possible, that by the time it has risen it is with the wind, and that, moreover, it is the long run at the finish which is one of the greatest benefits. It is clear on such a reckoning that there is an enormous balance of forward power in favour of the second period of flight.

The situation is clearly somewhat complicated when it is the second shot that is being played (or the tee shot in the case of a long one-shot hole), and, while the putting green is within range, there is a bunker guarding it on the side on which it is desired to come in either with the pull or the slice. It is then a question of calculation as to how, if at all, the hazard can be circumvented while still getting the length that is available from the wind and the special stroke. If the risk is too great there may be nothing for it but to play short, and in this event perhaps straight. It is a matter for individual judgment upon the precise circumstances which exist at the time ; and the game would not be what it is if a rule-of-thumb could be formulated in advance for every conceivable situation, or if there were never any difficulties which are apparently insurmountable. But let it be remembered that if it is the second shot upon which the player finds himself in this dilemma, as it will most frequently be, there will probably have been something wanting in the judgment with which he played his first, for it should have been so played that the ball was placed in such a position that this difficulty would not have been presented, or, at all events, would have been presented in the least difficult form. A golfer should always look a shot ahead, and if he did so he would be spared many of the difficulties in which he constantly finds himself. As a set-off to the failure of the pull or slice with the wind to help us out of such difficulties as this, there is the fact to be remembered that it happens frequently as the result of these long swerving balls, hazards which are placed directly in front of the green may be played round, when they would probably catch a straight shot that had no wind to help it.

We have thus considered the cross-wind as a factor in giving us a long run and increased length, when used in conjunction with the pull and the slice ; but there are times when the combination arranged differently may be made to be of equal service, cutting short and sharp the flight and run of the ball, that is, by slicing into a wind from the right, and pulling into a wind from the left. The possibilities can best be illustrated by imaginary cases. Suppose you have the wind coming from the right, and the hole well within full-shot range with a bunker in front of, or to the right of, the green. This bunker might very easily be carried either by a simple shot with mere wind allowance, or by a pull with the wind, as the case might be ; but if the hole were only just beyond, or even some little way beyond, even the best player would hardly be able to keep his ball from running past the green, and he would have a second approach

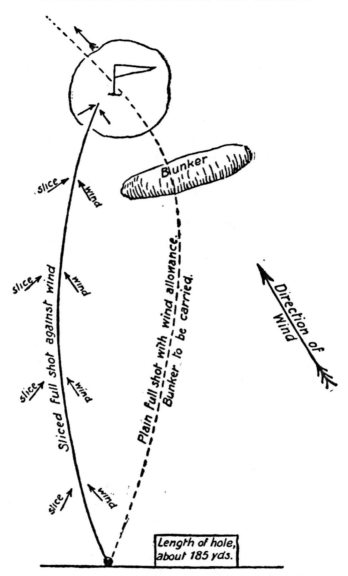

slice

slice

slice

slice

wind

wind

wind

wind

Sliced Full shot against wind

Bunker

Plain full shot with wind allowance.
Bunker to be carried.

Direction of
Wind

Length of hole,
about 185 yds.

SHOWING HOW THE WIND MAY SOMETIMES BE USED AS A BUFFER IN
ORDER TO STOP A LONG SHOT DEAD WITHOUT RUN. *See page* 85.

shot to play back to it. The shot that exactly suits his purpose in such a contingency is a slice against the wind along a line well out to the left. Thus the ball will be brought to draw in towards the green on the open side, and will come down from its flight dead with very little run. In the same way a pull might be played against a wind from the left with a similar purpose. The diagram shows exactly what is meant. This facility for getting a fair length, and at the same time pulling the ball up dead as soon as it comes down, when the necessary cross-wind is blowing, is of considerable value in approach play; for it may frequently serve the purpose in hand much better to play such a shot with a club a power above an iron, say, than by going straight with the iron, when the run of the ball could not be so well controlled and limited.

However, as a last word, learn to pull and slice well, and play these shots when necessary; but remember the straightest shot is generally best, so use them very sparingly. I said this at the beginning of this chapter, but I feel I must say it again.

CHAPTER VI

DIRECT WINDS AND WET WEATHER

A FIRST-CLASS player will not generally play a quite plain shot when the wind comes from one side. On the other hand, the straight shot is usually—not always—the thing when the wind is either blowing straight up or down the course. With some young players it may be the impression that these winds are the simplest and easiest to deal with, and that from the following wind, at all events, the best results may be achieved. This is not so—at least, it is not so in the case of the man who has the command of all the recognised strokes, such as those which we examined in the last chapter. Less science and less resource can be brought to bear in playing with straight winds than with those across, and there is often less pleasure in the result. However, all winds are in the game, and we have to consider the best ways of playing with them. Generally speaking, the golfer in the course of his experience will encounter winds entirely with him or those entirely against him less frequently than cross winds, for the simple reason that when a course is wisely laid out, it is made, when possible, so that the prevailing winds are more from the side at the majority of the holes. To be constantly fighting one's way to the turn against a strong wind, and having it right behind all the way back, affords variety of a kind, but it is dull work, and it is not a good thing for one's golf.

The man of only a few months' experience in golf has some general notion of the principle on which to play shots in direct up and down winds, even though it generally happens that until he is very experienced he has not the courage to act upon them, and commonly trusts to what we may call standard strokes. His simple ideas are that when playing with the wind in his favour he must use his utmost endeavour to get the ball well into the wind, so that it may take the fullest advantage of it; and that when it is dead against him the object must be to keep the ball as low as possible so that it may be cheated. Assuming that in each case the maximum of length is required, this is quite right, and the only question remaining is that of ways and means, which may be considered very briefly.

Let us take the adverse wind first, as being the one that generally causes the most trouble, inasmuch as a really strong breeze blowing dead against the ball is often enough to take half its normal length off it, and generally makes a great risk of finding a bunker. In such circumstances, and when there is a long carry to be faced, the question of playing short should always be seriously entertained, particularly if the play for the time being is by score in a medal competition. I mention this point because the average really good player is a little inclined to be too headstrong, and constantly to try shots which he is almost convinced are beyond his powers. I am no believer whatever in pawky play, and in the majority of cases I would condemn any playing short; but it is not the game— only mere folly—to attempt the quite impossible.

However, when going for as much length as we can possibly get, our object, as already indicated, is to keep the ball as low as possible, in order that it may to the fullest extent escape the force of the breeze. Unfortunately for the game of the majority of players, they have but the roughest notion of how thus to keep the ball down, and how generally to play the up-wind stroke. Their usual ideas of a low tee, and a stroke carefully aimed so as to produce something in the nature of a half top, are not good enough, and it is not surprising that in course of time they give up trying to play this particular kind of stroke. As a matter of fact I think that to get a low shot it is best to tee the ball fairly high, and then take it quite cleanly. The chief thing to be remembered in playing this shot is that the weight of the body should be kept well forward, but at the same time the ball must be over towards the right foot. Ball towards the right foot, weight on the left—that is the simple rule; and the next point, that is of at least equal consequence, is that the right shoulder should be kept high up, certainly higher than when playing an ordinary stroke. The throwing of the weight on to the left foot will help to keep the right shoulder up. In the upward swing it is advisable that the wrists should not be turned quite so much as usual; and therefore we should say that at the top of the swing the toe of the club need not be—and, as a matter of fact, should not be—facing the ground, as it always ought to be at the top for an ordinary full shot with any wooden club. The consequence is that when the club comes down on to the ball the face is turned over a little, and the combined effect of all these variations—with the weight of the body kept well forward the whole time

TOP OF THE SWING WHEN PLAYING FOR A LOW BALL AGAINST THE WIND

—is that the trajectory of the ball is decidedly lower than usual, and when the shot is properly played according to these directions it will be quite as low as is consistent with proper carrying capacity. If a low tee is fancied, by all means have such a one; but one should guard against any extremes in this direction; and it must always be borne in mind that when playing the driver with an extremely flat tee there must necessarily be a considerable risk of not taking the ball as cleanly as is necessary for the perfection of the shot.

One of the results of all these special preparations for playing against the wind is that there will be a tendency to hook the ball—in fact, a little hook is almost inevitable. It may be disregarded, or even welcomed, as the pulled ball will be found to be a very good traveller in circumstances of this kind, boring its way through a head wind in fine style, and showing no tendency to get up. Also the player, if he has to do much of this hard work against the wind, will find himself getting into the way of what may be best and sufficiently described as punching the ball. In this there is no harm either, so long as it is not forgotten that there is never more value in the follow through than when playing against the wind, where all the driving-forward capacity that it is possible to impart to the ball is urgently needed. North Berwick is a windy place, and I should imagine that it is this circumstance that has been chiefly responsible for imparting a somewhat strong characteristic, as of punching, to Mr. Robert Maxwell's play with his wooden clubs.

Having said so much about playing against the wind, instruction in full for playing with it may be

offered in a word—reverse.   In the first place, satisfy
yourself that it will be quite to your advantage to get
all that extra length that you are anticipating in
consequence of the favourable wind, that you are not
running any unexpected risk, and that it will make
the rest of· the play to the hole easier, even if it does
not result in the gaining of a stroke.   In playing the
stroke throw the weight more on to the right foot,
and arrange the stance or the tee so that the ball
is brought more towards the left one.   Neither in
this case nor in the preceding one is the position of
the feet changed in relation to each other and to the
proposed line of flight of the ball.   This is to say, the
stance is just the same as that for an ordinary full
shot, but the ball is moved to the right or left of its
usual position according as to whether the wind is
against or with, and I might add that in my own
practice the variation is generally about three inches
each way.   Whereas when playing the shot which
we have first described, the importance of keeping
the right shoulder up was emphasised, it has now to
be said that when playing with the wind it should be
let down ; and it will be clear that with the ball
forward, the weight behind, and that shoulder down,
it is certain that the player will get more under the
ball.   He may, if so disposed, assist himself in this
direction by having a high tee, but it is not essential
nor always advisable that he should disturb his usual
arrangements in this respect.   The small diagram on
next page shows the relative positions of the ball and
the relative distribution of the weight of the body
when playing with the wind and against it.

There are a few further pieces of advice to be
given, which have been reserved for the end of this

section, because they apply equally to playing with
the wind or against it.   For the first I would say that
in either case it is well to make the upward and
downward swings with measured exactness, and, if
not exactly slowly, certainly not quickly.   Whichever
way the wind is blowing it will exert a tendency
towards ungearing the normal swing, and making it
a little quicker than usual, with the general result

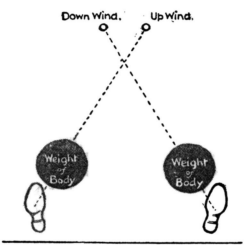

DISTRIBUTION OF WEIGHT AND POSITION WHEN PLAYING UP
AND DOWN WIND

that the ball is, so to speak, hit too quickly, and a
comparatively poor shot is the usual result.   Very little
is lost in length by the speed of the swing being
reduced a little, and I am confident that much is
gained in the exactness of the stroke.   Particularly
when the wind is against you there is a tendency to
hit quickly at the ball, due to a kind of idea that in
so doing you are fighting the elements better.   This
tendency is natural, but it must be checked.   The

fact is that for driving power against a strong head wind there is nothing like a comparatively slow, well-timed swing, which seems to have a great amount of force and determination about it. A quick swing is soon finished ; a slow swing in a case like this means a determined follow through, and a better result.

A second point is one that I touch on with some hesitation, as the professional golfer in a case like this likes to keep himself clear of all questions that may seem to have anything to do with commercial interest ; and it might be imagined that in speaking of the different qualities of balls, his opinion is one that should not be accepted without independent consideration ; but let me say at once that I have no intention of mentioning the names of any particular brands, and therefore it will not be suggested that I am making advertisements, or attempting to influence the choice of golfers. There are several brands of balls on the market at the present day, all of which may be fairly described as good and reliable. They have slightly varying characteristics, and partly on this account, and partly because of mere unexplainable fancy, many of us have tastes in favour of one particular ball, and are convinced that it is the best one for our game, as no doubt it is. I have a strong fancy of my own in this direction, and I should be slow to admit that it is not well founded. But the business I have in hand at present is to emphasise that nowadays the most important consideration of the golfer is not that some balls may be better than others, but they are different from each other in some of their most important characteristics, so that a variety of possible results of any particular stroke is afforded to the golfer by this means. In

the old days of the gutta all the balls were much
the same, and the differences that existed among
them, save in their markings, were mostly imaginary.
But now that balls are made consisting of two or
three different parts—and there is no rule and no
limit to the way in which these parts may be pro-
portioned—there is no doubt whatever that some of
greatly varying characteristics and capacity may be,
and are, produced ; and it is often not more correct to
say that the A ball is better than the B ball, than it is
to say that one sort of bait is always better than
another sort for catching fish, when each may be
the best for its own special line. Each ball is best
in the special circumstances to which it is most
closely adapted, and as it seems that we are to
continue with this variety of balls, and perhaps even
to have the variety increased, I think the golfer would
do well—when he has gone far enough on in the
game—to study these characteristics of different balls,
and see how he can profit by them, as he should
be able to do. Mind, I do not think that the game of
the moderate player is good enough to enable him to
gain any advantage in this way—rather the reverse—
and I must not be understood to be advocating the
use of two or three sorts of balls in the same round,
or of a player constantly changing the one upon which
he chiefly relies. The man who did this would soon
get into a great confusion, and his game would suffer
terribly, particularly on the putting greens. It must
be left to each player's common sense and discretion
to discover how exactly he may safely attempt to
gain a trifle by a change of ball ; and, in the
meantime, all that I wish to do is to point out
how the variety that exists at the present time

may be of service in grappling with these wind difficulties.

Classifying them broadly, some balls are soft and others are hard, some are highly resilient, and others have a quite low resiliency, and the chief difference between these kinds is that the resilient balls are best in the long game, where great distance is needed, but are frequently, by the very fact of their being so resilient, and consequently "jumpy," not quite so trustworthy in the short delicate game. Another difference which frequently counts for something is in the marking, and even though all balls are now stamped in the bramble pattern—which experience has proved to be the best—this pattern in itself varies, and good judges have often noticed that the size of the pimples and the clearness with which they are cut, considerably affect the flight. How exactly they do so is rather too large a question to inquire into here.

Now the idea that comes from experience—and I have not the very slightest doubt that it is the fact—is that in normal circumstances, and with a player of average strength of stroke, the best results are obtained with a medium soft ball, one in which there is plenty of rubber core with much spring in it, and cased with material that allows the club to get at the core at once. Everybody knows what kind of ball I mean, for there is no mistaking the feel of it on the club. This ball answers eagerly and quickly to a full shot with any club, and generally what the ambitious but imperfect player most wants is that length which it gives to him. On the other hand, many players—though certainly not all—find that with a harder ball they cannot get quite so far, but that this ball is much steadier in the short game and in putting than the other one, as, theoretically as well as practically, it must be seen to be. Therefore it becomes a question as to which is worth the most to a man—a gain in the long game or in the short one. This point, in so far as it concerns general play, I shall leave alone; but we may consider the characteristics of the two balls in their relation to straight winds, because I think that the majority of players make a mistake in the matter. If they are playing with a wind they might say to themselves, "Well, this wind will give me all the length I want, and it will therefore pay me to concentrate all my attention on the short game, so that I had better take out a hard ball, which will give me the fullest advantage on the greens." On the other hand, when they have a wind against them which is likely to cause a lot of trouble and reduce the length of the shot to a most dangerous extent, they might think to themselves, "Here I want every yard of length that I can get, and therefore I had better use the ball that will give it me—the soft ball. It is more important that I should get over the bunkers and scramble on to the green somehow, than that I should be down in less then two putts. "

This reasoning seems quite sound, but some other characteristics of the balls are being overlooked in the process of it. It is the soft ball that should be played down or with the wind, and the hard one that should be brought into service when the game is up or against the wind. The reason is simply this, that while the soft ball is certainly a fine traveller when the conditions are favourable to it, it does really require those conditions to be favourable, for it is what

7

you might call a bit of a coward, and does not like hard work.   There is something delicate about its flight, and even as it goes off the club, when it is starting against the wind, you feel that it has not got a great amount of fighting power in it.   The soft touch on the face of the club seems to mean hesitation.   But the hard ball is generally regarded as having a lot more "devil" in it, and if a hard stroke is applied to it, it has most certainly a greater boring capacity through a head wind than the other ball.   In this matter it is slightly assisted by the circumstance that it is generally a little heavier than the soft ball, though not bigger, and this difference in weight, though extremely trifling, counts for a great deal in the flight of a ball in such circumstances.   And another most important difference is that the soft ball has an unmistakable tendency to get up and soar, owing perhaps to its flattening more on the face of the club and getting more underspin, while the hard one almost invariably preserves a low trajectory throughout.   This characteristic of the soft ball is an excellent thing when it is a question of picking it up with a brassey from a bad lie ; but it is not good when a head wind is being faced, and this is just the very time when it is shown in most prominence, for against such a wind a very soft ball, unless treated in a most perfect and scientific manner in the playing of the stroke, will slide upwards against the wind and waste all its length in making direct for the sky. But the hard ball, with its low trajectory, escapes as much of the wind as it is possible to escape, and shows no inclination to rise, and in this way it stands a far better chance of getting a good length than the other one.   I would play the soft ball down wind when it is desired to take the very fullest advantage of that wind. It will rise into it and travel with it so well that a very big piece of a stroke may often be gained, and the advantage is such as to neutralise any difficulty that may be experienced with the ball in the short game.

A matter of the greatest importance when playing with or against a strong wind, and one which is too frequently overlooked, is consideration of the effect of the wind on the very short shots. The utmost pains are taken to gauge the wind in the case of the long shots with the wood and the full irons, and to play particular shots to suit the circumstances ; but directly half-iron shots, mashie approaches, and putts come to be done, it is as if there were no wind at all. Yet the effect of wind on these shots, played with much more delicacy than the others, is enormous, and of even greater consequence than in the other cases. Experimentation for five minutes would teach the golfer a great deal upon this subject. Let him do a pitch shot of fifty or sixty yards up-wind towards the pin, and play the same kind of shot from the same distance on the other side, and notice what a remarkable difference there is in the results. In the same way I think that not one player in half a dozen has a sufficient appreciation of the effect of wind on a long putt ; but concerning this matter I have something to say in a subsequent chapter.

There is nothing in the way of special instruction to give for the playing of the short game in windy weather, as so much depends on particular circumstances ; but it is generally the safer thing to play the very lowest shots, such as run-up approaches, in preference to the more lofted ones when going both up and down wind, as so much more control can thereby be preserved over the ball. When against the wind it is to be remembered that pitches should be bold, and that more than ever are they short on such occasions than past the hole. When the wind is really strong one can almost afford to pitch right up to the pin in the comfortable assurance that there will be practically no run whatever on the ball when it comes down on to the green. Pitching with a strong wind at your back is generally a very awkward business if the object is to get anything like near the hole, and at no time is the ability to cut the ball with the mashie of greater service.

There is only one other word to say regarding play under such conditions of wind as those we have been considering, and that is about playing for position. A golfer should always be playing for position, and he should never put it to himself that he has the whole course at his disposal in the long game. But it is, above all things, necessary that he should give the very closest thought to the question of position when there is a strong wind blowing up or down, for the effect of it is practically to change the whole character of the course, the placing of the bunkers, and everything else, so that the second shot is never the same as at other times. Yet the player who does not think enough does his utmost to place his tee shot in just the same place as he would be able to do if there were no wind, regardless of the fact that that place may be one of the most difficult on the course from which to play the second in the existing conditions. If there is a hole of, say, 320 yards length, which becomes a drive and a short approach when playing with the wind, a well-lofted pitch ·to the green may be necessary if the tee shot is sent away to the right, but a run-up may be possible if a little length is sacrificed and the ball is steered to the left. Of course, one cannot be very exact in giving directions about cases of this kind, and everything depends on the precise nature of the circumstances; but in the case thus very briefly presented it would often seem that the run-up shot would be by far the safer of the two, and is the one that ought to be played for as far as possible. Again, though the wind may be blowing straight down from the tee to the pin, it should be remembered that it may often be converted into a cross-wind for the second shot, and that such cross-wind may then be used for approaching the hole in one or other of the ways that were described in the previous chapter. This is of some importance. Thus, suppose you deliberately slice away far to the right, you then have the wind as a partly forward, partly cross from the left when you come to make your approach; and if the hole is nicely within range—and the chief consideration is to lay the ball as dead to it as possible—you will naturally play your second with a pronounced pull which will hold the ball up against the wind, and have the effect of stopping it fairly dead, as has already been explained. The variety of ways in which position may be played for to the very greatest advantage are too numerous to mention, but these suggestions may serve to put on the right way any player who has hitherto neglected consideration of the point.

At the conclusion of this chapter one may appropriately deal with the special circumstances which exist when it is raining, or when the course is wet.

When it is actually raining, the power value of

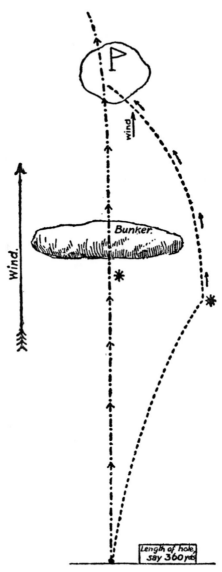

USING THE WIND IN PLAYING FOR POSITION. THE ASTERISKS
INDICATE THE PLACES FROM WHICH THE SECOND SHOTS
ARE PLAYED IN DIFFERENT CASES. *See page* 101.

any particular shot is reduced as much as a third
sometimes, for there are the raindrops beating down
on the ball during every inch of its flight.   Little as
their individual effect may be, it must be perceived
that in the aggregate they count for very much, and,
leaving all questions of wind on one side, the man
who expects his ball to go to exactly the same places
with the same stroke as when it was not raining, is
expecting more than he can get.   One can do nothing
more than remind the player of the difference, and
leave him to make allowances as he thinks proper.

Players generally are now alive to the great disadvantages of rubber grips in wet weather—so great,
indeed, as to make golf almost impossible with them
at such times, in consequence of the hands slipping
every time the club is swung.   Many players find
such grips delightful in dry weather, but they should
always be prepared for contingencies of this kind.   No
matter what is on the handle, a club is always difficult
to grasp with security when it is raining, and I would
offer the hint that one of the very finest things in the
world for effecting a secure grip in such circumstances
is a cotton glove.   This is not generally known ; but I
have used these gloves on many such occasions, and
have been extremely grateful to them for the way in
which they have helped me through trying ordeals.   It
might be added that too many players pretend to be
indifferent to the cold that they feel in their wrists
and hands in the winter time.   I think that it is of
particular importance to see that the wrists should be
kept protected and as warm as possible.   For this
purpose there is nothing better than knitted cuffs or
mittens.

CHAPTER VII

ABNORMAL STANCES

ONE of the best tests of the skilled golfer is his ability in playing full shots from difficult stances. The player of moderate skill is not so certain of the ordinary, straightforward shots that he feels disposed to make experiments at times like this; and even the cleverer man, who knows exactly how they should be done, gets so little practice at them that they are more or less in the nature of an ordeal each time. It does not make it any easier for the player to accomplish these strokes because he has frequently an idea that he is hardly treated in having to play them at all, inasmuch as lies which call for abnormal stances occasionally result from good shots straight down the course. Where the ground is of a rolling character, it is simply a matter of luck whether a flat and level stance is obtained, or one of the abnormal varieties. Yet it must be regarded as the best and most enjoyable golf where such lies and stances are constantly met with, for to a good golfer it must always be a pleasure to encounter any problem requiring a special amount of thought. Indeed, nothing in the game is so satisfactory as achieving a good result from trying conditions. On the very best courses you will find this rolling ground, so that the man who has only been bred and trained to a kind of park golf, when his feet and the ball are always level with each other, is at a serious disadvantage. Once across the Swilcan Burn on the way out, and you will find the way of the old course at St. Andrews rolling and rolling, with huge mounds and hillocks here and there, and the man who cannot play good shots from abnormal stances will never be as happy in this fine piece of golfing country as he should be. Rye is another course which is of a very rolling character, and Deal is a third fine example. At those last four famous holes, which are of the best golfing character, a man is just as likely as not to be called upon to stand askew to his ball, so to speak, after he has played his tee shot, all the way up to the putting green. There are, in fact, plenty of places where he may even be denied a level stance when he is putting. For example, on the first green at Deal, if on no others, there is a huge knob which considerably complicates the question of how best to hole the ball, when that ball settles itself upon it or near it; and of other greens that one calls to mind with such pronounced knobs, there is, notably, the home green at Northwood. Perhaps it is a point whether such exaggerations are quite wise on the putting greens; but at all events their tendency is to make putting more scientific and more difficult, and they are to be commended in place of the dull and uninteresting flatness to be found on some other greens, where there is one reckoning only to be made when the putting is being done, and that is the reckoning of strength.

However, it is not my object in this place to discuss abnormal stances for occasions when there is anything less than a long shot to the hole—for where the player is within the limit of length that may be attained by a shot in golf, even a difficult shot, the player will naturally adapt himself, perhaps by choosing another club, to the circumstances in the manner which will give him the most confidence. It would not be to his advantage, therefore, to lay down any set rules for his guidance in the short game; his instinct and his experience must be called to his service. The shots we shall deal with are those of full length, or nearly, when it is a matter of almost vital necessity that distance shall be obtained with the stroke. They are wooden-club shots; but there is at least one case, as we shall see, when it would be too dangerous and difficult to employ a wooden club.

A moment's consideration will indicate that these abnormal stances are to be divided into four main varieties. First there is the case when the feet are level but the player stands below the ball; then there is the exact reverse of the position, when the ground is sloping the other way—down from him—and the player, though he can balance his body properly as regards the distribution of weight between the feet, is perched up several inches above his ball. Next there is the time when we come to play, as it were, up a steep hill, the left foot being much higher than the right one, and the weight, consequently, being thrown right back on to the latter; and, fourthly, there is the opposite of this, when the left foot is the lower, with the weight upon it, and the ball is on a downward slope, giving it what is generally termed a hanging lie. Each of these shots has its own peculiar difficulties; but that which is perhaps dreaded most by the golfer is the last one, when the hanging nature of the lie is very pronounced.

STANCE AND ADDRESS WHEN STANDING WITH BOTH
FEET LOWER THAN THE BALL

There is one piece of advice which may be given by way of preliminary, applying to all four classes of stroke, and that is that in each case the player should make the stroke as easily as is compatible with the obtaining of a fair amount of length—not a full amount of it. When he comes to view the situation, he should realise that there are exceptional difficulties presented, that the stroke as played will almost necessarily be less certain in its execution than others of the simpler kind ; and that even if it were played to perfection, and with the fullest confidence, the very nature of the lie would prevent such distance being obtained as could be if the whole of the surroundings were level. The difficulties being what they are, and there being manifestly an increased risk of a failure, it is of the utmost importance that the whole effort shall be concentrated on accuracy and cleanness of the stroke ; and since the weight of the body is distributed in a most unusual manner, and the whole swing is more or less unconsciously changed as the result, it will be found that such accuracy and cleanness are next to impossible if the swing is quite full, and the force that is exerted is the maximum. Yet in actual play the golfer is generally so overcome by the difficulties of the situation, that, to maintain his position in the game, he is tempted to press, and the chances are then decidedly against any successful result of his stroke. Instead, he should make up his mind that a certain penalty has to be paid for the lie, and that it is his game to sacrifice a little length—not necessarily much—and to take the stroke easily, making dead certain of getting the ball off cleanly and finishing his swing as he ought to do. In a word, every time you get an abnormal stance be on your guard, and play the shot very easily and with extreme care. Swing slowly, and keep the club absolutely under control.

Now to take the particular case when the ball is some inches above the stance. Like the others, this is a very difficult shot. The player suffers from a cramped position, the wooden club which he wants to use is evidently too long in the shaft, and there is no sort of freedom in the arms for the swing. Besides, it seems as if there is a very grave danger of the club not lying evenly to the turf as it comes on to the ball. The question whether it would not be wiser to play with a powerful iron, or at least a short spoon, at such a time—if the sunken stance is an exaggerated one—should always be considered. However, when the wooden club of full power is used, there is generally a natural disposition to grip it lower down on the handle than usual. This disposition is entirely justifiable and proper, as it keeps the hands to their correct level. It has to be remembered, though, that what with the shortened grip of the club and the elevated lie of the ball, the circle of the swing is necessarily much shorter than usual, and with the head of the club feeling lighter in the hands also, there is a tendency towards making a very quick, nippy swing with no follow through — a sort of swing which gives nothing but failure. This tendency has to be watched for and guarded against. And another, which is equally dangerous, and largely the result of an effort to give a hard hit at the ball, is the tendency to fall back—away from it. This will be fatal every time, and a fairly slow swing with most careful timing is the best remedy for it. The circumstances of this stroke generally produce a very flat swing with a little pull as the result, and the best

STANCE AND ADDRESS WHEN STANDING WITH BOTH FEET
ABOVE THE BALL

TOP OF THE SWING WHEN STANDING WITH BOTH FEET
ABOVE THE BALL

thing to do in this matter is to make the necessary
allowance for it ; while another point that should be
looked to is the strong tendency that exists to hit
the ball off the toe of the club.   This should be
largely corrected in the address, and it may be taken
for granted in doing so, that whatever allowance is
made, it will be next to impossible to hit the ball with
the heel.   Remember, finally, that one of the surest
ways of making a failure of this stroke is to hold up
the hands above their normal position, with the idea
that you will thereby bring them to their proper
position in relation to the ball.

In many respects the case where the player has
such a stance that he is elevated considerably above
the ball, is just the reverse of the preceding one.
Here the club is, as it were, too short, and there is a
natural inclination to grip the handle at the end,
which, again, is a proceeding quite justifiable.   But
here also the swing, though slower, is generally made
too full, and one's particular counsel to the player
must be to keep it short, and be most careful in the
timing.   Just as there was a tendency to fall back
when the ball lay above the stance of the player, so
now there is a strong one to fall forward when coming
on to the ball, and the utmost care should be taken to
prevent this happening.   In playing either this shot
or the one that was described before it, if it is found
to facilitate the maintenance of a secure balance, the
player might very well forego some of the body twist
in the upward swing which is usual in full shots.   He
may lose a little in power and length, but there will
be a considerable gain in certainty.   In playing from
a low lie like this the swing is inevitably of an upright
character, and the ball will frequently be sliced, for

which allowance may be made when there is particular reason to think that this will happen. In his effort to reach down to the ball the player is generally disposed to bend his whole body down archwise from the hips; but he will find his movements very much less restricted, and his situation one of much greater advantage, if, instead of doing so, he will let the whole of the bend, or as much of it as possible, be in the knees.

In the third and fourth varieties of abnormal stances, as enumerated already, the situation, as has been suggested, is complicated by the uneven distribution of the weight on the feet. Another great difficulty is that the path of the club-head, in coming on to the ball and in following through, must follow to some extent the slope of the ground if the ball is to be properly taken. If the slope is upwards, and the swing is kept the same as when playing the ball off the flat, the natural result is that you get far too much under the ball. Moreover, the club has no sooner got on to the ball than it digs into the turf just beyond, and a weak kind of jerk shot, with the ball soaring upwards, is the result. On the other hand, if you play horizontally on to the ball when a hanging lie is presented, the almost certain result is a bad top and no rise or distance. These are the things that have to be watched for. In regard to the swing, the simple rule is that you must swing to the slope of the ground; that is to say, when the ball is facing up hill you must approach it lower with a flat swing, and the head of the club must rise up quickly after impact; and when the lie is a hanging one, you must come down on the ball with a more upright swing, and keep the club as low down as possible in the follow through. One of

STANCE AND ADDRESS IN THE CASE OF AN UPHILL LIE

TOP OF THE SWING IN THE CASE OF AN UPHILL LIE

the most difficult full shots to play in the entire game of golf is that in which the ball is to be made to rise properly from a very hanging lie, and it commonly happens that the penalty for failure is the severest, since too often the hanging lie is part and parcel of a gradual slope of the course down to some big bunker or dreadful pit.

Beyond this instruction the player, when he has an up-hill lie, may be well advised to stand a little more closely to the ball than usual, and he should be particularly careful to secure a very firm stance, and to keep his body as rigid as possible, even to the sacrifice of some of the twist of it. As in the first case, there is a tendency to pull again, and it may be advisable now to check it by making the stance a trifle more open. Important things to remember are that the body, though brought well forward to the ball in the matter of stance, should be held well back or behind it, and that the very utmost pains should be taken to see that after impact the arms swing well and easily through, with a long sweep up the slope of the hill.

The fourth and last case is the most trying one. When the lie is only moderately hanging, the manner in which the ball should be treated has already been sufficiently indicated. Get well under it, and let the body and club follow it, as it were, down the slope, having it in mind also that the ball's inclination will be to go off the club with a slice on it. It will be remembered, also, that if the slope is pronounced the turf will be rising, as it were, behind the ball, and that an upright swing will be necessary in order to keep clear of it in going back. But when the lie is very hanging, when, in fact, the ball is at rest on a quite steep hill,

it is time to go in for a very unusual kind of shot, and
to forsake all standard methods of getting length.
Many players in such circumstances are tempted to
"play for safety," but unless it is tolerably certain
that there will be no loss in doing so—as will very
seldom happen—or unless the player is in a winning
position—I am all against such a course of procedure. This is not the same as playing against
a wind which makes full distance absolutely impossible. Here you have a shot on, although an
exceedingly difficult one, and it ought to be played.
The man is expected to play it.

A moment's consideration of the situation when
there is such an exaggerated hanging lie as that, will
show that a wooden club is quite useless this time.
It would not get sufficiently under the ball at impact,
and would not lift it enough. The steep angle of
the ground immediately behind the ball would be
enough to prevent its doing so. Therefore an iron
should be taken—not a cleek, which in this situation
would be little better than a brassey, but an iron,
and the heavier and the more powerful the better.
Check the tendency to slice by having the ball close
up to the left foot. In the process of the upward
swing it will be found that the body has to be drawn
up (look at the photographs of this stroke), and the
player must guard carefully against the whole of the
swing becoming ungeared in this process. Slowly
upwards is the watchword. The downward swing
at a time like this is different from any other that
has to be employed in the game. It is simply a
plunge down on to the ball, and something in the
nature of a loose dive after it. The club must
have a downward follow through, and that follow

STANCE AND ADDRESS IN THE CASE OF A VERY HANGING LIE

TOP OF SWING IN THE CASE OF A VERY HANGING LIE

FINISH IN THE CASE OF A VERY HANGING LIE

through should be as complete as possible ; but the main feature of the stroke, which has to be a forceful one, is the plunge forward. It is not a pretty shot ; but it is the only one that stands any chance of being effective in a case of this kind. Examine the photographs bearing on these points of instruction very carefully. The utmost care was taken in preparing them, and they are admirable illustrations of what I mean.

8

CHAPTER VIII

DIFFICULTIES THROUGH THE GREEN

WHAT golfers of limited experience are oftenest
short of, are special strokes for special
circumstances. They may be good at the
ordinary strokes of the game; and they apply these
strokes to all kinds of situations, with which they are
sometimes ill fitted to deal. When a really serious
difficulty is presented—when even the same kind of
difficulty repeatedly arises—there seems to be no
proper and reasonably certain way of overcoming it.
The result is that for years, perhaps for a whole life-
time, the man goes on playing these strokes in a
haphazard, blindfold sort of way, trusting chiefly to
luck for any good result that may ensue, instead of
having a particular stroke for each particular difficulty.
There are such strokes for all, and they should be well
practised and established as a part of the golfing
system. I will describe a few of the most useful.

It almost goes without saying that the difficulty
that is most constantly encountered in playing through
the green is that of delivering the ball with as much
certainty and power as possible from the rough
into which it may have been sent as the result of a
crooked shot. There is a working arrangement
between the unintentional pull and slice and the long
stuff which fringes the fairway on most courses; and

on inland courses, in the summer time especially, the long grass sometimes presents problems of the most troublesome character. The first word of advice to give about playing from the rough is to observe the strict letter of the rules in doing so, and one is obliged to think that in far too many cases the rule on the point is much distorted to the advantage of the player. Many golfers take too little trouble to ascertain the wording and the meaning of the rules in cases of this sort, and have an erroneous idea of their privileges through something that they have heard said by some other player. No fallacy is commoner among them than that, according to the rules, they are "entitled to see the ball" when playing it from long grass, bracken, and the like. In this belief you will sometimes see them carefully bending sideways all the covering and obstructive matter, removing little pieces of dirt, stones, twigs, and pressing down with their feet all that surrounds the ball, until at the finish it is scarcely in any rough at all, but is lying so very fairly that some such club as a cleek may be taken to deal with it. All this is in direct contravention of the rules ; and it is not a fact that the player is entitled to see the ball when playing it. Something was done by the authorities at St. Andrews, not very long ago, to dispel this very common error ; but it is to be feared that it is still entertained by a large proportion of even experienced golfers. Replying to a question which was put to it by the Aldeburgh Club, the Rules Committee of the Royal and Ancient Club answered that the player is "Not entitled to a sight of his ball when addressing it, but only to remove long grass, bracken, etc., sufficiently to enable him to find it." It is clear, therefore, that the instant that the player discovers his ball he must cease all disturbance of the grass or other obstruction in its immediate vicinity.

Now there is the question as to which is the best kind of club with which to play the ball from fairly long grass in general circumstances—grass which is, say, two or three times the height of the ball. To my mind there can be no doubt that a fairly well-lofted iron, broad in the face, or a mashie iron, is far and away the best club for the purpose. The average mid-iron is a good club, as it affords nearly the maximum of delivering power in these special circumstances, and at the same time gives as much length as anyone has a right to expect. Many people will prefer the mashie iron, for the reason that with its deeper face the risk of going right underneath the ball is reduced.

There are some golfers who pride themselves that they habitually take their brasseys when dealing with lies of this character, and get the best results from them, while others have a partiality for playing the long grass shots with their cleeks. Well, sometimes the results may be satisfactory, but there cannot be any doubt that, however skilful the player, the chances are heavily against such success, and the occasionally satisfactory results are almost entirely due to the player being blessed with a wonderful amount of luck. The only time when play with the brassey or cleek from long grass is justifiable is when the hole seems to be as good as lost, and when the length to be obtained from an iron shot would be useless. On the other hand, a mashie is no better than a niblick; in fact, of the two I think that on the majority of occasions I should prefer the niblick, the lie being so heavy that there would be danger in taking the iron. The chief advantage of the iron or mashie iron, apart from its right amount of loft and its good-sized face, is the cutting power which is possessed by its sole. You will always find that a good iron will shear its way through grass as no other club will, and thus it gets at the ball in the quickest and most effectual manner. It is unnecessary to add that whatever the club that is taken, the shaft should be strong and unyielding.

A point to be remembered in playing the stroke is that if there is any length at all to the grass, it generally displays a tendency to wrap itself round the blade of the club as the latter is coming on to the ball. Besides doing much to kill the force of the stroke, the effect of this is to turn the blade slightly over, and by this means to knock the ball down, instead of getting under it and lifting it up. I am confident that this is the reason in a large number of cases why the ball is not moved when it has appeared that the club got at it sufficiently to release it from its position. The moral is plain. The grip should be of the most vice-like character, and, furthermore, it is strongly advisable that the body should be kept as rigid as possible, and that as much as possible of the stroke should come from the wrists and arms. Many players aim at coming down two or three inches behind the ball, having the idea that they are thereby going to get well under it and make the more certain of effecting a clearance. Getting under it is well enough in its way, but it must be remembered that in circumstances of this kind, where the resistance of the thick stuff is so considerable, a great danger of not getting properly to the ball at all is created. I suggest, therefore, that instead the player should do his utmost to come down as close to it as he possibly can—that is, as close as he dare without running any risk of topping it. Another thing to be borne in mind is that as there is a tendency for the club to be turned over, so there is a corresponding one for the ball to be pulled if it is got well away. If it had originally found the rough on the left, or if there is any danger threatening on the left ahead, it will be just as well to bear this in mind, and possibly make some small allowance, though, as a general rule, when the ball has got badly into the rough, there are other things to think about than the checking of a little pull.

When the ball has found either thick heather or gorse, the case is altogether different. It will seldom be considered that such a light iron as that which we have recommended to be used in grass will be of any avail. There is generally only one thing for it, and that is the niblick. In playing this shot there is one governing consideration, and that is as to whether you can get a proper back-swing in or not, for it so frequently happens that when the ball is in such trouble as this there are so many other impediments about that the player's movements are very considerably restricted, and he is reduced to attempting to get the ball away by means of a short swing, or a kind of little push, which is not likely to do much more than move the ball for a yard or two, if it does that. If you can get in the back-swing it is wonderful what you can drive the ball through with a heavy niblick; and as for the method of it, there is little to say save that the grip should be very tight, and that again the club should come down as close to the ball as possible, for even an inch of this thick, wiry stuff is enough to take all the sting off the stroke and make the direction wrong. It will generally happen that a

pure hard hit, a kind of jerk shot, is the one which
will be most effective in results.

Now there is the water hazard. To be able to
play anything like a shot when the ball is floating
in water, results in the clear gain of a stroke, or nearly
a full one, according as to whether the green is near
or far away, since there is generally a stroke penalty
to be paid for lifting. As water hazards are fairly
numerous on inland courses in these days, it will be
to the advantage of the player to practise playing
from them. It is surprising to find what poor and
timid efforts are generally made in this direction.
The first thing to do is to make up your mind whether
it is essential that an attempt should be made to play
from the water, or whether the hole may be saved
if the penalty for picking out and dropping is paid.
If the latter is the case there is no sense in wading
into the water to play the stroke, which in the very
best of circumstances, and with the application of the
best skill, must still be a risky one. Not by a single
word would I detract from the merit of a golfer's
determination to play the ball from any place whatsoever in which he may find it, regardless of any
personal inconvenience to which he may be subjected;
but it will frequently be found that this determination
is not carried through as it ought to be, and that,
while the early preparations for the stroke are all
that one could wish to see, what ought to be the
most effective part of it is decidedly spiritless. It
is no good wading into water and being wretchedly
wet about the feet for the remainder of the round,
unless there is a firm and serious intention to make
the best possible job of the shot, and unless there is,
also, an advantage to be gained.

In wading into the water the golfer should be on his guard against so disturbing the surface as to cause the ball to move appreciably.   The law in this matter is somewhat uncertain, and it is better not to run the risk of argument.   I remember that when Harry Vardon and I were engaged in a foursome for a considerable stake, not long ago, and our ball found water, it was a great question with my partner as to what risk he would run if he attempted to wade into it, particularly as the ball was already moving slightly, and eventually we determined on picking up and dropping, so as to be on the safe side.   In playing the stroke the best advice that can be given to the player is that he should try to imagine the water as being fine sand.   If he can deceive himself to this extent the chances are that he will make a good shot of it, for in so far as the methods of play are concerned, the water is just what fine sand is.   The club should be brought down on to the water just about an inch behind the ball, certainly no more than an inch.   A common and most unexplainable mistake is made by most players in coming down on to the water far too much behind the ball, with the result that the club goes clean underneath and comes out at the other side without having moved it.   Let it be remembered that the resistance of the water is exceedingly small.   It would require no particular effort on the part of a man to drive his club through six inches of water, but it would be a very severe task to force it through so much sand.   If the club is brought down about an inch behind the ball, and with an upright swing, it will just nip under it and lift it up, and then if the follow through is properly performed, away it will go.   There is, unfortunately, a strong tendency in players not to follow through at all, and it is quite impossible to get the ball away when this is the case. This happens through their instinctive fear of getting badly splashed. It is not that they are really afraid, but seems to be the assertion of the instinct of self-protection, and some men find it difficult to overcome the instinct. The first indication of it is the closing of the eyes just as the club is coming down, and this is followed instantly by a sudden pulling in of the arms, so that for all practical purposes the stroke ends there. It is unnecessary to say that either fault will kill the stroke, and that it might be worth while to make some serious effort towards the cure of them. One or two of the most historic shots ever played in the game were made from water, perhaps the most celebrated of all being the fine and most successful one that the late Mr. F. G. Tait made from the then waterlogged bunker at the seventeenth, or Alps hole, at Prestwick, when the Amateur Championship Tournament was once being played there.

A most difficult and tantalising kind of shot through the green is presented in the late summer time on most inland courses, and even on many at the seaside, when the turf is baked quite hard and does not yield at all to either wooden or iron clubs. There is only the one thing to be done in either case, and that is to take the ball quite cleanly. If this is not done perfectly, the shot is almost certain to go wrong, for the very hard turf stops the club and twists it the moment the two come into contact. The difficulty is least in playing the short and medium short games, despite the fact that turf cannot be taken as it is sometimes desired to take it on these occasions. But it will generally be found that the best thing to do is to keep the ball quite low, thereby minimising the danger of its getting a bad kick as soon as it pitches, and to keep it low no turf need be taken ; in fact, a plain low pitch and run should be resorted to whenever possible.   However, this is a point that is best discussed in the chapter after this.   Nothing can be more difficult or demand greater perfection of eye and hand than the making of a full shot with a wooden club through the green when the turf is baked, and it is necessary that the ball should be taken cleanly.   Not only is the shot being played in an unaccustomed manner, but the very least deviation from correctness proves fatal.   If the club comes down on to the turf it is askew before it reaches the ball, and has also been jerked upwards so that at the moment of impact it is often actually rising, and the ball is topped.

No special directions are possible in the matter of playing the stroke, though a hint as to the best club to play it with may be serviceable.   A deep-faced brassey should be avoided in playing shots of this kind ; the difficulty is to pick the ball up when it is taken so cleanly, and the best club for this purpose is one that is as shallow as is consistent with its driving power. One is disposed to recommend for this shot that round-soled brassey whose special business was set down as the playing of shots in wet weather and on soft-bottomed courses.   It would seem that it is the best adapted for taking the ball cleanly ; and the more one considers the number of the occasions when this club seems the most useful for particular purposes, the more indispensable does it appear.

From some points of view there cannot be con-sidered to be much of advanced golf in bunker play, since the beginner soon comes by a large

STANCE AND ADDRESS FOR A NIBLICK STROKE WHEN PLAYING FROM A BAD LIE IN A BUNKER

FINISH OF THE SAME NIBLICK STROKE

experience in that play, although it frequently fails to make any improvement. It is remarkable how few players of many years' standing play their niblick shots in the proper way, and how constantly holes are lost in consequence. The average number of strokes taken by players generally to get out of bunkers is probably much nearer to two than one, and this is more a consequence of the improper way in which the strokes are played than the extreme difficulty of the position in which the ball is found. I would therefore venture to impress upon my readers a few points that may benefit them. In the first place, let them be slow to risk playing with anything but a niblick, but if the lie is so good as to justify the hope of obtaining some length, let the club chosen be the iron, which is far better adapted to this purpose than any other. As between the mashie and the niblick in certain circumstances of fairly good lies there is this much to be said for the former, that when not much sand is being taken, and an extra yard or two in clearance length is an advantage, the flatter sole of the mashie is less liable to dig and go deeper in the sand than was intended than is the niblick with its rounded sole. What is wrong with the way in which most bunker shots are played is the stance. It is generally much too forward, and the swing is not sufficiently upright, while many players would be surprised if you were to tell them, what is the simple truth, that they do not keep their feet as firm as they ought to be kept, and even let the left one slip right back when they are in the act of making the stroke.

Just let us consider the whole stroke when the lie is, say, a rather bad one, the ball lying low down

with a steep face close in front of it.   The ball has
to be made to rise very quickly.   A real bunker
shot has to be played.   To play it stand quite behind
the ball, which should be in a line with the left toe.
The right foot may be forward a little, giving an open
stance.   See to it at the beginning that the stance of
both feet is absolutely secure, the feet having been
worked into the sand, if necessary, for this purpose.
An insecurity of the stance is often not suspected until
the swing is in process of being made.   It is then too
late to do anything.   Grip the club fairly firmly,
though not in an absolutely tight and unyielding
manner, such as would be recommended when playing
from heather or gorse.   The reason for the distinction
is just this, that we want a little play in the wrists,
and some slackness of the muscles, in order to nip
the ball up and screw it out of its place, as it were,
at the moment of impact.   This screw-jerk, with very
much the same kind of wrist action as is employed
when a man is engaged in uncorking a bottle with a
corkscrew, is a very necessary feature of the well-
played niblick shot.   Another point is that the hands
should be kept quite low down, so that the heel of
the club may cut in under the ball, the whole face of it
getting underneath very much more expeditiously
when this is done than if the sole came evenly to
the sand.   The swing should be of a quite upright
character.   Of course when the ball is quite close to the
face of the bunker, and it has to be made to rise up
almost vertically, it is necessary to get very well
under it and to take a great deal of sand; but I
think that generally players make the mistake of
taking the sand too far behind the ball instead of
under it, with the result that there is really no lifting

TOP OF THE SWING WHEN PLAYING THE BALL FROM A FAIR LIE
IN A BUNKER

FINISH OF THE SAME STROKE

power left in the club by the time it gets to the ball.

More thought should be given to bunker shots than is done : there are scarcely two of them quite alike, or two that call for the same treatment.   A shot upon which many players come to hopeless grief is that which is presented when the ball is lying in a shallow pot bunker quite close to the green.   Here the ball has only to be raised a little, only just made to clear the intervening few feet of sand, and the great mistake made by the majority of players is in thinking that the way to play this shot is to take the ball cleanly and give it just a gentle little pitch with either the niblick or the mashie. This is a most uncertain course of procedure in the circumstances, and one that quite commonly ends in complete failure, while even when it does not there is no sort of control over distance as there is imagined to be, the truth being that the anxiety to get quite clear of the bunker prevents that concentration on accuracy which is desired in the circumstances.   The proper way to play this little shot is not gently, but with tremendous force, and not cleanly, but by taking a lot of sand.   Come down heavily two or three inches behind the ball, and the result is that it just jumps up as if a mine had been exploded underneath it ; indeed, almost all the force that is applied to it does practically come from underneath, and the ball flops heavily on to the green with scarcely any run on it. After a little practice it will be found that the length gained can be adjusted very accurately by the amount of sand taken, and the beauty of this shot is that, despite all the strength exerted, it is really a delicate one, and the direction and distance can be regulated to quite a fine shade. A good player will get the ball dead from a bunker more frequently in this way than in any other.

As a last word in this chapter I would say this, that it is the capacity to recover effectively from difficulties that distinguishes the fine golfer from the good one more frequently than anything else. It is impossible to avoid getting into difficulties at this game; the thing is to be able to get out of them again with little or no loss. Many golfers who can play most of their shots beautifully fail badly when they are in difficulties, and this fact is in the way of their progress. To them and to others I would say, that time spent in the practice of " recovery shots " is time well spent.

CHAPTER IX

VARIATIONS IN THE SHORT GAME

IT is a common thing to find a man who is a first-rate player with his wooden clubs, and whose game in this department leaves little to be desired, who is yet almost absurdly weak, as one might say, with his irons. On the other hand, it is not often that you find a man who uses his irons well who is not at the same time a capable player with his driver and brassey. The fact is that iron play is very generally misunderstood and not appreciated. One frequently comes across quite experienced players who hold to the idea that it is the same thing as wooden club play, except that the clubs are designed to lift the ball up more and carry it a shorter distance. This leads them into all kinds of mistakes. They play their irons with the same style of swing as their wooden clubs, and very frequently they play them with a full swing every time.

It must be realised that the game with the irons is different throughout. Their objects and their methods are different. With the wooden clubs length is everything, and direction, within reasonable limits, comparatively little. With irons, direction is everything and length nothing, or at least length never ought to be anything, for a man should never have any doubt that the club that he is employing will take the ball as far as is required with the greatest ease. When such a doubt occurs, it should always be removed by exchanging the club for one more powerful.   But with the mind relieved of all anxiety upon the question of length, it must tackle that of direction, and consequently the entire end and aim of play with all iron clubs, except sometimes the niblick, is to get as near to the pin as possible.   So essentially different are these two varieties of the game, that it would be a great assistance and advantage to a player who was endeavouring to cultivate his game with his iron clubs if he could for the time being forget everything about driving and brassey play, and bring to the short game a mind and muscles uninfluenced by any other habits.   It is in the short game alone that a player can put that finish on his play which will stamp him as a golfer of the first class.   You may be in doubt as to the quality of a golfer when you have merely seen him drive ; but are not generally so much so when you have seen him play with his iron clubs.

The chief mistakes—all of them really serious— that are made by players who have had some seasons of golf, but are still evidently and knowingly weaker than they should be in the short game, may now be stated.   They play to the full value of the club, and make swings that are too long, being very much like those swings made with wooden clubs.   Their swings are nearly always full ones, and they never take the care to cultivate anything else.   A full swing should seldom be made with any iron club, for when it is made that necessary control over direction is lost.   Of course we often speak of "a full iron" and "a full mashie," but in doing so we mean really a full swing for an iron and a full swing for a mashie, which I would set down as being a three-quarter swing in relation to that for the drive. This is to say, that a three-quarter swing should generally be the limit for any iron club, and if there is a doubt about its giving enough length with the club that has been taken, that club should be exchanged for the next one more powerful. So in this sense I do never believe in playing to the full value of the club ; but, on the other hand, I think it is quite essential that a player should cultivate not only three-quarter swings, but what are to many the more difficult half-swings.

He cannot do this properly until he abandons at least two other faults with which a far too large proportion of golfers grow up in their iron play. As the swing is shorter, and as direction means so much and length so little, it is necessary that the swing, such as it is, should be, as it were, less free and loose and more compact. For all iron shots there should be less twist of the body, less bending at the knee, and particularly less pivoting on the side of the foot. A large proportion of players of considerable experi-ence seem to think that the pivoting is essential to a shot of any kind that is longer than a putt, and that accordingly it is the proper thing to pivot. But their object should be to pivot as little as possible in iron play, and to do their utmost to keep the left foot fairly steady the whole way through. Of course, for, say, a three-quarter swing with an iron, it is necessary to release it considerably while the backward move-ment is in progress, but for shorter shots it should always be the endeavour to keep the heel as low down as possible. This in itself does a great deal towards steadying the body and making the player concentrate himself on direction almost unconsciously ;

9

it tends to make the shots come chiefly from the arm and wrist, where what we may call direction shots ought to come from, and not from the shoulders and the body.

The other point of error is in the speed of the swing. Generally speaking, iron shots, and particularly the shorter iron shots, are played too quickly, and there is far too much hurry at the turning point of the swing. This is obviously a fault which was created when the player was learning to drive, being then most seriously told that there must not be the slightest suspicion of pause at the top of his swing, or he might just as well not have swung his club backwards at all. As in so many other details, his swing with his irons then became modelled on his driving swing. Anything in the nature of a pause at the top of the swing for a full drive kills all the force of the stroke; but in iron play it is not the same. It is necessary that there should be the most careful deliberation; and therefore one is almost inclined to say that the slower the stroke is, until the club is actually coming on to the ball, the better, and I certainly believe in there being so much of a pause at the top of the swing as the player can at all events feel and be conscious of, even though it cannot be seen, and the shorter the stroke that has to be made, the greater should be this pause within reason, as one might add. To some people it may seem very wrong thus to counsel the stoppage of the club at any point from the time that it is started on the backward swing until it has finished the follow through; but I am quite certain that this one little hint is often sufficient to convert bad iron players into something very much better. The effect of the pause is to steady the player, to enable him to adjust strength and direction to the utmost nicety, and to come to a clearer understanding with himself as to how the stroke is going to be finished, than he would otherwise be able to do, for in the case of all iron shots from the full three-quarter iron to the smallest chip with a mashie or run-up from just off the green, it is most absolutely necessary that the finish should be quite right, the character of the shot being generally entirely decided by the finish.

Now, to come down from the general to the particular, the player needs to realise what iron shots he has at his disposal for all the different distances and positions with which he may be confronted in the area that lies between the putting green and 150 yards from it. Farther away than that, and either the cleek or the brassey is needed. It is within this 150 yards' range that the real iron play begins. Then it should be quite as much a question as to what kind of shot to play as what club to use, for it is too often not realised on these occasions that there are two distinct types of shot that may be employed on most of them, particularly when the range is short, and that there are even considerable variations in these types. You have the pitch and run in one class, and the run-up in the other. The former may be subdivided into many different kinds, from the pitch with so much stop on it that there is practically no run, to the pitch and run in which a fairly long run-up to the hole is a feature of the shot. The run-up is capable of many variations, even though all of them are subject to the same principle and the same style of play. And then, of course, there is the full three-quarter shot with the iron, which, to some extent, is in the nature of a pitch and run without any definite regulation of either.

What the player needs to realise more than he does is that there is not, and never can be, anything that is in the least orthodox in the short play to the hole. On a good course, one may play often without having two approach shots that are in all respects exactly alike. The approaching game is particularly one in which the player is left entirely to himself, and is called upon to exercise his powers of thought and judgment ; and while the shots of the short game need most careful execution, and are in many respects most difficult, it is hardly too much to say that most players of a little experience lose more through their faults of choice of shot, mere errors of judgment, than they do in any other way. I think that perhaps the course architects of a past generation were to some extent responsible for so many golfers regarding the approach play as a rule-of-thumb sort of business, since so many courses were made on a fixed plan in which there was a long bank kind of bunker immediately in front of the putting green, and it was the golfer's business, as a rule, to do a pitch shot over this bunker. Generally speaking, this was not good golf, and indicated an entirely wrong idea of the possibilities of the game on the part of those responsible for such course construction. Practically these people disregarded the run-up as a shot in golf, treated it with contempt, and would not permit it to be played ; while, on the other hand, they called for pitching at every hole.

Time has proved the mistake of this view, for to-day these hazards enjoy little of their old popularity, while all are agreed that the run-up is one of the prettiest shots in the short game, calling for the most perfect judgment and skill, and by which the greatest results can be achieved. It is the duty of most golfers, therefore, to revise their views in regard to this stroke if they have not already done so, and cultivate it most thoroughly, not regarding it merely as a kind of big putt which may be done almost anyhow, so long as the ball is run along the turf. The run-up is not merely a shot to play when one is on the edge of the putting green. It is most effective at distances of 50 or 60 yards right up to 100 yards, and even sometimes beyond that, the ball being given a little lift up to begin with to help it on its way. There are times, of course, when the ball must be pitched, and the golfer who cannot pitch well is in a very difficult position ; but I would lay it down that whenever circumstances permit, it generally pays best to approach the hole with a low shot. This is particularly the case when there is a wind.

Some people believe that when the ground up to the putting green is bumpy the run-up is too dangerous a shot to play, and that the ball should be pitched to get it clear of most of the bumps. If the green is so big that the ball may be pitched right on to it there may be some value in this view ; but it seldom happens that the golfer is favoured to this extent ; and if it is a case of pitching on the bumpy ground short of the green, and of running up over much more of it, I think that generally the running-up shot is decidedly the one to play and the safer. It may be true that if the ball is pitched it may have only a single one of the bumps to encounter ; but it has to be remembered that with the ball falling down so vertically, it may, and very often does, kick clean away at right angles on alighting, especially if the turf is hard ; or, on the other hand, is impelled forwards or stopped almost dead, according as to whether it pitches on a slope forward or against one.   Therefore there can be no certainty in such a shot, and the experienced golfer who plays it must often feel that he is taking his life in his hands and placing an enormous trust in his good fortune.   Against this there is this to be said for the run-up, that though the direction of the ball may be affected by the bumps, the extent is generally quite small, and to all intents and purposes may be disregarded.   And again, when the ground up to the green is quite flat and smooth, what can there be more reliable than the run-up ?

Plateau greens are constantly an anxiety to the player who is approaching them, and he is frequently in a great state of doubt as to what is the safest shot to play.   To my mind there can be no question as to which is the right one, unless the green is in quite a soft state.   Considerable judgment may be necessary in estimating the effect of the bank on the run of the ball, and particularly what change it will make in its direction if the bank is being taken at an angle, but nevertheless the run-up is generally the best shot in the circumstances.   To attempt to pitch on to a plateau is nearly always fatal, unless the player is aided by luck to a far greater extent than he has any right to expect to be.   To take cases in point, the twelfth, the long-hole-in, and the seventeenth at St. Andrews, where the greens are all on plateaus, it is very much better to approach with a low run, if the player is within easy distance, than it is to pitch.   More disasters have been caused by attempts to pitch on to the seventeenth when the course has been hard, probably than at any other hole anywhere. Of course if the green is really soft, so that from any kind of a lofted shot the ball can be depended upon not to run much, a pitch-shot may be played. A hint that it will be useful to remember when playing run-up shots to plateau greens, is that the bank on the edge of the green is generally softer than the level part of the course, and that if the bank faces the south-west it holds more moisture than any other and will be softer still. Things of this kind make a difference.

If a pitch shot has to be played, why is the mashie so generally regarded as the only club with which to make it? The cardinal feature of a good pitch shot is the control that is exercised over the ball immediately on alighting, and the amount of stop that can be placed on it. Very frequently when the pitching is at very short range, the niblick is superior to the mashie for the purpose in hand; yet, though the virtues of this club have been preached by many players of the highest class, the golfer who employs it for the purpose is often regarded as being somewhat eccentric, and as departing from the proper principles of play. I would not recommend the niblick for pitching at a longer range than 40 yards, but for that and under it is certainly a most effective club, for by its means the player can afford to pitch his ball almost right up to the pin with the comfortable assurance that it will stop almost dead on reaching the turf.

Now I will indicate some of the points to which the average player needs to give more particular attention than he does in the making of particular shots with particular clubs. Take, to begin with, the fullest shot that should be made with the iron, a three-quarter shot from a range of, say, 150 yards, in normal circumstances of wind and weather. If much wind is against the player the stroke will probably need to be made with a cleek, but if it is at his back a mashie will be taken instead of the iron. In each case the same shot will be played, and the description of it will apply to each club. The mistake that many players would make in the case of the opposing wind would be that instead of taking the cleek and playing the same three-quarter shot with it, they would be disposed to persist with the iron, lengthen the swing with it, and attempt a hard forcing shot about which there would be no reliability, and of which the club is not really capable. For this and all other shots with iron clubs the grip should be slightly tighter than the grip that is given to the driver, and the wrists should be held as taut as possible, with next to no flexibility in them. The length of the shot must be regulated entirely by the length of the backward swing within the limit indicated. The longer the swing the greater is the velocity of the club when it reaches the ball. As to what the extent of the back swing should be in particular circumstances of length to be obtained, no definite rule can be laid down, as everything depends on the natural power of the player, and what will be a full three-quarter swing for one man will not need to be more than a short half for another. The player will find out for himself his own capabilities in this respect, and will adjust his shots accordingly.

I have already indicated the advisability of his swinging more slowly backwards than is the general custom, of there being the slightest suspicion of a pause at the top of the swing, and of the necessity of

FAIRLY LONG APPROACH WITH AN IRON CLUB—MASHIE, MID-IRON OR
CLEEK ACCORDING TO CIRCUMSTANCES

FINISH

FAIRLY LONG APPROACH WITH AN IRON CLUB—MASHIE, MID-IRON OR
CLEEK ACCORDING TO CIRCUMSTANCES

keeping the left foot thoroughly firm. In the case of this extreme shot with the iron there must necessarily be a little pivoting on the left foot, but not nearly so much of it as when driving, and the shorter the shot becomes the less there should be, until at last it is reduced to the least possible give of the heel. While the swing should be of an upright character, the shot should be played low down right through. The hands should be kept low, and above everything they should finish low, for it is the great mistake of a large proportion of players that they finish their iron shots with the hands up as when finishing a drive, and with the club pointed right up in the air. Except in the case of a full cleek shot where length is wanted, and which does not come within the present category of iron shots, there is only one in which the club should finish with the shaft in a vertical position, and that is when a pitch pure and simple is being played. For an iron shot, even one of the fullest type, the club at the finish should be very little above the horizontal. I invite the attention of readers to the illustrations of these shots which are presented on special pages, remarking that the finish for the iron shot represents the most powerful stroke with that club that the player ought generally to call upon it to make. When he points his club up at the finish he has inevitably raised his hands in order to do so, which is not only wrong in itself, but brings about another mistake, which is the unconscious raising of the body. This lift of the body at the finish of iron shots is one of the commonest faults to be seen on the links, and it is more frequently than anything else the cause of topped balls. Let the head of the club seem to go straight forward towards the hole and stop there. Only in this way can certainty of direction and cleanness of execution be made sure of. If the circumstances suggest that the shot should be played fairly well up to the hole, and that there should be some drag on the ball when it comes down, a little turf should be taken from under the ball at the moment of impact, and not behind the ball before the club gets to it. This is a most important point, and one in regard to which mistakes are commonly made.

The shot just described is simply a long iron shot up to the hole. When the range is shorter, say, within 120 yards, with no adverse wind to encounter, and the ball is thus within comfortable distance of the green, it is a well-defined pitch and run that is generally called for, and such a shot needs to be very carefully calculated. The common error is that the place of pitching and the proportion of pitch and run are never properly determined. If the ground is fairly even I generally play the ball to carry three-quarters of the distance and to run the rest, and I think that this proportion should be the basis of the calculation in most cases. There is a considerable difference between the manner of playing this shot and the one which has already been described. In the first place the player should stand more in front of the ball, and the club should be taken a little farther out in the back swing, with the arms rather more extended. The wrists should not be turned up so much, and should be held a trifle more stiffly. All this helps towards controlling the club, and full control at the top of the swing is the most essential quality of this stroke. A careful comparison should be made of

STANCE AND ADDRESS   TOP OF SWING

PITCH AND RUN OF MEDIUM LENGTH

FINISH

PITCH AND RUN OF MEDIUM LENGTH

the different sets of photographs of the various iron
shots which will serve to emphasise the points I here
remark upon, and I might add at this place that for
this particular shot the club should never be carried
farther back than as shown in the photograph, where
at the top of the swing it is as near vertical as
possible. What most players lack is the ability to
control the club completely when the back swing is
stopped at this point, and the way in which they can
best improve it is by practising the work of their
wrists and forearms, and particularly by cultivating
the habit of the little pause (we will still call it the
suspicion of a pause) at the top of the swing. In
this case, run being wanted after the pitch, the ball
should be taken quite cleanly. No turf should be
taken. At the finish of the stroke the wrists should
be slightly turned over, and should be fairly stiff.
In all these iron shots the left foot should be pointed
more towards the hole than in the case of full shots
with wooden clubs, and the more open does the stance
become in accordance with the nature of the shot and
the requirements of the case, the more is the left toe
turned in the direction of the hole. Generally one
will play this stroke with an iron or mashie, but when
a low ball is favoured—and I believe in such a ball
whenever the circumstances permit—there is nothing
so good and reliable as the approaching cleek which
I described in the chapter on the selection of iron
clubs, and which I use chiefly for running-up
purposes.

For the run-up shot the stance should be taken
so that the ball is almost opposite the right foot, and
the swing should be considerably more of a round-
the-body swing than in the case of any other shot

with an iron club. It should be just a little gentle
round swing, in which the club should never be taken
to a higher point than that shown in the photograph.
One of the most important points to attend to in
the playing of this stroke is that the stance should
be taken very much closer to the ball than usual.
This will make the man *very* firm on his feet,
which is essential, and he will be well over his ball,
and therefore in the best position for controlling its
direction. At the finish of the stroke the arms and
club should be straight and stiff, pointing in a line
directly along that in which the ball is travelling, or
ought to be travelling, and this can only be brought
about by the player standing close in. In the back
swing there must be less turning of the wrists and
more stiffness than ever, and at the moment of impact
the hand should be slightly turned over, that is to say,
the right hand should be disposed to turn palm downwards. While I would not absolutely insist upon
this in ordinary circumstances, I think the movement
is most useful and really necessary on a windy day,
serving, as it does, to give very much more control
over the ball. Everything depends upon the ball
being hit absolutely truly. True hitting is as important in this case as when putting, and the majority
of run-up shots go wrong simply because the ball has
not been hit properly. When the player gets to
within a short distance of the hole and makes a run-
up shot, he often finds his normal tendency to take
his eye off the ball too soon to be greatly increased,
and therefore when practising this shot it might be
well for him to make it a rule that he sees the place
where the ball was after the stroke has been made.
It may bring about much cleaner hitting, and make

STANCE AND ADDRESS   TOP OF SWING

A LONG RUN-UP

FINISH

A LONG RUN-UP

a considerable difference in his play. The stroke and the finish thereof, which are shown in the photographs, represent a fairly long run-up played with the approaching cleek. For a much shorter stroke the swing will of course be shorter, and the finish will not be so high; in fact, the shorter the run-up the more closely will the stroke resemble a long putt in the manner and method of playing it, until at last, when the ball is only a few yards off the edge of the green, the putter itself may be taken, and the stroke is then really nothing but a long putt.

Now for pitching there are a few special and very important points that need to be insisted upon more than they generally are in the early days of a golfer's experience. Pitching is not nearly the difficult matter that so many players often fancy it to be; they would usually find it not in the least difficult if they did not very regularly disregard the principles of it. The stance, of course, must be a very open one, with the ball fairly well towards the left heel and the hands held a little more forward than usual and low down, so that the heel of the club, and the heel only, is resting on the turf. Then the player should, so to speak, sit well down to the stroke—that is to say, both legs should be very perceptibly bent at the knees, and the general position should be something in the nature of a crouch. This, in itself, exerts a strong tendency towards lifting the ball up in the desired manner; it is impossible to get it up properly if the player maintains a position which is at all erect and stiff. Above all, bear in mind that this bent position must be maintained until the absolute finish of the stroke, for by far the commonest fault in pitching is the raising of the body when the club is being raised in the finishing of the shot. The back swing should be a very upright one, and there should be considerable underturn in the action of the wrists, although those wrists and the forearms should nevertheless be kept fairly rigid. The player must never lose the sense of power and control in them. As soon as he does that it is all over with his pitch. Turf is most usually taken with this stroke — a very fair amount of it sometimes, which will vary somewhat according to the particular kind of pitch that is wanted—and the concluding feature is the upright finish, in which it differs from any other approach stroke with an iron club. No matter how short the range may be, if the ball is to be made to pitch properly the club must be brought very nearly to the perpendicular at the end of the stroke. If this is done, and the ball is taken as it ought to be, there will never be any difficulty in getting it up properly, and it will be found, also, that there is as much stop on it as is generally required. Very rarely, indeed, do I consider it to be necessary to adopt any special measures to put what is called cut on the ball. When the thoughts turn towards such a necessity the use of the niblick may very confidently be recommended. It is hardly necessary to say that the stance all through must be very firm, and that while the left knee bends in a little towards the right, and the left foot a little over in order to allow of the movement, the heel should only just leave the turf.

The greatest difficulty is usually experienced with half shots, and this is entirely due to weak work with the hands and wrists, and to the player losing control of his grip at the turning point of the swing. Once

STANCE AND ADDRESS   TOP OF SWING

PITCHING WITH THE MASHIE

FINISH

PITCHING WITH THE MASHIE

again I would mention that little pause as the most satisfactory remedy.

Finally, I must again impress upon the player the necessity of bringing all his keenest thoughts to bear upon the playing of an approach, and I might specially make mention of a point that is too often neglected, and that is, the question of the side of the green towards which he will approach. Frequently the man plays straight at the hole without any consideration whatever of this matter. If he lays his ball dead this is all right, but it is perhaps unlikely that he will do so, and it may happen that the putting is very much easier from one side than it is straightforward, and that on one particular side it is easier than from the other. Thus if there is an appreciable slope of the green in any direction, it goes without saying that it is easier to putt up it than down it, and it is better to have this point fully in mind when playing the approach shot than to complain inwardly about the situation when the time for putting comes. Also, when the hole is in a corner of the green it frequently happens that it is in very close proximity to uneven or rough ground, or even a bunker, and on such occasions it is obviously the safe game to play to the other side. I only mention such points as this by way of suggesting the need for the most exhaustive consideration of the surrounding circumstances when any approach stroke is being played, and that as these circumstances vary considerably almost every time, there is not, and never can be, what we may call fixed methods in the short game, the golfer being left to himself and to his judgment every time. Thought and judgment are everything in the short game.

CHAPTER X

PUTTING STROKES

THE majority of golfers certainly do not take their putting seriously enough; if they did they would be better golfers. One wonders how many of them constantly reflect that of the total number of strokes that they use up in the course of a round a good third or often even a half are taken on the putting greens, and appreciate the moral that is conveyed by that reflection—that if they were good putters, instead of the indifferent ones they often are, their game would probably be improved to the extent of a good third. It takes a great deal of extra skill for a man to gain six strokes in a round in the long and medium and short games, but when he is really on his putting he can do that frequently. Nor do golfers remember, as they should, that while their physical deficiencies may be against them in the long game— and if they are now they will very likely always be so —such deficiencies have not generally any appreciable effect in putting, the best qualities for which are a power of calculation, a delicate sense of touch, and reliable nerves. Thus practically any man has it in his power to become a reasonably good putter, and to effect a considerable improvement in his game as the result.

Of all ways, then, of becoming more advanced in

golf this is the surest, and the fact is perhaps best
understood when a player comes to think of it after
he has been three or four years at the game, and has
obtained some amount of skill in it generally. In
the early period of a golfer's experience there are
generally two things which prevent him from giving
that study and care to putting that he ought to do,
and which he must do some time if he is ever to
become a fine player. In the first place, he often
starts golf with an entirely wrong notion of what
putting is, and what it is meant to be, and this notion
clings to his mind sometimes for years. It is that
the real game of golf is played from the tee and
through the green, and that it is only " real golf "
when you have to make a swing, have to hit more or
less forcibly, and have to run a risk of some sort of
not hitting the ball as it ought to be hit. The idea
of the beginner takes that form, and his view of
putting is that it is a kind of formality to be observed
near the hole, that the ball has just to be stuffed in
at the finish to complete the job, and that the green
is made nice and smooth so as to make the task as
simple as possible. Very often it does not seem to
occur to him that it matters very much whether he
takes two putts or three on each green ; and, in fact,
he may have been encouraged in this ignorance of the
true importance of putting by the circumstance that
in his early play against opponents of the same class
as himself it did not generally make much difference
as to whether an extra putt was necessary or not, and
it was only when his golf and that of his opponent
became so much better that he came to realise that a
putt gained on the green is often enough a hole
saved or won, and that a putt lost generally means a

10

half or a hole gone the wrong way.   When he knows this he begins to study putting in earnest, or ought to do, and he comes to realise that though the play is so gentle and delicate, and there is no earthly reason, so far as the player's age, experience, and physique go, why the ball should not be hit properly every time, putting is still a most scientific and even complicated business, and that there is as much to study in it as in any other department of golf.   A player who wishes to improve in his golf has done much when he has brought himself to these thoughts, and the object of this introduction to the subject is to help him towards that definite conclusion, so that for the future he may give his mind more whole-heartedly to the study of the very short game than he has done in the past, in the satisfactory knowledge that he will be sure of his reward.

Of course, they say that good putters are born and not made ; and it is certainly true that some of the finest putters we know seemed to come by their wonderful skill as a gift, and nowadays constantly putt with an ease and a confidence that suggest some kind of inspiration.   But it is also the fact that a man who was not a born putter, and whose putting all through his golfing youth was of the most moderate quality, may by study and practice make himself a putter who need fear nobody on any putting green. I may suggest that I have proved this in my own case. Until comparatively recently there is no doubt that I was really a poor putter.   Long after I was a scratch player I lost more matches through bad putting than anything else.   I realised that putting was the thing that stood in the way of further improvement, and I did my best to improve it, so that to-day my critics

himself to the way of making an accurate calculation
of the effect of different varying factors, and how they
balance each other ; otherwise his attempts at reckoning will end in a frightful muddle, and his mind will
be in a very unhappy state when he comes to make
his effort.   If he goes about this business properly he
will find putting become a real pleasure, and perhaps
the most interesting part of the whole game, the part
where mental cleverness, together with a good eye
and a steady hand, count for everything, and where
the little slender man may be the superior constantly
of the tall, muscular man, who rarely fails to drive his
two hundred yards off the tee.

I have just said that what I call the mechanical
part of putting—the hitting of the ball—is simple and
sure in comparison with the other difficulties that are
presented when a long putt has to be made ; yet it is
hardly necessary to say to any experienced golfer that
there are absolutely thousands of players who fail in
their putting, not because of any lack of powers of
calculation or a good eye, steady hand, and delicacy
of touch, but simply because they have fallen into a
careless way of performing this mechanical part, and
of almost feeling that any way of hitting the ball will
do so long as it is hit in the right direction and the
proper degree of strength is applied.   These players
give their very last thought to something else, and not
to the way in which they hit the ball, as they ought to
do.   The careless way of hitting the ball is a very
easy one to get into by young players, since, differing
from all the other shots in the game, the club is
now under complete control, and the hitting of the
ball in exactly the way that you want to hit it is
apparently the easiest thing in the world.   The result

are kind enough to say that there is not very much wanting in my play on the putting green, while I know that it was an important factor in gaining for me my recent championships.

So I may be allowed the privilege of indicating the path along which improvement in this department of the game may best be effected ; and what I have to say at the beginning is, that putting is essentially a thing for the closest mathematical and other reckoning. It is a game of calculations pure and simple, a matter for the most careful analysis and thought. On every putting-green there are generally about half a dozen different factors affecting the strength and line of the putt which have to be carefully weighed and balanced against each other, and not until this has been accomplished to a nicety does the golfer stand a good chance of holing his putt. Many a man can putt properly and with certainty if he knows the line and knows the strength. The mechanical part is comparatively simple. Putts most generally go wrong because the strength or the line, or both, were misjudged, and they were so misjudged because the different factors were not valued properly, and because one or two of them were very likely overlooked altogether. How often do you hear, after a putt has been missed, the player exclaiming, " Oh, I never saw that little slope there ! " or " The green round about the hole seems to be quite woolly ! " and others to like effect ? In these cases a factor of supreme importance, one the proper reckoning of which meant all the difference between success and failure, has been completely overlooked, and there is no excuse for such neglect. The player must study everything that there is for him to study when he comes to putt, and he should train

STANCE AND ADDRESS

BACKSWING

FINISH

A SHORT PUTT

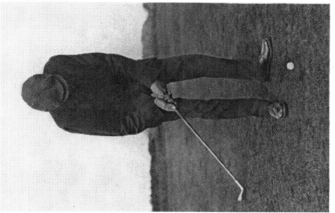

STANCE AND ADDRESS

BACKSWING

A LONG PUTT

FINISH

is that as often as not they do not make the stroke
exactly, or, to use the general expression, they do not
hit the ball truly. Absolutely everything depends on
hitting the ball truly, and the man who always does so
has mastered one of the greatest difficulties of the art
of putting. A long putt can never be run down
except by a fluke when the ball has not been hit truly,
however exactly all the calculations of line and
strength have been made. Hitting the ball truly is
simply a question of bringing the putter on to it when
making the stroke to exactly the same point as when
the final address was made, and of swinging the putter
through from the back swing to the finish in a straight
line. The former depends largely upon the latter, for,
taking it for granted that the ball was finally addressed
by the exact part of the putter with which it was
intended to hit it—be that point the centre or nearer
the toe or heel—it follows that if the swing is quite
straight and true that part will come back to the ball.
It is clear that if another part, either nearer the toe or
the heel, comes back to the ball, there has been an
unintended deviation in the backward swing, and this
will be in operation during the time of impact and
the follow through, and the whole stroke correspondingly upset. The ball is either toed or heeled,
and it is sent off in the wrong way. A large section
of players fail also to hit the ball truly because they
do not always bring their putter on to it on the proper
level, or even consistently on the same level. The
sole of the putter should generally just skim the surface of the green, that is, it should be as low down as
is consistent with none of its speed or direction being
in the least degree affected by contact with the green.
The usual error is that of hitting the ball with the

putter too high up, and thus virtually half topping it. When this happens the ball goes away with a very heavy, unsatisfactory, and uncontrollable sort of feel. I am sure that true hitting is easier with the aluminium and wooden putters than with putting cleeks.

In making these observations I have in mind the fact that a few very fine putters always play from the toe of their club, but it is to be pointed out that there is a great difference between addressing your ball with the toe and playing from that place, and addressing it with the centre and playing from the toe. A ball that is truly hit is possible in the one case, but not in the other. As to the merits or otherwise of putting from the toe I can hardly be expected to say anything. Those who adopt this system presumably like it, and are satisfied with it, but nevertheless it is an eccentricity, and it is not a thing to cultivate. Another "fancy" way of putting which has been adopted by a few excellent players is one by which they give a short, sudden lift up to the putter at the moment that it comes into contact with the ball. The obvious tendency of such a movement is to give a little forward spin to the ball, and it is claimed for the practice that it gives an even run which will send the ball quite a long way, and yet keep it under control, so to speak, so that it will drop in the hole when it comes to it. One might say that the idea is that you get increase of running power without increase of speed and momentum. I do not doubt the wisdom, and certainly not the skill, of the fine players who putt according to this principle; but it seems to me a little doubtful as to whether there can be any gain by giving forward spin in this

way over the common practice of hitting the ball a
little harder; and one would imagine that all this
running power must increase the tendency to run
round the rim of the hole if the ball does not enter
exactly in the middle, while the lift-up must surely
make true hitting a trifle more difficult.

There are a few words that I consider I should
say here with reference to the choice of putter,
although the matter was touched upon briefly in an
earlier chapter. The question of pattern is not of so
much importance as the question of principle; and
when people are inclined to condemn what are
generally described as "novelties" in putters, it has
always to be remembered that with some of the most
fantastic of these, some players regularly achieve fine
results in putting which they have found themselves
quite unable to accomplish with any other clubs. Of
course, it is a matter of fancy and confidence, and
therefore one has no right to say—and, indeed, would
be wrong in saying—that any particular putter which
is fancied by a player is "a bad putter," or that he is
unwise for using such a putter. I do not like these
fantastic models myself, and even the sight of them
is often a little offensive to some players; but it has
to be borne in mind that some very excellent golfers
can putt better with them than with any others, and
that settles the question so far as they are concerned,
and silences anybody who may be disposed to criticise
their taste in such matters. The balance of a putter
counts for more than the shape of it.

Generally speaking, the favourite models in these
days are the aluminium putter, which is shaped something like the old wooden putters, and the simple
putting cleek, and while nobody can have a word

to say against the latter, I would like to state what I consider to be a great advantage of the former in the case of all golfers who do not come within the descriptions of "born putters," and who are subject to periods of very faulty putting, when their work on the greens proves very expensive to them.   There is something about the big block of aluminium which seems to steady the stroke very considerably, and the majority of players who putt with aluminium clubs play a more even, steady, following-through shot than they do when playing with iron putters.   I am sure that in a large proportion of cases those who putt with putting cleeks make more of a hit at the ball than a nice swing putt, and this circumstance has been considerably accentuated since the rubber ball came into general use.   On the other hand, it is very seldom that you see anyone "hitting at the ball" when playing with an aluminium putter, if for no other reason than that they very soon find it will not do.   With wooden and aluminium putters you must swing and follow through.   I am quite certain that I have been much steadier in my putting since I have used the aluminium club.   One of my chief faults when I used the putting cleek was that I was constantly "knuckling in."   There may be times when the little tapping stroke may seem to be advantageous; but I think it will be generally agreed that better and steadier putting does come, and must come, from the swing and follow through.

Golfers generally make a too slavish attachment to one particular kind of putter which may be their fancy, that is to say, they stick to a club when they have gone off in their play with it, and have lost all confidence on the greens.   I think that is a mistake.

A change of putter will do more than anything else
to bring back both confidence and success. Perhaps
it is as well that the change should not be to a new
putter, but to a kind of second favourite. There is
such a thing as getting tired of one's best club, and
for my own part, no matter how well or how long I
have been putting with my favourite club, at the first
sign of going off it I make a change. But there are
other and stronger reasons why players should not
look to one club only to carry them all through their
golfing lives, and the chief of them is that I do not
think that one putter, however much of a favourite it
may be, can be the very best suited to all circumstances. In saying this, I am, as may be supposed,
thinking more of the loft on the face of the putter than
of anything else. It can hardly be disputed that there
are times when it would pay better to take an iron
with only a very little loft out of one's bag to make a
putt with than to trust to one's ordinary putter; and
there are some fine players who, in the course of their
experience, have used nearly every iron club that
their bags contain, to make their putts with. This
does not show that they are too changeable and
eccentric in their tastes so much as that they think
more than others, and are not bothered by any
regard for custom. Probably more than half the
total number of players would be surprised at the idea
of their putting with anything else than the putter,
and if they attempted the experiment would consider
that they were doing a most dangerous thing; but
what if all these players were at the same time to feel
bound always to use their drivers from the tee, no
matter how short the hole at which they were playing
might be, or obliged always to use their brasseys for

their second shots, in spite of the bad lies that they may have found?

All that one can do is to suggest the need for occasional variation, and the manner and extent of it must be left to the player's individual judgment; but in one case, at all events, a principle may be set forth. For general use I am a strong believer in a putter having just a little loft. I know that some players like one with a perfectly straight face which does not impart the slightest drag to the ball, their theory being that such putters are capable of more delicate work than others, and that the ball answers more readily to the most delicate tap from them. There may be considerable truth in this, though obviously great skill and confidence on the part of the player are taken for granted. The difficulty that I and many other players experience with such putters is in keeping the ball straight with them. It is a very hard thing to do, and it is wonderful how much easier it is to be straight with a putter that has just the least loft on it—so much, say, as to enable one to see the face when one has taken the stance and soled the club. The advantage of such a shade of loft is most apparent when a little firmness is required, and also when putting from the edge of the green, when it is not only necessary to keep closely to a chosen line but to display considerable skill in the determination of strength. The strength of long putts can generally be more accurately regulated with a lofted putter than with a straight-faced one.

This is the kind of putter that I would recommend for what might be called a medium or an average green, if there can be said to be such a thing; but I wish to point out that the putter that is the best

suited to such a green is not so well suited to either a
very fast green or a very slow one, and that in each
of the latter cases the club best adapted to the circumstances is one with considerably more loft on it. A
very little consideration of each case will make this
matter quite clear, and' though the circumstances are
so different it will be seen that, so far as the player
is concerned, they create much the same kind of
difficulty. That difficulty each time is to gauge the
strength of the stroke. On a very slow green, perhaps rain-soaked or unusually woolly, one has to hit
the putt very hard ; in fact, in the case of a twenty
yards' putt up an incline on a stiff green, the strength
that would need to be applied to the putt might be
so great that nearly all that delicacy that enables a
player in form to reckon a putt up to a few inches
would be lost. The trouble is also that, while one has
to hit the ball so hard and start it off at such a pace,
it pulls up very suddenly when all the force that was
put into it has been exhausted. The result is that it
is quite easy to be either two yards short of the hole
or two yards past it, and that neither skill nor calculation will enable the player to avoid this liability under
such conditions—when putting with an ordinary
putter.

Then take a similar long putt on a very fast
green, slightly down hill, say—in fact, just the reverse
of the other conditions. By ordinary methods it must
be considered one of the most difficult things in
the whole of golf to control the ball in such circumstances, and the player's consciousness of the
enormous difficulty of the situation may be sufficient
to unnerve him. I remember that during the 1904
Open Championship at Sandwich, Mr. John Graham,

when right at the top of his game, and apparently
making a bold bid for the record of the course, fell
into great trouble on one of the greens on the outward journey when the conditions were just what I
have suggested as the most difficult. The greens
were sun-glazed and as fast as ever they could be—
far too fast for sure putting—and when Mr. Graham
came to putt on this particular green he had a
fairly long one presented to him, and it was down
a slight slope. Despite the difficulty of the situation it was the kind of putt that a man, playing
as this well-known player was just then, might expect
with a little luck to hole, and in any case it had to be
regarded as certain that he would be down in two.
But his ball slipped far past the hole, and lay not by
any means dead, and then, in putting back, it went
nearly as far past the hole as before. It came about
that either four or five putts were required, and what
looked like being a fine round was ruined.

Now in both these cases, when the greens are
very slow and when they are extremely fast, the best
putter for them is one with very considerable loft on
the face, and it will often be found that there is
nothing better than a fairly straight-faced iron or an
ordinary cleek, if it is big enough in the face to suit
the player. With this club and its great dragging
power the effect seems to be practically to reduce the
distance between the ball and the hole. Such is the
drag that the ball is simply pushed over a considerable part of the way, and it is only when it is
quite near to the hole that it begins, as it were, to run
in the usual way. The fact is that for the first part
of the journey the ball does not revolve regularly upon
its axis, as it does when approaching the hole, but

simply skates over the turf, and it will be found that
with a little practice the point at which it will stop
skating can be determined with very considerable
exactness.   When it does so stop, there is still so
much drag on it that it is very quickly brought
to a standstill.   Thus in both cases, of the very fast
and the very slow green, the ball can be played
without fear right up to the hole when the putter is so
well lofted as I have recommended.

A word may be said concerning the length of
the shaft and the place at which it is gripped.   Many
golfers grip very low down, even half-way between
the leather and the head.   If their putting, when done
this way, is first class, nobody can say anything to
them.   But if it is not first class, it may be pointed
out to them that the system is certainly bad.   It may
be allowed to pass for holing-out purposes ; but for
a putt of any length it cannot be good, for the club is
not swung in the ordinary easy manner by which
distance can be so accurately gauged.   The ball is
more or less poked along.   When a man putts in this
way he is putting largely by instinct, and even though
he may generally putt well, his work on the greens
cannot be thoroughly reliable.   No putting is so good
and consistently effective as that which is done with a
gentle, even swing, which can be regulated to a nicety,
and such putting is only possible when there is
enough shaft left below the grip to swing with.

As to the length of the shaft, many players,
because they find that they always grip their putters
a foot or so from the end of it, proceed in due course
to have the best part of that foot cut off, or, in
purchasing a new putter, they have the shaft cut very
short.   Are they quite satisfied that it is not better

to have a fair amount of shaft projecting up above
the place where they grip when that place is very low
down ? Often enough no consideration is given to
this point ; it is not imagined that the shaft above the
grip can serve any useful purpose. Yet it is constantly found that a putter cut down is not the same
putter that it was before, not so good, and has not
the same balance ; and, again, many players must have
been surprised sometimes, when doing some half-
serious putting practice with a cleek, iron, or driving
mashie, each club with its long shaft, to find out what
wonderfully accurate work could be done in this way.
The inference from all experience, having theoretical
principle to back it, is that the top or spare part of
the shaft acts as a kind of balance when the putter
is gripped low down, and tends materially to a more
delicate touch and to true hitting of the ball. A very
little reflection will lead the reader to believe that this
is so, and in some cases it may lead him towards a
revision of his present methods.

CHAPTER XI

PROBLEMS ON THE PUTTING GREEN

IT seems to me that people who depend upon holing their putts or laying them dead by science and calculation instead of by mere inspiration—which, at its best, would seem to be a rather uncertain quantity—have commonly six matters which they need to take into their close consideration when they come to make a long putt on a green presenting the difficulties which a golfer must expect to find, and without which putting would be far less interesting and trying than it actually is. Frequently the player seems to consider only three points, these being the upward or downward slope from the ball to the hole, the line, and the strength. It is not so often that the wind or the varying character of the surface of the green comes into the reckoning, although it often happens that these are factors of first-rate importance, and affect both the strength and the line to a very large extent, so that if the latter are calculated without taking account of these influences the results of the calculations must certainly be wrong and the putt cannot possibly be successful.

In the case of the most complicated, but still not at all uncommon, kind of putt, there are, then, six points for reckoning, and I would state them thus :—

(1) The distance of the ball from the hole, and

the strength needed to putt it over that distance if the green is flat, of average pace, and there are no complications.

(2) The state of the green as regards wetness and softness, or dryness and hardness, and the length and texture of the grass upon it, and therefore its relative speed.

(3) The extent and the character of the various inclines and undulations upon the green in the immediate neighbourhood of what, at a rough estimate, seems to be the line of the putt, how they will affect the run of the ball, and act and react upon each other, and therefore what is the true line of the putt.   (*N.B.* —The speed of the green, as already determined, will need to be taken into close consideration in making this calculation.   The faster the green the greater is the ball's susceptibility to slopes.)

(4) The exact nature of the surface of the green along the line of the putt as already determined, and how the character of the surface, and therefore its speed, varies along the whole length of that line, and particularly in the neighbourhood of the hole where the ball, with its motion almost gone, will be more susceptible to such variations than earlier in its journey.

(5) The direction in which the wind is blowing, and the extent of its influence upon the ball one way or the other.

(6) The question as to whether the green has just recently been cut or not, and, if it has been, the direction in which the mower was passed over it, relative to the line of the putt.

Taking these points in order, there is very little that need be said here in emphasis of the obvious

importance of the first one, except that in the case of
the player's unfamiliarity with the course upon which he
is playing, he must take care not to be deceived.   On
a course that is well known to him a player does not
usually experience difficulty in reckoning the distances ;
but in other circumstances he needs to be on his
guard against mistakes which it is very easy to make.
For instance, it may not be generally appreciated that
surroundings affect one's estimate of such distances
very considerably.   Thus a long putt often looks
shorter than it really is on a small green in a hollow
much enclosed by trees or other surroundings, while
a putt from the edge of a large green on an eminence
from which there is a wide view is in a sense dwarfed
and made to appear less than it is actually.   The
deception in each case may be very slight, but it is
sometimes sufficient to upset one's calculations.   This
point may be brought home better to the player by
reminding him how much longer a couple of yards
looks when measured on the floor of a room than it
does when measured on a lawn or road outside.   The
thing to bear in mind is that, though the player may
be deceived by surroundings and circumstances, the
ball never is.   The ball has to run the distance as it
really is, and not as it seems to be.

On the second point, the player will early on in
his game have the considerable advantage of the
experiences he has already obtained on the day ; but
he needs to remember that when the sun or wind is
drying a green that has been very wet through dew
or rain, it is often in a very puzzling state.   A green
that is quite wet and, at the same time, evenly wet,
is often fairly fast and quite easy to putt upon ; but it
is generally very much slower when it gets into the

11

medium and sticky state between wet and dry, the blades of grass then becoming very bristly and inclined to stick up and retard the progress of the ball. It will be borne in mind also that in the case of such rain or dew, greens that are in a very sheltered position, and also greens that are of the saucer shape, or which lie in hollows, naturally dry very much more slowly than others, and therefore their speed at a particular time of the day may not be the same as that of other greens at the same time. Another matter that makes a difference is the consistency of the turf below the surface grass, for when there has been recent rain that turf may be quite heavy and exert a retarding influence upon the green, even though to all outward appearances the green is dry and fast.

The third in our list of considerations may present considerable difficulty and call for close calculation. If the green is quite flat there is indeed no trouble to be met with under this head ; but, then, greens are not usually quite flat, and those that are so are becoming scarcer all the time, as clubs and green committees are becoming more enlightened upon the requirements of putting. When the slope either runs straight up or straight down towards the hole the case is simple, since the line, after all, is straight, and it is merely a question of strength. Also, when a player has to putt along the side of a slope the circumstances are not very puzzling, although more difficult than before. It is merely a question of how much borrow against the side of the hole has to be made, and, if so disposed, the player may slightly counteract the drawing tendency of the gradient by applying a little cut to his ball which will enable

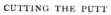

CUTTING THE PUTT   HOOKING THE PUTT

it to fight against the hill all the way. Putting with
cut, however, is at all times a difficult matter, and is
hardly to be recommended unless the player is very
confident of his skill or there are special circumstances, such as a stymie, which call for exceptional
measures. However, the reader may safely be left to
solve the problems of the one simple gradient unaided.
It is when this gradient changes along the line of the
putt, is less steep at some places than others, is
actually reversed from one slope to another in the
opposite direction, and is sometimes complicated by
being mixed up with a general upward or downward
slope, that the case becomes extremely difficult and
puzzling. The green is, as it were, twisted in many
different ways, and in such circumstances it is far from
being a simple thing to straighten out the calculation
as to the proper line of the putt.

In this case it is clear that one gradient will have
to be set against the next one and a balance struck,
and then a mean will have to be found between that
balance and the third gradient, and so on, all the way
up to the hole, and a point to be strongly emphasised
in these considerations is, that the nearer the ball gets
to the hole and the slower its speed the more is it
affected by such gradients. Thus a slope of, say, 1
in 10 may have five times the effect on the ball within
two yards of the hole as it would have if slope and
ball were twenty yards away and the ball had a
corresponding amount of motion in it. Anybody
can prove this for himself very easily by actual
experiment. Hit a ball hard because it has to go a
long way, and it will run across quite steep inclines, to
all intents and purposes unaffected by them ; but tap
it gently, as if it had to travel but a yard or two, and

in its almost lifeless state it will yield itself most completely to the gentlest incline, particularly if the green
is a fast one.   This matter has to be reckoned with
in dealing with such a complication of gradients as we
have suggested.   If you have in turn five different
gradients to encounter in the course of one long putt,
naming them in order, A, B, C, D, and E, of which
A, C, and E slope from the left, and B and D from
the right, each being of equal length and steepness,
it is evident that if the ball is travelling at the same
speed the whole way there will be a preponderance
in what might be called pulling-down power on the
part of the gradients A, C, and E, and that even on
that account alone an allowance needs to be made in
the way of borrow up the side of A.   Then the ball,
running at its top speed, will be very little affected
by the slope of A, and will be over B also before it
begins to show any great disposition to yield to the
influences upon it.   According to our assumption,
the last slope runs right down from the left side to
the hole, and the ball, then almost stopped and as
susceptible as it can possibly be to the incline, must
be brought up to a place from which it can run
straight down into the hole almost as the result of
the slope alone.   It is quite evident in a calculation
of this kind that the slopes D and E are the prime
factors, and that though slight allowances need to be
made for the others, the chief consideration is to be
attached to the last two.   A close study must therefore be made of these and of their probable effect
upon a ball running so slowly as this ball will be
when it encounters them, and particular notice must
be taken of the apparent speed of the green here-
abouts.   The point of direction which the golfer will

need to have in his mind in making such a putt as
this is not the hole itself, but a particular spot on the
slope E on the left-hand side of it. If the player
selects his spot with judgment, and then succeeds in
making his ball reach that, he will consider his work
as having been done, for if the ball does not then
drop near the hole it will only show that his calculations were out. To reach a particular spot on E in
this way it is evident that the most careful reckoning of D will have to be made, and there will be a
certain limited space on that slope through which it
will be necessary that the ball should travel if it is
to get to its right position on E. What I want to
impress upon readers is that while the early slopes
have influence, it is those that are to be found in the
last three or four yards of a 20-yards' putt that
have the most. Of course the case just presented is
a very exaggerated one, but at the same time it is far
from being an impossible one. Its special duty on
the present occasion is to drive home the hints I
have to offer, and to impress upon the golfer that the
calculation of the line of the putt on a sloping green
is not a matter for guesswork. No rule of thumb can
be given as to what allowances and borrows must be
made, since everything depends upon the particular
circumstances and the state of the green; but the
player who trains himself to make such calculations
as are necessary, though he may find them difficult at
first and frequently unsatisfactory, must almost inevitably improve in his putting, and will certainly
derive greater satisfaction from it.

Regarding the necessity of closely examining the
surface of the green all along the chosen line of the
putt, one must observe that no assumption is so com-

mon and so fatal as that the green is just the same all
the way from the ball to the hole. When the greens
are naturally good, and are in their best condition,
there may be little or no variation ; but such variation
is often considerable after a spell of drought, and
particularly in the case of inland greens. It has to be
remembered that a few inches of moss will act as a
tremendous brake on the speed of a putt, and that
clover, which is much commoner than moss, has a
more retarding effect. Putting greens ought to be of
the same grass throughout ; but Nature having something to say in this matter, it sometimes happens that
they are not, and that, indeed, there is some variety
of grasses on the greens, particularly if the green when
made was sown with a foreign grass, while though in
the majority of cases the putting differences may be
only small, it may sometimes happen that they are
such as must be taken into account.

Very few golfers take any wind that may be blowing sufficiently into their consideration when putting.
As often as not it is not reckoned at all, and even
when it is the player seems constantly afraid to make
full allowance for it. It would probably do the putting
of many golfers much good if some time, when a
good breeze is blowing, they were to take a few
balls out on to a putting green and mark the different
effects of putting with the wind and against it. Let
them putt from one corner of the green to the opposite
one with the wind, and then putt the ball back against
it, and the result of this simple experiment must inevitably be to give them a much fuller appreciation of
wind influence for the future, with corresponding
advantage to their putting. On a keen green especially, the effect of wind is most marked, and a side

wind, under such circumstances, will constantly baffle the player. Yet even then many people have the rashness to disregard it. One is rather inclined to think that the golfers of the old days studied such matters as this more closely than players generally do now, since the very slightest effects of wind variation, such as may be brought about by a player changing his position while a ball is on its way to the hole, is duly allowed for in the rules.

Concerning the last of the six points, it may be remarked that a newly-cut green is in alternate sections of fast and slow speeds, according to the way in which the machine-cutter has been taken over the various sections. The player sees these stripes in different tints, but he does not always reflect that the tints represent different speeds. They do so in this way : According to the direction in which the machine has been pushed, so are the blades of the grass bent down, that is to say, they are bent forward in the way in which the machine goes, and as the machine, when it has arrived at one side of the green, is taken back to the other in the opposite direction, it follows that the grass is bent down in opposite ways in adjoining sections of the width of the machine. It will very easily be understood that the ball will find more resistance when running against all the points of the blades of grass than upon the perfectly smooth carpet which has not such a point upon it—that is, that the green is much faster when you are, so to speak, putting along with the machine than when you are putting against it. The points of grass facing you give a dark complexion to the green, so that the light stripes represent the fast sections of green, and the dark ones the slower sections. Of course, if your putt was from the other side of the green the speeds would be reversed—that is, the fast sections would have become the slow ones, and *vice versâ*. The shades of colour would also have been changed, so that there would be no doubt upon the matter.

There is one other matter that I would like to mention near the close of this chapter on putting, and that concerns the question of the treatment of short putts when the greens are exceedingly keen and tricky. Too many players do not seem to believe, or to have the courage to act upon their belief, that the best thing to do with such putts is to bolt them, unless, indeed, the case is so free from anxiety that there are two for the hole.   There are times every season when, the greens being at their keenest, there is nothing more uncertain than a 2-feet putt, when the ball is merely trickled up to the hole.   It has such very little way upon it that on the slippery, and often gritty, surface it is most irregular in its run, and is susceptible to the slightest influence, yet with the green being so fast the player seems exceedingly afraid of putting any more strength into his stroke.   But it is certainly his best policy to make dead certain of his line to the centre of the hole and to play boldly.   By so doing the ball will at least keep to the line, and, as on a keen green it generally runs low down with very little jump on it, the chances are that if it goes to the middle of the hole it will go in, despite the circumstance of its extra speed.   If the hole is not taken dead at the middle it is extremely likely that the ball will run round the rim and stay out.   What prevents most players from having the courage to bolt these short putts when circumstances demand this policy, is their constant fear that if they miss the hole they will run so far away as to be not at all dead for the next attempt. Upon this point there are two things to be said, the first being that they ought not to miss the hole, and ought hardly to take into consideration the possibility of their missing it; and the second, that in anything like good golf it ought to be of far greater importance that the hole should be won than that it should be halved, which represents the only other contingency of any value. It frequently happens that the greens on the championship courses are extremely fast about the time of the championships, when there has been a fair spell of fine weather, and you will generally find that those competitors fare best who adopt the bold policy of bolting their short putts.

In any detailed consideration of the problems and possibilities of putting, a place must be given to stymies, though there is not much that can usefully be said on the matter in any work of instruction. The successful playing of a stymie, when it is possible to play it successfully, is chiefly a matter of confidence, and this is particularly the case when it is the pitching method that is resorted to. Players bungle their stroke and fail in their object because for the time being they are overcome with a sense of the difficulty and responsibility of the venture, just as they fail at other strokes through the same cause. Given complete confidence, the successful negotiation of a stymie is a much less difficult matter than it is imagined to be, though in the nature of things it can never be very easy.

I need not say that the pitching method is only practicable—and then it is generally the only shot that is practicable—when both balls are near the hole, and are so situated in relation to each other and to the hole that the ball can reach the latter as the result of such a stroke as enabled it to clear the opponent's ball. A player must decide for himself when this shot is on and when it is not. Assuming that it is the kind of shot to be played, it is just an ordinary chip up, with a clean and quick rise, the fact being remembered that the green must not be damaged. To spare the latter the swing back should be low down and near to the surface, which will check the tendency to dig. The thing that will ensure the success of the shot, so far as the quick and clean rise is concerned—and often enough success depends entirely upon that—is the follow through. Generally, if the club is taken through easily and cleanly, all will be well; but it is on this point that the confidence of the player most frequently fails, and the shot is foozled and the ball knocked hard up against the other—perhaps even sending it into the hole—because the man jerks and hesitates with his club. The confident follow through will make the shot, and there is really nothing more to be said about it. I think the mashie is the club best adapted to the purpose; but some players prefer the greater loft of the niblick.

As for the negotiation of a stymie by going round the other ball, this is obviously a question of the possibilities of putting a little cut or hook on the ball and borrowing from convenient slopes on the green, chiefly the latter, and the circumstances of each case must be left to suggest the most suitable methods. Whichever way I wish to make the ball curl, either round the other ball from the left-hand side, or from the right, I hit my own with the toe of the club, drawing the club towards me in the former case so as to make a slice, and holding the

STANCE AND ADDRESS

BACKSWING

THE STROKE SUCCESSFUL

PITCHING WHEN STYMIED

THE BALL HAS JUST LEFT THE CLUB

PASSING THE OPPONENT'S BALL

RUNNING TO THE HOLE

face of it at an angle—toe nearer the hole than the heel—in the latter, in order to induce a hook. You cannot do anything by hitting the ball with the heel of your putter. But remember that you can never get any work on the ball if the green is stiff. One need only add that at these times the green in the immediate neighbourhood of the hole should be most carefully examined for the slightest suspicion of undulation, for the very least of such can be of the greatest service, and, in fact, it is the least that is the most helpful. The existence of such an undulation is generally the only chance of a golfer who is stymied at long range, and too often he decides that no such chance is left to him without having made any proper examination.

As a last word, when you are off your putting— or if you have never been properly on it—ascertain whether you keep your body and head absolutely still when making the stroke. On the whole, I think this is the most frequent fault in putting, and it is one which is generally unsuspected or ignored; but any accurate putting is quite impossible when the body is swayed. It must be absolutely motionless—all quite still except for the swinging of the wrists and the arms. And keep your eye on the ball, not looking forward anxiously to the hole just as the club is coming on to the ball. This is a very human but a very fatal fault, and it costs many holes to those who make it.

CHAPTER XII

SYSTEMS OF PRACTICE

THE chief reason why most golfers fail to get on in the game as fast as they would like, or even as fast as they ought to do, is that they do not practise sufficiently. This may appear a rather simple and easy thing to say, and that the same thing could be said of other players in other games, but it may not be realised without a moment's reflection that the average golfer does not practise at all; that is to say, considerably more than half the men who have played the game for some years never undertake any systematic practice with the direct object of improving particular strokes in their game. The most that many of them ever do in this direction is occasionally to putt with a few balls on the green nearest to the clubhouse, or practise a few swings with the driver while waiting for their turn to start off. Their general programme is to play their two rounds a day in match play either against one man in a single or as one of a partnership in a foursome; this being varied occasionally by a medal round in a competition. The frequent result is lack of confidence in playing almost every shot that has to be played, and a nervous hesitation at every address. It almost seems sometimes that the player has forgotten several of the strokes since he last played; he has the feeling himself that he has done so, and another result is that he has no definite system, and you will find his stances and swings for the same sorts of shots varying to a very great extent. Playing one tee shot he will have the open stance, and at the next one it may be almost square; while in one case the ball may be brought opposite the left toe, and in the other it may be back again much nearer the right. Some of this constant chopping and changing about is unconscious sometimes, but at others it is simply the result of general uncertainty and lack of confidence, in which mood the player wants to try pretty nearly everything he can think of, and see which comes off best. At such times it seldom happens that any of the shots turn out very well, and it need hardly be said that a good golfer is scarcely ever made in this way. It often occurs that when a player has gone to a course in the hope of getting a match and fails to do so, he does not play at all, preferring no golf to golf without an opponent. This is a great pity, because these are particularly the times that should be devoted to serious practice—that is to say, practice alone, and with only one club, or a few. It is such practice as this that makes the quickest and surest improvement in a player, and it will often be found that a couple of hours spent in this way makes a difference to the game of a player, the effect of which may never be lost, and he will frequently find out in that short space of time more about the play with one or other of his clubs than he would ever do in any other way. At the present time he may have clubs in his bag with which, though he has to play with them in every match, and has done so for a long time, he is still not very familiar. He hardly knows what they can do ; he is not sure as to the best way of playing with them ; and, generally speaking, they are still more or less like strangers. This is just because he never takes the opportunity of having a little quiet play with them all alone at times when there are no other considerations to distract the attention from the complete study of their peculiarities.

There is nothing new in this advice in favour of one-club practice, but there is certainly as much need as ever there was, or perhaps more than that, to insist upon it, for in these days there is not generally the same painstaking study given to the improvement of the game as there was in the past generation. Therefore I am the strongest possible advocate of this kind of practice, and if the player goes about it in the right way it need never be the dull business that he may imagine it beforehand ; indeed, those who have cultivated it have often found it more interesting than ordinary play, and in some respects a great deal more satisfying. A man may have a couple of hours' practice with one or two of his clubs, and at the finish of it he will almost certainly feel that his game is considerably the better for it, and that though a little of the extra skill that he has gained that day may have disappeared by the next time he comes to play, still some of it will probably remain, and that anyhow he has learned a few things that he will never forget. The man who feels this at the finish must have pleased himself, whether he has played a match or not.

Now one-club practice should be done on a system, and the player who goes in for it had better mark out a proper scheme for himself, and adhere to it as closely as he can. He ought to go through the entire list of clubs that he has in his bag, or at all events those that are most necessary to his game, and which are in constant use, and he should have one or two days' practice with each of them separately, and after that he may make combinations of twos and threes. There are two ways of practising with a single club. One of them is to take out a number of old balls and play them with the club from the same position, and the other is to take out just two or three balls and wander over the links with them, playing them from place to place as they are found. There are distinct advantages and disadvantages to each of these systems which may not have been thought about. In the first place, the player who finds a quiet part of the course quite off the ordinary line, is generally secure from interruption while he remains about the same place and continues his practice from the same spot ; and this is not such a small matter as it may appear, for there is nothing more irritating than to be continually having to move out of the way of matches that are coming along, and not only having one's own practice spoiled but knowing that one is making a nuisance of oneself. If a more or less retired spot is found, the private investigations into one's system can be carried out in the most thorough and satisfying manner. Another great advantage of practising with one club from the same place, hitting several balls one after the other, is that one is able to make another shot immediately with a more or less adequate knowledge of the mistakes that were made with the one that was played just before, and with the result of them fresh in the mind. Corrections or variations in methods can be made instantly, and changes in effect noticed and compared. It is wonderful how quickly the impression of all the various circumstances that attended the playing of a shot will fade away while one is walking from the place where it was played to that where the ball has run to, until by the time the ball is reached it is only a vague one that is left.   The one great disadvantage of standing-still practice in this way is that the player almost necessarily plays rather too quickly, and the result is that he tires and becomes careless.   In the actual playing of a match you have an average of about a minute between each stroke, and this is used for the complete recuperation of the body and mind from the effects of the previous one.   Some people may say that the efforts are not so great that any recuperation of this sort is necessary ; but those who say that should try the effect of standing in the same place and making, say, a dozen full swings with a driver at an imaginary ball.   By the time the turn for the twelfth arrives, most men of average strength will feel thoroughly dead-beat, and incapable either of swinging properly or of giving the mind earnestly to the details of the stroke.   After an experiment of this kind they will not generally make light of the expenditure of physical force in playing golf; and at the same time they will realise the danger of too much practice from the same place with the one club. In a little while it will become very careless and hurried.   On the other hand, the comparative merits and faults of walking part way round the links with only one club and two or three balls will be clear from what we have already said.   It gives the best opportunities for the really thoughtful study of the game, and the player makes every shot with the utmost care and attention to detail.

Now the best thing, in my opinion, is to combine both systems; and, in the course of a morning or afternoon, to do a little practice from one place with many balls, and also to go partly round the course with two or three. This can be done in a particular and easy way. If the man is practising the long game, or the semi-long game with his driver, brassey, or cleek, let him play, say, half a dozen balls from one of the tees, and then go forward, pick them up, or perhaps play second shots. From the next tee he can do the same thing, and so on. If, on the other hand, it is the short game that is being practised, and the player has out with him an iron or a mashie, he can play two or three balls through the green until he gets well within range of the hole, and has a definite mark to try at, when he can drop a few more. Even in the case of the long game, I believe in the practising player aiming at a definite mark for some of the time, partly because this cultivates accuracy, and partly because such a change in the idea of the practice greatly relieves the monotony of it. He should practise long shots to the same mark from various positions. By means such as this the best sorts of practice are obtained at the same time, and the player is not unduly tired.

As I have said, the whole bag of clubs may be gone through in this way, and it may often pay very well to give two or three successive days to one club. Begin with the driver and go right through the list, giving extra time and extra practice to any club with which particular difficulty is experienced. After you have had days with two or three clubs, go back for a day to the one you had out first. Thus, having got as far as the cleek or driving mashie, go back to the driver; and in the same way, when you have got down to the mashie, go back for a spell or two with the cleek, and in fact keep reverting after a short interval to any club about the quality or accuracy of play with which there may still be grave doubts. One positive rule may be laid down, and that is that practice with any particular club should never be given up while there is still doubt and hesitation as to what is the proper way to use it.

It is difficult to say what club is best to practise with in this way. Of course there is the outstanding rule which has already been suggested, that one should practise most with the club one has least confidence in, even if this is not the most pleasant form of practice; but leaving this on one side, I think the average golfer will derive most benefit from putting in plenty of time to practising and experimenting with his cleek and iron. I say this for the particular reason that while the average player has only one shot with most of his other clubs, and does not generally need more than one, he has often only one with these chief iron clubs when he certainly ought to have more, and can obtain them with a very little practice. It is with such clubs as the cleek and the iron that most of the fine finessing work, as it might be called, is done, and it is by their aid that he gets up to the hole from medium long range through all kinds of difficulties and risks.

Just think of the position. When a man is from within 80 to 100 yards of the hole, and has just an ordinary approach to play with his mashie, it is, barring accidents, certain that he will be on the green in one stroke and then down in two putts—a total of three. With a little luck either in the pitch

or with the long putt he may be down in two, but
he cannot in the least degree reckon on this, and
it is not likely. Three is his number, and three
is almost a certainty unless a mistake is made.
Now think of the case where an approach shot
has to be played from a distance of 130 to 160
yards. An iron or a cleek has to be taken; there
has to be a slightly greater expenditure of force;
and, however skilful one may be, it cannot but be
more difficult to get on the green when the mark is
so much farther away, and is none the bigger for
that, and the difficulty is increased by the fact that the
shot has to be played for a fair amount of run.
There may be many other points to consider, such
as the effect of the wind, the lie of the ground, and so
forth : so that in this case the player is not so certain
to be on the green in one and then down in three ;
yet at the same time that is the number, and he is
expected to be down in it, and will probably lose
the hole if he does not. You often hear many players
say that they would as soon have an approach with
an iron or a cleek as with a mashie, and this may be
so if they are unable to do any sort of good with their
mashies, and usually hit nice crisp shots with their
irons ; but in the absence of any glaring defect in
one's system of play, this certainly cannot be the
case.

When the distance from which these medium
long approaches have to be played varies so much
as it does, and when the circumstances in which
the shots have to be made are constantly so very
different, it is clear that exactly the same kind of shot
cannot be quite as good in all cases, and that it will be
far better for the player if he can make such variations

as will suit the different cases rather better than the
ordinary stroke. These variations are chiefly of three
sorts. There is, firstly, the regulation of the different
lengths of swing in order to get various distances ; and
this is worth weeks of practice in itself, because it is
only by playing ball after ball, and changing the
length of the swing continually, that the player can
arrive at a proper understanding as to what length
of swing gives what length of ball. Secondly, there
is the matter of controlling the amount of run on the
ball after it pitches, which resolves itself into the
question of how much cut one can give to it when
necessary ; and thirdly, there is the matter of altering
the trajectory of the ball to suit special circumstances.
The chief thing in this section is the cultivation of
some kind of a push shot—a low, forcing shot in
which the ball is taken rather high up, and the turf
cut after it has been hit, and in which the body and
club go forward at the finish of the stroke, the club
then being pointed straight out in the direction of the
hole. There are many advantages to this stroke, and
it is particularly useful when playing long approaches
against the wind. All players of experience should
have these various strokes with the clubs at their
disposal, and when they have them it is almost
as if they had three clubs for each one. Thus the
player's game is rendered much stronger and more
resourceful than it would otherwise be, and there is
no feeling of pleasure better than that of knowing that
one can do several different things with one's favourite
iron, and that each time a shot has to be played with
it one picks out that which is the best for the time and
the situation.

There are other minor variations of iron play that

one has to practise as well as the three that have been mentioned. For example, there is the way of slightly varying the angle of loft with which the club is laid to the ball. The player should not get into the way of doing too much of this sort of thing, and unless the circumstances do call clearly for a variation he should let the club have just its natural and proper lie. The risk of something going wrong with the shot when its lie is interfered with in this way must always be slightly increased. Nevertheless there are times when nothing will suit the purpose in view but a slight laying back of the face of the club, or, on the other hand—and this more frequently—a slight bringing forward of the hands and turning the face of the club in somewhat, so as to impart a little hook to the shot. It is generally fatal to try to do these things for the first time in a match, or when one has only tried them on a few other occasions, and that in the course of serious match play also; whereas, when they have been practised well beforehand, they are comparatively simple things to do when wanted, or at all events the player has plenty of confidence in attempting them, and does know how to go about them. That is everything.

By such one-club practice as this with an iron, not only will the player get several different strokes from each club, but it very frequently happens that he also gets one or two of his own, to all intents and purposes his own inventions, strokes that he plays in some peculiar way with some special little trick in the laying of the face of the club to the ball, in the stance, the grip, or in the swing of the club. The man suddenly finds one day by accident that as the result of doing his stroke in some peculiar way a certain result is brought about, and quite a good one at that, and he finds that he can do the same thing again in the same way, and that, in fact, he has got a new stroke. Now, I am sometimes asked whether a player ought to stick to strokes of this kind which he makes for himself, which are not generally reckoned in what might be called the standard strokes of the game. I can only answer that there is no rule saying what kinds of strokes shall be played and what shall not, and that the player will do well to get as many of these specialities as he can, and to stick to them all, always making sure that they are really good and reliable strokes, and that they do not take the place of something simpler and more generally understood.

With such constant and thorough practice as this with one's iron clubs it is next to impossible for any man not to become a greatly improved player, and to find that there are possibilities in the game and its science, even for him, that he had never dreamt of.

Approach play with a mashie is, of course, a thing in itself, and the man who practises it will do well to try approaching the same hole with a number of balls from several different points ; and, to make this practice all the more valuable, he should choose a hole that is on a slope, and then approach it with a number of balls from the downhill side, again from the uphill side, and then from different angles, and if he previously knew how to play his mashie properly he may learn more about the science of the short game . in an hour spent in this way than he would in a year of ordinary play. Pitch and run have to be varied shot by shot ; sometimes a great deal of cut is wanted, and at others none at all, and different allowances have to be made for the lie of the land

and the slope of the green. Another most useful
sort of practice in approach play is to play in the
same line at the hole from different distances, beginning at, say, sixty, and then increasing it by ten
yards after every half-dozen shots. It is a very good
thing also in practising approach play to have by one
at the same time the club with which one does the
running-up shots, and to practise these at the same
time, or in a separate spell afterwards. A comparison
of ways and results is especially valuable in a case of
this kind, because it will teach the man when exactly
he ought to play the running-up shot and when he
ought to pitch his ball—a question upon which in
actual play he is frequently in much doubt. After
a little practice of this sort he will see at once what
is the merit of each shot, and with which he can
depend on getting nearest to the hole under certain
circumstances. There is, of course, not the same
objection to practising large numbers of shots from
the same place or close by it, of this pitching or run-
ing-up sort, as there is in the case of practising drives
or fairly heavy shots with iron clubs, because there
is little expenditure of strength ; but the player should
be careful to stop at the first sign of tiring or of carelessness. In mashie play this is generally indicated
by constant failure to get the club through at the
finish of the stroke.

I have still a few other things to say about this
one-club practice, so advantageous and important do
I consider it to be. In the first place, for the sake
of the course, do not practise iron shots from the
tees, because it is wrong that you should thus run
the risk of spoiling them in this way, particularly as
the ordinary fairway will serve your purpose just as

well. In practising play with the driver it will generally be a good thing to carry a rubber tee in the pocket; and, after having played the shot from the proper teeing ground, to tee the ball again at the place where it is found. This will give you the advantage of more tee-shot practice than you would otherwise obtain; and, after all, if you have your driver out it is driving practice that you want, and not brassey play. Another point of advice is, that until you have had a full course of practice with the different clubs separately, it will be better not to take them out in twos and threes, much less take the whole bag of them out for a round. Many players who want to do a lot of practice with just one club only, nevertheless will always take a putter out with them also, just to putt out with and finish off the play at the different holes. The effect of this is to distract their attention from the proper subject and to do a lot towards spoiling their practice with the other club.

That brings me to another point, which is, that for the sake of variety, and also for the advantages that it gives, it is a good thing sometimes to play a whole round with one club, if that club is of the right kind, namely, one with which a fair length can be obtained in shots through the green. What I mean is that a whole round of quite a satisfactory character can be played with a cleek or an iron; but a mashie is hardly suitable, as one would be so often tempted to try to get more length with it than one ever ought to do.

I suggested at the beginning of this chapter that this kind of practice ought not to be dull and un-interesting, and it need never be so if the player goes about it in the right way with a desire for the improvement of his game. There is no reason why he should not give it a little competitive interest all its own in order to make it still more interesting. For example, he may count the number of strokes that he takes for a certain number of holes with one club, and also with the other clubs of the bag ; he can try to beat his own record for the number of successive shots with which he reaches the green from a distance of, say, 160 yards when playing with his cleek, the same with his iron from 140 yards, and in the case of pitching practice he can take the number of successive shots with which he manages to place the ball within a particular radius from the hole—representing just that very useful sort of pitch which leaves the player with a good chance of getting down in one putt. He can compete against himself at running-up in the same way, and in the case of short shots of this kind, from not far off the edge of the green, it should be the object of the player to get within a yard or so of the hole. Of course this represents a very well-judged shot, and one that will not come off every time, but it has to be remembered that a very short run-up of this sort really cannot be considered a complete success unless the ball is laid fairly dead. In this and other ways which may suggest themselves, the player may make his practice thoroughly interesting, and constantly give himself some special object to try for, the achievement of which will give him scarcely less satisfaction than winning a match.

This sort of self-competition is just serious enough, but not so much so as to interfere with the proper working of the player's ideas and his system. He is never so desperate as to trust blindly to some old bad method, with which he has long been familiar, just to try to bring off one particular shot. Instead of that he will go on playing them all as he ought to do, and he has the very great advantage of being able to play the shot over again if it has not resulted as he expected, and in this way to find out exactly the right way of doing it. This is where there is all the difference between this kind of practice and its value, and ordinary play. Now and then at the beginning of a match the man may make a shot according to some idea that he has, and it may fail because of some little trifling thing that was wrong with his stance, his grip, or his address to the ball. But he has no opportunity of trying it again immediately, and satisfying himself that this was so, and proving that the shot could be done properly in the way that he thought of. He has to let it go until exactly another shot of the kind is presented, and by that time he has either forgotten about the old one or thinks he would rather not experiment any more, or at all events not this time. As the game goes on, and the issue becomes more critical, he is less and less inclined to try different ways of doing things. In this he is generally wise, because at the most serious part of a game it is generally better to do a thing in the way one really knows how to do it, even if it is not a good one and is rather uncertain, than it is to try a way with which one is altogether unfamiliar, but which one believes is the right one. The risk is too great. Thus, what with one thing and another, the man who only plays his matches, and never goes in for a thorough course of one-club practice, is always in some kind of difficulty, always afraid to make some shot or other, and gets into certain bad systems of play that he never gets out of, for the simple reason that he does not dare to try the right ways in his matches.

I have written at great length upon this question
of practice, and practice particularly with one club ;
but I am sure that I have not said a word too much,
because some system of this kind must be the basis of
the programme of every player who wishes to make
himself throughly proficient. If he not only devotes
the times when he cannot get a match to practice of
this kind, but also gives up definitely one morning or
afternoon a week to it, and sometimes in the summer,
when the days are long, makes this kind of practice his
occupation instead of playing a third round, he will do
his game far more good than he could in any other way.

Of course there are other aids to progress. One
of them consists in watching really good players, and
an earnest student of the game should not miss any
good opportunity of this kind that comes his way. It
will always be well for him to remember that most of
the best players of the day owe much of their success
to watching and studying the methods of others. One
or two hints may be offered in this matter. In the first
place, the majority of people who go to see the golf that
is played at championship meetings, open competitions,
and exhibition matches, make the mistake of watching
the ball and its flight too much, and not giving
sufficient attention to the player, that is if they are
students of the game who want to learn something, and
not mere sightseers whose chief concern is as to who
will win. This is a time when it is not a good thing
to keep one's eye on the ball, in fact the less it is kept
there the better. Even when a watcher is anxious to
find out the player's methods, he often defers his
examination until the shot is made or almost made,
and then it is too late. The time to watch the player
is from the very moment when he goes up to his ball

to play the shot, noticing how he takes up his stance, how he grips his club, how he addresses the ball, and then every detail of his swing the whole way through. It will generally be impossible to notice the whole of a swing in one stroke, and therefore one should content oneself with an examination of the up-swing one time, and the down-swing another, and should always try to connect any peculiar effect of the stroke with some distinguishing feature of the method. Unless this can be done the watching is after all very nearly worthless, because it is not much use knowing that a man does a particular thing if one does not know why he did it and what effect it has. The aim of course is to see all that is done by these good players, and copy anything that really seems to be a good idea or a good point of style, being at the same time one that is well suited to the game of the watcher. He must remember that everything that he sees may not be good for him, and in fact he would do well to pay most attention to the game of players whose style is most like his own, or the ideal that he has set himself. If he does not do this he may get himself into a rather bad mix-up. At the same time he may remember that the man who always does everything right is not yet born, and never will be ; so if the watcher is anything at all of a player himself he need not always take it for granted that the man he is watching does the shots in the best way, or the way that is better than his own.

Another great help towards the improvement of any man's game is plenty of foursome play. There is scarcely anything like it, provided it is backed up by a proper amount of one-club practice. It will generally be better for the player if he gets himself partnered with a player who is better than himself, because that will serve to increase the sense of responsibility, and at the same time encourage him to do things as they ought to be done and in a good style, which is the chief advantage of foursome play from the point of view of the good that it does to one's game.

If the player means to go in for golf at all thoroughly, he should never miss opportunities of playing the game and practising it under conditions that are more trying than they generally are. A man who is merely a fair-weather golfer is generally in serious difficulties when he is put to play a round in a high wind or when there is a lot of wet about. Even if he does not seek these opportunities, he ought at least not to avoid them. Besides, golfing in a wind can be thoroughly enjoyable when the player goes about it in the right way, and studies playing the shots in the manner that is best adapted to the circumstances. But particularly is one-club practice a fine thing on a windy day. Most players fail in a wind, not because they have not often played in one, but because they have never practised in one. They have only made their shots when it was necessary to get the ball away in some fashion, and at such times they have not had the courage to play the ball as they have been told it ought to be played at such times, and in the way which they themselves believe is the right one. Consequently they never have enough confidence. An hour's practice with the driver and the cleek now and then on a windy day would make a world of difference in a matter of this sort.

It is just the same with bunker play. Every player is in some bunker or other almost every time he plays—or he is very fortunate if he is not—and yet how very few players do you find who really play their bunker shots in the right way, or, what is more, from their point of view, how comparatively few get out in one stroke. Why is this? They do not know how to play bunker shots because they have never practised them. The sight of a man with half a dozen balls in a bunker trying to get them out from different and difficult positions may not be a very fine one of its kind; but that is the man who will go a long way. The average player gets into a bunker and then plays some sort of a shot out as best he can. He may know, or think, there is a rather better way, but at a time like this he feels he must not experiment; and so he sticks to the old defective method. This goes on from match to match and from week to week, and so the player in a case like this never knows how to play a bunker shot; yet there is scarcely one in the game that is better worth knowing or that pays better, and any man must be convinced of this who reflects upon the number of holes that he has lost in important matches through his inability always to get out of the bunkers in one stroke. What too few players realise, also, is that there are more clubs for bunker shots than niblicks, and also that the niblick is for other things than bunkers. Let them just think over the fact that Mr. John Ball frequently, if not generally, plays his bunker shots with an iron, or a mashie.

My last remarks in this chapter must be on the question of change—change of all sorts, opponents, links, system, and so on. Sometimes it is good, and sometimes otherwise. Of course it is a bad thing for a player to keep to methods and to a system of play that he knows to be wrong. The sooner he gets out of it the better; but at the same time it is well to remember that it is not generally wise to give up a system, even if one has doubts about it, until it is proved to be both bad and a failure. What I chiefly want the reader to avoid is the continual chopping and changing about, one system one day and another the next, the open stance this week and the square one the week after, that is characteristic of the play of some golfers, who never seem to have the patience to persevere properly as they ought to do with one settled system. Do not adopt any particular method or system in the first place just because somebody of perhaps no great authority has told you that it is a good thing, but only when you have thoroughly satisfied yourself that it is really good, and also that it seems to be well suited to your own game. Then when you have adopted it, give it every chance and do not discard it quickly just because it does not do wonders for you at the very outset. Every new shot and every new system need a great deal of practice before first-class results can be got from them, or else there cannot be much good in them.

So with clubs. Some players are never satisfied unless they are buying new clubs, and directly they go off their game they come round again to the belief that their clubs do not suit them, or at all events they feel that they have never got the iron, or mashie, or cleek, or whatever it is, that they really want. So they make another purchase, and discard one of the clubs in their bag to make room for it ; but in the course of a few days it is quite likely that the discarded club will have returned, and that the new one will have been added to the store of others of its kind that were given a brief trial and were not afterwards wanted. This is not good for the player, but it is quite good for the clubmaker.

I am far from saying that it is not a very good thing indeed to make a fresh start with a fresh club at times when it seems that the shot can never be done properly with the old one. It has happened in hundreds of cases that a new club has given new confidence, and has suited the player in a way that his old one never could have done; and it is one of the best ways of getting a player out of difficulty when other means have failed. But a new club should not generally be chosen impulsively at a time of great disappointment, and one should seldom go into a shop making up one's mind that a new club shall be bought whether it is exactly the thing that is wanted or not, particularly as the exact thing can nearly always be got by waiting a day or two. The purchase of a new club should be regarded in a way as a serious matter, and it is one that should be thought over carefully beforehand, and done with great deliberation.

Then there is the question of changing one's opponents. For that there is a great deal to be said. Sometimes you come across players who make a point of playing in each other's company whenever possible. It is always the same match with them time after time. No doubt this sort of thing has much to recommend it in some ways. It may be very convenient in the matter of arranging dates and times, the players know each other's little ways and habits, and the play between them is very pleasant from the social point of view. But it may not be the best thing for the golf of these men. When they play together time after time, and the victory of either over the other ceases to be anything at all of a novelty, it is thought nothing of, and the next thing is that the matches are played more or less carelessly, and there is indifference to the result, which ought never to be the case. Of course this is not always the state of affairs, and it depends largely on the temperaments of the individuals ; but in the nature of things there must nearly always be some sort of a tendency in this direction. On the other hand it is, perhaps, not wise to play too much with complete strangers. In a general way one does not play one's best at such times, and sometimes one is over-anxious. You never know what the temperament or the keenness of the other man is, and what are his views on certain matters, and the doubt may affect your play. Most golfers have a fairly large circle of golfing friends, and the best plan is to play with a fair number of them in turn, avoiding playing with one man almost exclusively, and in the same way taking complete strangers on as little as possible, except when circumstances of courtesy and the consideration of others who may be without matches render it obligatory.

Finally, there is the question of change of courses, and for a golfer who is getting well on to something like a good game there is nothing that will help it still more than playing on a course that is comparatively new and strange, and the better that course is as a test of golf the better will be the improvement in the play of the man who visits it. Most golfers play too much on one course, and in these days, when it is difficult to move about anywhere without coming across one, they do not take sufficient advantage of their opportunities to visit strange ones, where they will be called upon to play shots of quite a different kind from those which they are accustomed to

13

play. When a man plays over the same course day after day and year after year, with only a change on the occasion of a long holiday, he gets into a very mechanical way of playing all the strokes on that course, particularly if it is not really a very difficult one, or the holes are not laid out in the very best way. He has often got to know too well that he can get his 4's at certain holes, no matter what sort of a shot he plays from the tee. Besides, even when a course is really good, it is seldom that it has all sorts of shots on it, and therefore the golfer who goes away always gets something new and has something taught him. Also, it is necessary to get into the way of playing at strange holes amid strange surroundings. The man who never goes away from his home course often feels utterly at sea and unable to bring out anything like the game of which he is capable when circumstances make it necessary for him to play on some other links. It is partly for this reason that many players who keep to one course are very often handicapped lower than they ought to be, because they have got into a mechanical certain kind of way of playing their own course, and win medals on it from time to time, but are quite unable to do that kind of thing on any other links. A man's real golfing form is represented by his ability to adapt himself to any links, or his average game over several, which amounts to the same thing, and not the game that he can play over the one course that receives nearly the whole of his attention.

CHAPTER XIII

HINTS AND IDEAS

HERE I have a few things to say on various matters that have been more or less unavoidably omitted from other chapters, and first there is the question of what may be regarded as some minor points of the player's equipment. It is sometimes a difficulty with players to know whether boots or shoes are best suited to their game, and this is not by any means such an unimportant matter as it may seem to others who experience no such difficulty. To my mind it is not altogether a mere question of taste, although those golfers who have a strong preference in either direction (preference generally meaning confidence) will do well to abide by it. It is all-important in the playing of every shot that the man should feel a sense not only of perfect security but of strength in the feet, for, as we have already seen, the feet, though they do not move, or only bend over, have not a little to do with the proper making of the stroke. Every player must have experienced the great difference that there is between playing in a pair of boots or shoes that are not only comfortable but fit well, and another pair that are the opposite in these points. In the one case there is that feeling of firmness that means everything, and in the other there are doubts arising at the moment that the stance is taken up, and the player wriggles about from one position to another, not finding any that completely satisfies him in the degree of security that he obtains. He does not generally suspect that some, if not all, of this difficulty may arise from the fact that his footgear may not fit him properly, but he would often find a wonderful difference to be effected merely by changing it to something that fitted better. Therefore one is inclined to say that it is of the utmost importance that a golfer's boots and shoes should suit exactly, and it is difficult to understand why so many men should treat this part of their outfit with so much neglect. You sometimes find golfers who consider that any pair of old boots or shoes that may have been discarded from their original use are good enough to play the game in, and sometimes when they come to buy new ones for the purpose they reflect that appearances do not count for much in playing this game, and this feeling leads them to the purchase of something very inexpensive, and perhaps too much so. It might be different if they would remember that the average player does a great deal more walking in his golfing boots and shoes than he does in any others that he possesses. Thus if a man plays, say, only three rounds a week, that means, with the extra walking that he does in the neighbourhood of the course, and perhaps in getting to it as well, at least fifteen miles a week, or getting on for a thousand miles in the course of a year. Surely, then, it is necessary that boots and shoes upon which the man may be dependent for his comfort for so long should be well-fitting, as well as it is possible for them to be, and that the leather of which they are made should be at the same time strong and pliable. Therefore I may be excused for suggesting that it is better in every case that these things should be made specially for the individual, to fit him as well as it is possible for them to do, and that no trifling expense should be spared in order to make them as good as they can be. There is another point, however, beyond that, to mention, and that is the one already hinted at, as to the respective merits of boots and shoes, which, as I have said, is not to my mind a mere question of taste. A player who has feet and ankles that are very strong may quite well play in shoes, and perhaps in such a case he will be all the better for them. But if his feet have not this golfing quality I think that in many cases he would do better to play in boots, for they certainly promote security, and with it confidence.   I think that a small man of no great physical strength is generally more " at home " when playing in boots.   However, though this is generally the case, it is, of course, a matter upon which no definite rule can be laid down.

It should be added to the foregoing, that many players find it a difficulty to know what to wear in the summer time when they not only wish to dispense with the nails in the soles of their boots and shoes if possible, on account of the weight that they feel from them in the warm weather, and in the soreness which they sometimes cause the feet when the turf has got baked very hard, but also because when the turf is in that state it is often difficult to maintain anything like a firm stance by means of these nails, which are very much apt to slip.   There is, then, a natural inclination towards rubber soles, and these are excellent so long as they are adopted in a wise and thoughtful fashion, and in conjunction with proper boots or shoes.   You

sometimes find players going from heavy leather to a
thin pair of canvas shoes, and then wondering why
they suddenly find that they cannot hit any sort of
a tee shot, not generally suspecting the real cause,
which is nothing more or less than those canvas shoes,
which not only give a most unaccustomed feeling to
the player, although it may seem a pleasant and
comfortable one, but afford no proper support to the
feet while they perform the work that they have to
do during the making of the swings, and particularly
the pivoting.   It must surely be the exception for a
player in his game to be quite unaffected by changes
of this sort, which are extremely important.   It is not
only that this sort of shoe gives no support to the
feet, but, to make matters worse, it is often enough
without heels of any sort.   This is altogether bad.
Rubber soles are best—and then they are very good—
when attached to leather uppers, or at all events
uppers that are made of some strong and binding
material, and the soles should be quite thick, and
have heels as large as those on the pair of boots or
shoes that are most generally worn by the player.   For
myself, I have a preference for the aerolite rubbers let
into a leather sole, giving, as they do, the maximum of
comfort and security.

Then there is the old question of gloves or no
gloves.   If a player has very tender hands, or hands
that must be preserved for other things that are more
important than golf, and he feels that he cannot do
without gloves for this reason, that ends the matter
so far as he is concerned.   He must wear them.
But, if it can be managed, I think it will generally be
better for the game of any man if he can dispense with
gloves, for they interfere rather with the grip and the

work of the fingers, and they naturally diminish the delicacy of the touch, which is a matter of some importance even in the long game.

There are two trifling things that a player might be recommended to carry in the pocket of his caddie bag, particularly when he goes golfing any distance from his head-quarters. One of them is a piece of chalk, which will do very well in the form of a square of billiard chalk, coming in very useful for chalking the faces of the wooden clubs on a wet day. Some players who have not had a very large experience may think that this is one of those special attentions given to clubs which may be left to the very best golfers, whom it would be affectation on their part to copy ; but this is not at all the case. The chalking of the face has the double effect of keeping the wet out of the grain of the club, and so preserving its life much longer than it would otherwise be, and at the same time of assisting the club to grip the ball properly under conditions which are not by any means so favourable to doing so as they usually are, but which on the other hand have a strong tendency to induce skidding. Many a time on a wet day, when the face of the club gets into a thoroughly greasy state, the ball slips off at a sharp angle, and the shot is believed to have been badly sliced, when one of the reasons for the failure was skidding due to the wet. The other thing to carry is such a small tin of vaseline as may be bought for a penny, which will serve to grease the iron clubs after the day's play is over, particularly at such a time of the year or under such special conditions that the likelihood of their rusting in a short space of time is considerable. In spite of all their promises, caddies are not generally to be relied on to give the necessary attention to the oiling of the clubs at times like this, and even when they do oil them the task is not always done well enough. Iron clubs rust very quickly at the seaside in the summer time, and there is nothing more disagreeable than starting a morning round with one's clubs all dull and brown with the overnight coat of rust. These matters of wet and damp remind one also that every player who does much golfing should have a caddie-bag with a hood attached to it, this hood being kept tucked away inside when the weather is fine and it is not wanted, but brought out for the protection of the clubs when it is raining. There can be no doubt that the life of a set of clubs is considerably lengthened by this means, and besides that the player is enabled to get considerably more satisfaction from his game at a time when he wants all that he can get.

I am often asked the question as to whether it is a good thing to do any sort of training for an important golf match, or whether, in other words, one ought to train if one wants to play the best golf. That all depends, to my mind, on what is meant by training. The point is, that I do not think it is in the least degree possible to play golf well any more than it is possible to play any other good game well, one involving considerable physical exertion and demanding steady hands and nerves, and the steadier the better, unless one is in really good physical condition, and the general health is good. But there is some difference, one may think, between being in good general health for most of the time, and being in that peculiar state of physical fitness which comes to a man who has trained for a period, but who at most other times neglects many of the best rules of health, and is then not at all in good condition. In the latter case the man might do better in a contest involving a great physical strain for just a short period, as in a footrace or something of that kind ; but I do not think that that sort of training would do a golfer any good. You cannot train to play good golf, that is rather better golf than you generally play, in a week or two. The man who wants to play the best game that is possible in his case, needs to keep himself in training always, or, in other words, never to need training. His habits must always be fairly regular, without making his life a misery to him, and he should take particular care to avoid anything that may have a tendency to disturb his nerves, such as excessive smoking and short hours of sleep. However, some golfers seem to be able to stand these things without its making the slightest difference to them, when others are very soon wrecked by them, so there is really no fast rule in the matter. I consider that it is a good thing, when a golfer has a period of golf just in front of him to which he attaches special importance, not to go in for any special training or make any pronounced difference in his mode of life, but just to accentuate somewhat the regularity of it. By this I mean that it could hardly fail to be a good thing to be very moderate in what one ate and drank for two or three weeks, to see that a proper amount of exercise was taken every day, and above all that plenty of sleep was obtained, particularly by the means of going to bed in good time at night. I believe that this is the best sort of training of all for the golfer—plenty of sleep, that makes him keen and keeps his nerves steady. If this is to be called training, then I think a little of it is a good thing when it is wanted ; but not many experienced golfers have any belief in such a course of procedure as is generally understood by the term.

This suggests what a player might sometimes do with advantage to his general game at times when an off season becomes necessary to him, as in the winter time when he may find it impossible to get down to a course for a game for days or even weeks at a time. It is said sometimes that a man plays better for such a rest as this, and it may happen occasionally that this is so. He is not likely to forget in such a little while all that he has learnt about the game ; but he does generally suffer from unfamiliarity with the feel and touch of his clubs when he takes it up again, and for this reason it would probably be quite a good thing if, during the off season, he were to make a practice of handling his driver for a few minutes either in a garden or a large room, and having just a few practice swings with it. It need only take a very few minutes, and such exercise would generally be pleasant, while it would certainly help to keep him in touch with his clubs, so that they would not be so strange to him when the time came to play with them in real earnest again. We hear sometimes of men who practise pitching strokes with their mashies and balls made of paper, playing their shots from coarse door mats, which are a very fair substitute for turf. As to the advantage of this form of practice I know and can say nothing ; but it cannot fail to be a good thing to keep one's self in some sort of acquaintance with one's clubs, and if possible to keep the golfing muscles supple and ready for work.

It is often asked what amount of play is the best

for a man's game ; but this is rather a useless sort of question to put, for there are very few players who would be guided by any rule of that kind. Those who are very keen on the game will generally play as much as they can, while those who are not so keen will do so just as often as they are disposed. Still, one might say that too much golf is not a good thing for a man's skill, because it will tend to make him stale, and that induces carelessness. However keen a player may be, however good his condition, and whatever time he may have at his disposal, it will generally be a mistake to golf more than four days of the week as a regular thing. Any more than that will have a tendency to reduce a man's keenness. It is generally a good rule only to play the game when one is really keen. Players are very apt to overdo it at holiday times. There may be no great harm in a third round once in a way ; but it is a very bad thing to make a practice of. It is too much golf in one day, not only for the limbs, but, what is often forgotten and is quite as important, for the eyes.

A hint might be given that it is not generally wise to be in too much of a hurry to give one's old clubs away, especially if they are in good condition and they are clubs which were carefully selected when they were bought, and were afterwards used for a considerable length of time. It often happens that a player goes off one of his clubs, and at such times his thoughts frequently fly back to one of the old ones which was put on the reserve list some time previously. Such a club will be more familiar and generally better suited to the player than one that is entirely new, and it is often the case that after a spell of rest in this way it seems to suit its owner better than ever it did. It is always quite a good thing to have plenty of reserve clubs in this way.

I have had no good opportunity elsewhere of remarking upon two points of general play, the neglect of which is often the cause of failure on the part of the player when he is in difficulty to know what the cause is. Every detail of his stance, swing, and everything else may be all right, and yet his shots are continually failures, and his game seems to go from bad to worse. How is this? In such a case the player will do well to ask himself whether he keeps his eye on the ball as he ought to do, and not merely to ask but to test himself on the point, because he would be inclined to say at once that of course he does, having been taught to do so when he first took up the game, and not being likely to disregard such a simple but important maxim. Yet the fact remains that many golfers of some little experience get into a rather careless way of looking at the ball. They certainly look at it, but they do not concentrate their attention on it hard enough, and they are very apt to let their sight wander off it at the critical moment, particularly when they are playing short approach shots. What it amounts to is that they seem to look at the ball in a vague general sort of way, and this is not enough. The player must rivet his attention on it as he never does on anything else, and he should not take the ball generally into his view, but a particular part of it, being the one to which he is directing his stroke. In the case of play with his driver or brassey, he often needs to be reminded that the place to look at is the side of the ball, and not the top of it. This hint and advice about keeping the eye on the ball is by no means superfluous. It is one of those little rules that one gets so much used to, and takes so much for granted, that one is inclined to forget them.

The second of the two points I referred to at the beginning of the last paragraph is as to always being very decided about the club that one is going to take for any particular shot, and the way in which the shot is to be played. Hesitation is a very bad thing in golf. Let the player think as much as he likes before he comes to a conclusion as to what he is going to try to do, and what club he is going to take for the purpose ; but, having taken his club, it will be far better for the prospects of his shot if he dismisses the question of any alternatives absolutely from his mind. Unless there is very good reason indeed for the change, a club should always be used for the shot it was taken out of the bag for, once the ball has been addressed with it. Changes at the last moment nearly always result in the golfer making his shot in a half-hearted sort of way, as if he were still not satisfied that he was doing the right thing. A good shot seldom results, and it is almost better to stick to the original club. There is no harm, of course, in making a change once in a way.

One feels that at the end of a chapter like this one ought to say just a word about the rules, and the necessity for knowing them thoroughly and always playing according to them. It would take too much space to go through the whole code, and point out how players are constantly wrong in their interpretation of many of them, or how in some cases they have even quite clearly never taken the trouble to read and understand them. There is no excuse for this, even though in some cases the rules are not very clear, and need a good deal of thinking about. But if the rules are not clear there are always the interpretations and official rulings to fall back upon, and these leave no doubt about the meaning of the different clauses. The rules about casual water, about the penalties for lifting and dropping, about what may and may not be done in bunkers and on putting greens, are those which are most frequently misunderstood and misapplied. So many curious situations arise in golf, and there are so many possibilities for more, that after all golf law can never be very simple if it is comprehensive and detailed, and the first thing a player does at the very beginning of his experience ought to be to make himself a thorough master of the regulations for the playing of the game.

CHAPTER XIV

MATCH AND MEDAL PLAY

IT almost goes without saying that a man has a great deal more to learn besides the strokes of the game and the best way to play them in all kinds of circumstances before he can be considered to be a good player of golf. He may play golf well—alone—and yet play it very badly when he has an opponent against him fighting out every hole all the way round the links. It makes all the difference. Again, the man who can play the shots very well indeed when alone, and play them as well or perhaps even better when he is engaged in match play against an opponent, may be a poor player when he has a medal round to do. But some men are good at this kind of game, when they are not at all good match players. In their case it seems to need the great responsibility of the card and pencil to bring out their real capabilities.

It is altogether a question of temperament. Any kind of a temperament may do to play the shots alone, but a man must have a good one, specially adapted to the game, in order to make him successful in his play against others on the links ; and while it needs one kind of temperament for the best match play, another kind, with special characteristics, is needed for the score game. As to which is the best golf, or the real golf as some people call it, is a question which need not be discussed. Match play is the more pleasant; but there can be no question as to which is the more difficult, and which is the severer test of temperament, skill, and judgment. That is medal play. The test is as hard as it can possibly be. In match play you have one man to beat, and you see what he is doing all the time, and what you have to do to beat him. It may happen that the task he sets you is one of extreme difficulty, but it would be an unusual match in which you did not now and then have a comparatively easy shot to play. It might so happen that you had quite an easy time all the way through the game. But in medal play you are playing not against one, but many; you do not know how well or how badly they are doing; but you do know that it is extremely likely that the man you have to beat in order to come out on the top is doing extremely well, since a bad score does not generally win a medal competition. Therefore, while moderate golf is often good enough in match play it is hardly ever anything like good enough in the stroke game, and the man who is competing is not given any really easy shots to play from start to finish, for if the ordinary shot is easy, then he will often feel he must try for something a little more difficult that will pay him better. Thus he is severely on the strain the whole time, and it rarely happens that a man who wins a medal competition has not thoroughly deserved to win it.

It is difficult for one with the wrong kind of temperament to become a first-class player, and to a large extent the temperaments are born with the players; but there is such a thing as training the temperament for the purposes of golf, and this amounts in reality to the application to one's game of various rules of what may be called common-sense. Therefore one can hardly teach a man to be either a good match or medal player ; the only thing one can do is to remind him of the chief matters for consideration in either case. They are the same game up to a certain point ; but there are times in each when a slightly different policy has to be pursued, according as to whether you are playing against a man or are out to do a better score than the field.

Now take match play first. It is true that you are playing against the one man, and that you have to beat him and him alone, and that while a 4 at a par 4 hole may be good enough in a medal round, and generally is quite satisfying, it may not be good enough in a match. Therefore it goes without saying that you have to keep a very sharp eye on what your opponent is doing, and that in a large measure your own play must be regulated according to his ; but there is such a thing as caring too much what he does, and struggling too much, to the detriment of your own game. Remember that you do not so often win holes as the result of your own brilliant play as by the mistakes that the other man makes. If he gives you no chance of winning a hole, it is not generally the correct policy to play desperately in order to make a chance for yourself. At such times the half ought to be enough, in the absence of a special piece of luck in your favour ; and the game must be to nip in and take every opportunity of gaining a point when the opponent makes a slip. When you look at things in this way you will see that it is not

14

generally a good thing to try to drive as far as the
opponent, when he is really a longer driver than
yourself, and is generally outdriving you.   By
pressing beyond your known capabilities you are
only spoiling your game, and certainly losing more
than you would do if you drove quietly and steadily,
and contented yourself with losing just a few yards
in the tee shot, which may very likely be made up for
afterwards.   So generally you should not mind what
he does until it comes to the short game, and there
is the last chance offered to either of you for winning
or halving the hole.   That is really the whole secret
of good match play—simply to play your steadiest
and best, and not to care about the opponent's game
until it is absolutely necessary to do so.   Simple as
such a rule may appear, it is a very difficult one for
anybody who has not got a perfect golfing temperament to abide by, and that is why match play is not
by any means such an easy thing in comparison with
practice golf alone, as it might appear to some who
do not thoroughly understand the game.

From this it is evident that no rule can be laid
down, as some people seem to think there might be,
as to what a player should go for and what he should
not.   Clearly, everything depends upon the circumstances that exist at the time.   It is not much use,
in fact it would be unwise, to play for a difficult
carry that is not by any means certain to come off,
and failure at which would probably mean a bad
case of bunkering, unless there is a decided advantage
to be gained.   At such times the steady game is
best, and undue risks should be avoided.   This,
however, is not by any means to say that a pawky
game should be played whenever you have just a

little in hand. There are some men who at such times will play short of a bunker that they would carry five times out of six, and this is a great mistake, for two or three reasons. For one thing, it very often happens that a shot played short in circumstances of this sort goes wrong, and then you are confronted with the fact that you have nothing whatever to give away if you are to win the hole. The result is a little anxiety, nervousness, and very often a failure with the next shot. Secondly, always remember that the other man is after all not done with, and he may quite possibly accomplish something very surprising towards the finish of his play to this particular hole, which will make you regret not having taken the chance you had. He may lay a long approach dead, or he may hole a long putt. Thirdly, constant playing short in the way I have spoken of reduces your ability in going for things when it is necessary to do so. You get afraid of quite easy shots, and quite the wrong sort of temperament is encouraged. What I say, therefore, is that you should play the steady game, and play short if it is best, when you have something in hand, but only play short when it would be risking too much to go for all that there is.

It is plain that all this applies more to the game that has to be played when approaching the hole than to any other part of the match. If both play steadily, there is not generally much to be won or lost in playing from the tee ; but it often happens in match play between two fairly good players that the second shot is the critical one, and it is at this shot that you most frequently have that awkward problem set which we have just been discussing, as to whether you shall go for a long carry or not. It is at a time like this that the longer driver has a great advantage, not merely in his being able to make the carry more easily, but in the fact that his opponent has to play first, and he sees whether he gets over or not, and what it is necessary for himself to do. In a doubtful case like this, when you are playing the odd you must generally give your opponent the credit for being able to do his best shot when it is wanted, and must go for everything yourself. Playing short with the odd must at all times be a very dangerous game. A thing to bear in mind most clearly in cases of this kind, is the distance that the green is beyond the bunker that has to be carried. It frequently happens that it is only a matter of some thirty yards or so beyond, and that the ball that carries the bunker will get on the putting green—a great gain. In such a case as this it is well worth any risk that there may be in attempting a long carry, for the success of such a shot means a clear gain of a stroke, and very probably will make all the difference in the result of the hole. Again, let it be remembered that even if the shot does not come off, and the ball gets bunkered, there will still be quite a good chance of getting out of the bunker on to the green in one stroke, so that nothing may have been lost as compared with playing short. It may be a different matter when there is a fairly long shot to be made after a long carry has been done; but if the long carry means getting on to the green, it may very likely be worth going for.

"Never up, never in," is a safe rule for the putting in every match, and a vast number of holes are lost when the player has two putts for them, and thinks he can afford to be almost anywhere with the first one. This generally results in his being short, when he may have cause to fear missing the next one ; for it is a thing to bear in mind that it is generally easier to putt back to the hole, unless it happens to be downhill, than it is to continue on the same line again with a putt that was previously short. Why this should be so is not quite clear, but nearly every player finds that it is so. It may partly be due to the fact that when he has to putt back from the far side of the hole the player has, at anyrate, the satisfaction of knowing that he gave the hole the chance that it was his duty to give it. Trifles of this kind make a considerable difference in the long-run. Mentioning the putting also reminds one that it is a bad habit to be always expecting a half to be given when neither ball is exactly what you might call dead, and that it is just as bad to propose the half when your own ball is slightly nearer the hole, but still not dead. In ordinary play there is rather too much of this giving of halves, and the consequence is that players lose the nerve and the ability that are necessary for the holing of short putts, and fail at them when they are made to putt. They are as much a part of the game as anything else, and halves ought rarely to be agreed upon unless the balls are so close to the hole that it is next to impossible for the putts to be missed. Not only in this respect but in all others it is generally better to play the full game, and to play it according to the strict rules. Then there can never be any misunderstanding or difficulty, and there can also be no after regrets, for a man who gives a rather difficult putt for a half when he is four up, may, however good a sportsman he may be, sometimes regret that he did so when it turns out that the other man becomes dormy one on him, and he has to fight hard to save the match.

You should always try to win every hole of the match ; any other policy is fatal.   You sometimes hear men say they do not like winning the first hole ; this is all nonsense.   A hole at the beginning counts as much as one at the end, and in moral effect it sometimes counts a little more.   Play for all you are worth at the start, and establish a lead, and, even when you have got it and are nearing home, never for a moment slacken, in the idea that you can afford to take it easily.   In a case like this the other man only wants a very little encouragement to make him play an exceedingly hot game, and at the same time the loss of even one hole out of the three or four that you may be up, sometimes seems like a disaster, and has a distinctly bad effect on your play.

Many matches have been lost by slackness of this sort after a man has been in a winning position. To consider the reverse case, it should never be taken too much to heart when the other man gets well ahead at the beginning of the round.   Of course he has an advantage then, but it should be considered that there are fluctuations in the great majority of games ; that you will probably at least have some good chances of getting on even terms again ; and that, after all, it is at the end of the round that matches are won, and not at the beginning. This is to say, that of the two things a brilliant finish is generally better than a brilliant start.   But much better is it to be brilliant all through.

In match play give nothing away that you can

help, either in the matter of the rules, the play, or in anything else, particularly in things that may tend to cause irritation or to disturb your mind from the serious study of the game.   There may be times when it is necessary to be very sociable and talkative in the course of a game, but one could hardly regard such a game as a serious one.   The very talkative golfer is more often a nuisance than not.   The game is played better, and, what is more, it is certainly enjoyed better, when there is as little talking as possible.   The time that is spent in walking from the place where the ball was last struck to that at which it stopped again, and from which the next shot will have to be played, had better be occupied in thinking out the problems of that next shot rather than in general conversation.   Too much thought can never be given to a consideration of the circumstances at times like these.   There is the wind question to reckon up, for unless the ball was hit quite straight towards the hole, the wind may not be in quite the same quarter with relation to the line of the next shot as it was to that just played.   Then there is the lie of the land to think about, and if it is an approach that will have to be played next time, there is the important question as to whether it shall be pitched or run up, which may be considered before the ball is reached, even if a final decision is not arrived at.   The state of the ground, and a dozen other details, can all be taken into account.   There is at the most a couple of minutes for all this thinking, and when the ball is reached only a few seconds will be left.   Besides, even if he thinks very little about his next shot, nearly every golfer will be the better and play the better for keeping his mind on the game right the whole way through it, and not talking about matters that have got nothing to do with golf, as some are so much inclined to do. It is always said that one of the great advantages of the game is that you can think of nothing else while playing it; but at the same time many players seem to try to think of other things, and to make their opponents do so also.

Very talkative golfers often prejudice their chances of winning the match in other ways than those mentioned. They explain their shots to their opponents, what they found out when playing them, and certain peculiarities of the situation that they had not suspected. " The ball caught the wind more just over that hill," or " I never noticed that little slope on the left-hand side of the hole," and things of that kind, are very valuable information to the opponent who has just to make the same sort of shot, and without it might easily have fallen into the same mistake. A sensible player would have kept silence and watched for the opponent committing himself in the same way; but he loses this chance through his talk. On the other side, always be ready to profit by any information given you in this way; and particularly get into the habit of watching your opponent's stroke, and what happens to his ball when he is playing from anything like the same position as you are in. You may find out something very much worth knowing about the way in which your own shot will have to be played.

Lastly, so far as match play is concerned, when the match is delayed in the middle, through a block in front or the slowness of the preceding couple, let it be borne in mind that during the period of waiting the eyes should be given as much rest as possible. It often happens that players occupy this interval by staring hard at the green in the distance, waiting for the couple ahead to hole out and get along. This course of procedure has two great disadvantages. In the first place, it is nearly always very irritating to the player, because the men who are putting always seem to be much slower than they really are ; and, in the second place, it will generally be found, when the player brings his sight back to his own ball, that he has difficulty both in focusing it and seeing it properly after the strain that his eyes have just been put to. This is a very frequent cause of missed shots. The best thing to do during a period of waiting is neither to look ahead all the time, nor at one's own ball, but just to turn one's back on the latter and look about. Then when all is ready one seems to come fresh up to the ball, without experiencing any of the usual disadvantages of waiting. I think that this is a most valuable hint. Of course, one could say a great deal more about the art of match play, and points that one does well to keep in mind, but these mentioned seem to me to be the chief.

Now as to medal play, the chief thing to remember is that one's moderate game, which might often win a match, will very seldom be good enough to win in a stroke competition. Your very best is wanted on these occasions, and that must be borne in mind from start to finish. Generally the cautious game will not pay. It is, of course, right to remember that if the ball gets into a very bad place in a bunker or elsewhere, once or twice, it may be quite enough to put the player out of the running ; but risks like this must be taken if there will be any gain resulting from a successful shot. Just as in match play it is not much use going for difficult carries, and all that sort of thing, if you

are not much better off for having performed them ;
but the case quoted in the argument for going for
a bunker guarding the green when playing a match,
applies with even more force to stroke play, for it
is the gain of strokes like this that makes all the
difference.   Always keep it in mind that while your
game can very easily be not good enough in stroke
play, it is impossible for it to be too good.   For this
reason any timidity on the putting greens is sure to be
fatal to one's prospects, for it is on the greens more
than anywhere else that success in these competitions
is gained.

The player must go for the hole every time, and
should never be short ; while in pitching and running
up, also, it should be the rule to get to the farther side
of the hole, unless there is some very good reason for
stopping on the near side.   You cannot afford to lose
the chance of holing with your approach, even though
it is such a small one.

A man does not generally win in a stroke
competition unless he is in the mood for winning,
that is, unless his temperament is in just the right
happy state.   He must try to make himself feel
comfortable all the time ; as soon as he gets fidgety
and uneasy his prospects will begin to diminish.   It
is therefore the finest tonic possible to make a good
start.   The man who plays the first two or three holes
really well has scored a great advantage, and it need
not be said what a heavy handicap a bad start is, and
how difficult it is to carry those lost strokes with you
all the way round the course, trying to get rid of them
here and there.   To win in a medal competition you
generally need a good start and a good finish ; but if
the former is denied you it must be remembered that a

brilliant ending has been the means of winning many of the most important tournaments. The player suddenly realises that if certain things happen for the best he has still a chance, and this last hope has a way of coming true oftener than one would expect. Once or twice I have been near winning a championship as the result of a strong finish, when at the beginning of the last round I had seemed to be well out of it.

I have said that a man must play the bold game in stroke competitions, with just a reasonable caution when necessary, and that his ordinary "moderate" game is no good. At the same time he must remember that he has no right to expect to be able to play better than his usual best, and that it is a mistake to attempt to force one's game with this object. One's entire golfing system is sure to go to pieces if this is done. Another hint worth remembering, is that it is not only good to try to forget one's bad holes as quickly as possible, but to take as little notice of what your partner is doing as you can. Of course, if you are out of it, and he is not, it is merely the good and proper thing to give him such encouragement (not advice) as is legal; but, while you are both in it, do not be put off by his brilliant holes, or by the fact that he soon gets an advantage of several strokes over you, remembering that points are sometimes more quickly got back in stroke play than in matches. Remember, also, when you have made a bad hole that there never was a medal round that could not have been a stroke or two better.

I realise that though stroke play is so difficult to succeed at, it is equally difficult to say anything about it that is not rather commonplace. The simple fact is that the man and his temperament, coupled with his best game and a little luck, are everything in a stroke competition. Steadiness, perfect control over the mind and the temper, and the ability to take chances when they are presented, are the best qualities, and if a man has not got them you cannot give him any set of rules for success in this branch of the game.

CHAPTER XV

THE SCIENCE OF THE STROKE

IT has been acknowledged for a long time that golf is a very scientific game ; but comparatively few players have any idea as to how really scientific it is, and it will seem to most people who have made a very brief study of some of the elementary scientific principles involved in such a stroke, for instance, as the drive, that the pleasure and satisfaction derived from the game are thereby much increased, and that it is desirable for every player to possess some such knowledge in order that he may have an idea as to why he does certain things, and what is the precise object that he wants to gain. At the present time most players know how they ought to be standing, and what the exact movements of their arms, wrists, and body should be in order to swing the club in the right way, and make the ball travel as far as possible ; but they do not all know, and in few cases, one suspects, have ever troubled to think, what is the process by which these movements when properly executed bring about the desired effect. They have the cause, and also the effect, but they do not often see the connection between the two. Of course, the ball in all ball games moves always according to scientific laws, but it has seemed to those who have studied these matters that the scientific problems involved in the flight of the golf ball are more intricate, but at the same time more interesting, than in many other cases.

The chief matter of this kind that it is desirable the golfer should understand is that concerning the character and effect of the spin that is given to the golf ball when it leaves the club. This spin is at the root of all the difficulties and all the delights of the game, and yet there are some players—one might even say many—who do not even know that their ball spins at all as they hit it from the tee. Some fifteen or sixteen years ago scarcely anybody knew that a golf ball ever had any such spin imparted to it by the player; and it was Professor Tait, the father of Mr. F. G. Tait, both now dead, who first studied the matter, and, having done so, proceeded to make many most interesting and scientific calculations as to the flight of the ball in different circumstances. These calculations were all of a very intricate character, so much so, in fact, that it would be next to impossible for an ordinary golfer, despite a good education in scientific matters, to follow them, and therefore the professor's conclusions must by most people be taken for granted. If this is not altogether satisfactory, there is this to be said for it, that these investigations have several times been gone through, and tested again in recent years, and have been found to be fairly reliable, and, moreover, they generally fit in with all that one may observe, and that is generally a good test. When Professor Tait first began to discuss these matters and suggested that underspin was given to the ball when it was driven, many golfers would have nothing to do with the idea, but they were very soon obliged to admit that it was true. Therefore, like most other golfers, I am content to accept the main scientific principles which the professor showed to be applied to the game of golf as correct, without being able always to follow him through his complicated arguments and calculations, the more important of which were made not before golfers, and for their benefit, but before scientific societies of which he was a member—so interesting from the purely scientific point of view did he regard these matters. I have read most of what he wrote on the matter, and I ought to add that for my understanding of the subject I am indebted chiefly to the lucid and interesting explanations of the professor's meaning that have been published by Mr. Henry Leach at different times and in different places.

It appears to be the proper regulation of the underspin given to the ball when playing it from the tee and through the green, at all events when length is what is most required, that makes success, and it is in this way that players of inferior physical power must make up for their deficiencies and drive long balls. Some very hard hitters get long balls in spite of their disregard of some of the well-understood principles of driving; but they do not get them much longer than the others who drive properly, although they hit much harder. Generally the man who trusts only to strength in this way is a shorter driver than the other man, and he is less certain. Professor Tait declared that in the hands of the former the ball is usually "a mere lump of dead matter, urged by sheer force," whilst by contrast it leaves the club of the more scientific player "in a quiet, easy, and graceful manner, almost as if it were a living thing and thought and acted for itself."

The chief differences, as they may often be observed, between the two kinds of drives, is that in the case of the hard hitter the ball leaves the club at a greater velocity, that it rises more quickly at the beginning of its flight, and that its carry is completed much sooner; in fact, it has been calculated that while the flight of the ball in this case often occupies no more than four or five seconds, it is as much as six or seven when properly driven—that is, with the aid of underspin. Professor Tait pointed out that what is wanted in order to make the ball fly a long way when hit with reasonable force is "time to travel," that is, some means by which the force of gravity might be discounted for the time being, and it is the underspin that does this and gives the ball a longer time in the air for its velocity or forward motion to act. It has always to be remembered also, that the resistance of the air to the flying ball being very much greater proportionally than any increase in the speed of the flight, it requires far more than half as much extra strength to be imparted to the drive in order to increase the distance gained by one half; in fact, if it is to be done by strength it requires a great extra expenditure of physical effort to gain as much as ten yards in the drive. Such a gain is more easily obtained in other ways, and players who want it would do well to consider the matter from this point of view. It is in the long game that the principles of spin are most interesting and important, but it must be remembered also that they are very prominent in their action upon the flight of the ball in the case of many other shots, and the peculiarities of different trajectories can generally be traced to this cause after a very little thought by one who has a knowledge of the scientific side of the matter as explained by Mr. Tait. This is particularly the case with high lofted approach shots.

Now let us see what this underspin is and what it does. The basis of the investigations made by the professor, as stated by himself, was an old scientific law, that when an object is poised in still air the atmospheric pressure upon it is equal at all points; and further, that, as had been known for a long time, since the days of Newton, or even before that, when a ball is made to rotate in a current of air, that side of it which is advancing to meet the current is subjected to greater atmospheric pressure than is that which is moving in the direction of the current. Simplified and applied to golf, this means that when a ball is sliced it spins from left to right, and there is then greater atmospheric pressure from the left, which forces the ball over towards the right. But when the ball has been pulled from the tee the spin is in the opposite direction, and therefore the extra pressure of the atmosphere is also from the opposite side, with the result that the ball is pressed to the left. When the ball has been topped, the spin on its front side is in a downward direction, and so the extra air pressure is downwards also, and as in this case there is the force of gravity pulling in the same direction, the downward movement of the ball is very quick and sudden. Lastly, when the spin given to the ball on the tee is that kind which makes the front side to move in an upward direction, that is to say underspin, the balance of the atmospherical pressure

15

tends to lift it upwards and in the contrary direction to the force of gravity. A very little thought will show that the result of this must be to keep the ball longer in the air than it would remain in it if there were no underspin, since it is the force of gravity that pulls everything down, and all the time that the ball is in the air it has some of the velocity that was imparted to it on the tee acting upon it until the other forces, chiefly air resistance, exhaust it. It will be seen, therefore, that pulls, slices, and balls that fly well all arise from the same cause, the rotation of the ball, and that the difference is the direction of the rotation, which is settled by the kind of stroke that the golfer makes.

Therefore the great authority concluded that good driving lies not merely in powerful hitting, but "in the proper apportionment of quite good hitting with such a knack as gives the right amount of underspin to the ball," and one of his calculations was to the effect that, in certain circumstances, a man who imparted underspin to his ball when driving it, might get a carry of about thirty yards more than that obtained by another man who hit as hard but made no underspin. There would, of course, be a great difference in the comparative trajectories of the two balls. In the case of the short one there is no resistance to gravity, and consequently, in order to get any sort of flight at all, the ball must be directed upwards when it is hit from the tee, or, to use the scientific term, there must be "initial elevation." This may be only very slight, but it is quite distinguishable, and in fact a player, who is only at the beginning of his practice and has little knowledge of the principles of the game, will generally be found trying to hit his ball in an upward direction, and by that means will make it travel farther than it would have done otherwise. On the other hand, the ball that is properly driven by a good player is not only not consciously aimed upwards, but, according to Professor Tait, is not hit upwards. For some distance after it has left the tee it follows a line nearly parallel with the ground, and eventually rises as the result of the underspin that is forcing it upwards all the time. Its line of flight thus becomes concave upwards, and there can be no doubt as the result of observation that a well-driven ball does make such a trajectory, which accounts for the fact that it often seems to be rising more and more when it had seemed to have got to the turning-point of its flight. An experiment that was made by the professor in the course of his investigations into the qualities of underspin, was very remarkable in its way. He laid a ball to the string of a cross-bow, the string being just below the middle of the ball, so that when it was let go it would impart a certain amount of underspin to it. When he shot the ball in this way he made it fly straight to a mark that was thirty yards distant; but when he shot it a second time, pulling the string to the same extent and laying it to the middle of the ball so that no underspin would be given to it, the ball fell eight feet short of the same mark.

Scientific calculations are so exact, and a man's efforts, particularly when applied at such high pressure as in driving a golf ball, are so much the opposite, and are also so variable, that it would be impossible for any scientist even to lay down a rule by which the longest drive is to be obtained, although if the conditions were known no doubt he might work out some formula for it.   However, it is well to bear in mind one thing that the professor said, namely, " The pace which the player can give the clubhead at the moment of impact depends to a very considerable extent on the relative motion of his two hands (to which is due the 'nip') during the immediately preceding two-hundredth of a second, while the amount of beneficial spin is seriously diminished by even a trifling upward concavity of the path of the head during the ten-thousandth of a second occupied by the blow.   It is mainly in apparently trivial matters like these, which are placidly spoken of by the mass of golfers under the general title of knack, that lie the very great differences in drives effected under precisely similar external conditions by players equal in strength, agility, and (except to an extremely well-trained and critical eye) even in style."

One very satisfactory feature of the thing, however, is that even if players cannot drive exactly like a machine, according to scientific calculations made out beforehand, they do at all events know when they are driving very nearly in the exact way that they ought to do.   This is partly the result of an instinctive feeling and partly of training and experience.   On the one hand an inexperienced golfer would know when he had hit the ball fairly in the middle of the club, and had timed the stroke correctly.   If he had done that there would be a sweet feeling, giving a great amount of pleasure even to a beginner, while otherwise there would be nothing but a nasty jar.   The good effect here is the result of clean hitting and accurate timing.   But then, of course, other qualities of the drive are necessary in order to get something approaching to the best ball obtainable in the circumstances, and these are chiefly the proper regulation of the swing, ensuring that the ball shall be hit not merely cleanly but in exactly the right way so as to ensure the proper trajectory being given to it in its flight. So far as I know, it cannot be stated in accurate scientific terms and figures and by lines drawn on paper what is the proper scientific swing in order to get the best drive. Besides, it must vary with the physical characteristics of the individual. What golfers have done, therefore, in the past has been to find out gradually which is the best way in which to hit the ball in order to make it travel far, and thus they have groped their way to the stances and swings which, if the truth were known, would probably be set out by science as the best possible ones for the purpose. It is clear that the instinct of the man serves him very well in this respect, because it is well known that when children are given a driver and a ball to play with, they very soon drop into a proper stance and swing without any teaching.

This is satisfactory in its way, even if, from the scientific point of view, one is driving, as it were, in the dark. However, there are certain things that the player should know about his drive when it is right, and which he should aim at producing, and they have been very well set forth by Professor Tait as the result of his investigations into the trajectories of golf balls hit under varying conditions of club-force, wind, and so forth. One of the first things to say—and this is really important in estimating their chances of making certain carries that are constantly set to them in the course of their play—is that some golfers have a delusion to the effect that the ball is at its highest point in the middle of its flight—that is to say, they think that just half-way between the point from which it was hit and the point at which it will touch the ground again, the ball is at its highest, and after that commences to fall again. In this belief when they have, say, a 140 yards' carry to make, they will reckon that their ball must then be coming down very fast towards the turf, having been at its highest some 50 or 60 yards before. They may think in such circumstances that they ought to hit up a little more and try to hit harder to make up for doing so. They would be wrong entirely, and that because they did not know what the underspin was that they gave to the ball, or what effect it had on its flight. Thus in the case just quoted, assuming that the ball had a total carry of from 150 to 160 yards, it would be at its highest point when it had travelled about 130 yards, and there would be no occasion to hit up, unless the object to be carried were very high.

The fact is, that a well-driven ball that has a total carry—that is, from the tee to the point where it touches the turf again, and not the distance of the obstacle that it clears—of about 165 yards, under normal conditions of wind and weather, is at its highest about 135 yards from the point where it was struck, and after that it begins to fall rapidly. This is chiefly the result of the underspin which is given to it when it is struck by the driver in the proper way, and it shows the importance of underspin to the golfer, for if there were none, then all our courses would have to be shortened, hazards brought closer to the tee, and the principles upon which the game is played would have to be altered in many respects. If there were no underspin, then the ball would have no help against the force of gravity, and the result would be that the highest point of its flight would be half-way between the point from which it was driven and that at which it alighted.

Now, in order to make all this clear, one cannot do better than reproduce some of the curious and most interesting diagrams that were prepared, after much study, by Professor Tait, in which he showed the comparative trajectories of golf balls hit under different circumstances ; and golfers would do well to examine them very carefully and think over them, for they may very considerably affect their views as to what they have to do and what is the proper way of doing it when playing, to say nothing of making their play far more interesting to themselves, knowing what curious scientific causes bring about the different results. Here, then, is one set of trajectories, and the lines were not drawn by Professor Tait by mere guess, but every curve and distance were worked out according to the scientific tables that he prepared :—

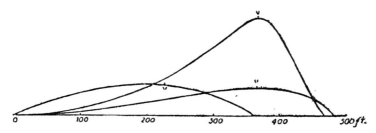

In each case the V at the top of the curve stands for "vertex," or the highest point attained. The ball which has travelled farthest, or rather the one that has been given most carry, is that which has been hit in the right way, and to which has therefore been imparted the right amount of underspin. This is, in fact, the ideal trajectory of a well-driven ball. It starts low, rises very slowly and gradually, the line of flight bending upwards slightly, and does not come down too quickly after the vertex has been reached. The other two trajectories both represent faulty drives. In the case of the short drive, which has not sent the ball much more than a hundred yards, no underspin at all was imparted to it, and if it had not been deliberately hit in an upward direction at the beginning to the extent, by the Professor's reckoning, of an angle of fifteen degrees—the other balls having been driven practically straight forward—it would have come down to the ground almost immediately. This is really, as Professor Tait said, what might be called a beginner's drive, when nothing of the knack of driving is at all understood.

The diagram indicating the high trajectory simply shows that too much underspin is a bad thing, but that it is better than none at all. Of course, as already indicated, the golfer does not know, and in one sense does not care, exactly how much underspin he gives to his ball when he drives it, only being aware that he has given too much or too little according to results, and knowing also that in either case the excess or otherwise was due to faulty stance or swing—most frequently this—or both. In the present case of this high trajectory, the exact amount of underspin given to the ball is half as much again as that given to the properly driven ball, and under the same normal conditions these would be the relative flights of the two balls. It follows from the height to which the ball attains, and its comparatively sudden and straight fall to the ground again, that it has very little run on it after alighting. It is a very unsatisfactory drive in most circumstances, and, if there were a head wind to encounter, it would suffer severely ; but yet it has to be remembered that this trajectory would be a most useful one in some circumstances, as for instance where a very long shot to the green had to be played with a wooden club, and there was a hazard in front of the green. Such a shot as this would be almost the only one that would keep the ball on the green if it were quite close to that hazard. Therefore, just as a pulled drive is a faulty one when a straight ball is wanted, while it represents a splendid feat of skill when the pull is just what is required and is tried for, so this high drive, with excess of underspin given to the ball, is a bad one at most times, but yet is caused by a distinct method, and it might be valuable to the golfer to practise the method, so that he can make the stroke when it is just the thing that is wanted. This is only said to indicate the possibilities of this game, and to show how much greater they are in the case of the golfer who will make a careful study of it, and, so far as he is able, a study that is scientific. Of course, a player will be getting very advanced before he can set himself deliberately to the making of fancy trajectories of this kind ; but, after all, it has to be remembered that when he deliberately pulls his ball he is deliberately changing the character of the spin applied to it, in order to accomplish a particular purpose, and in the present case he would only be doing practically the same thing, that is, he would be slightly increasing the underspin.

To supplement the idea conveyed in the block

of diagrams already given, Professor Tait worked
out another set, to show the trajectories, which he
described as "fairly representative of ordinary good
play by two classes of drives," one of these having
the benefit of underspin, and the other not. They
are as represented here :—

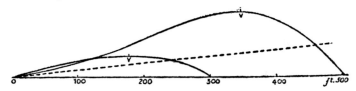

Our scientific authority remarks upon these figures
that "in spite of its fifty per cent. greater angle of
initial elevation, the carry of the non-rotating ball is
little more than half that of the other, and it takes
only one-third of the time spent by the other in the
air. The contrast shows how much more important,
so far as carry is concerned, is a moderate amount
of underspin than initial elevation, and it can easily
be seen that such initial elevation, always undesirable
unless there is a hazard close to the tee, as it exposes
the ball too soon to the action of the wind where
it is strongest, may be entirely dispensed with." The
dotted line shows the initial elevation that was given
to the ball in the case of the longer drive. The
club-force applied to the ball in each case was the
same, but a comparison should not be made with the
trajectories represented in the previous diagram, as
the conditions which were assumed were not equal.
The long drive in the first diagram represented very
nearly the ideal—a long, low one.

In the next drawing there are shown the trajectories which were worked out in the case of wind

resistance of varying degrees.   There was supposed
to be a head wind of a strength of seventeen miles
per hour contending against the longest of these three
balls, and it was hit from the tee at the rate of
275 feet per second.   The middle ball had a wind
of twenty-five and a half miles per hour against it,

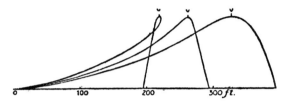

and the force with which it was driven was equal
to a speed at starting of 262½ feet per second ;
while in the case of the shortest ball of the three,
the windage was thirty-four miles per hour, and the
starting-speed, 250 feet per second.

There are two or three things to say here, on the
same authority as before, about these starting speeds
and the effect of winds.   The Professor came to the
conclusion that in the case of a good drive the ball
left the club at the rate of about 240 feet per second,
but that the very best drives by the best drivers
might start with a speed varying from 300 to 350
feet per second.   This was in the days of the gutta
ball, and it has been pointed out since then that the
rubber-cored ball with its greater resiliency must
start with a greater speed, so that it may be reckoned
that in most cases of good drives nowadays the ball
starts at a speed of about 300 feet a second.

Now as to the wind, a common mistake of the
golfer is pointed out in the following terms : " It is
well to call attention to a singularly erroneous notion

very prevalent among golfers, namely, that a following wind carries the ball onwards! Such an idea is of course altogether absurd, except in the extremely improbable case of the wind moving faster than the initial speed of the ball. The true way of regarding matters of this kind is to remember that there is always resistance while there is relative motion of the ball and the air, and that it is less as that relative motion is smaller, so that it is reduced throughout the path of flight when there is a following wind. Another erroneous idea somewhat akin to this is that the ball rises considerably higher when driven against the wind, and lower if with the wind, than it would if there were no wind. The difference (whether it is in excess or deficit will depend on the circumstances of projection, notably on the spin) is in general very small, the often large apparent rise or fall being due mainly to perspective as the vertex of the path is brought considerably nearer to or farther away from the player."

Another very important point to bear in mind, hinted at in one of the quotations already made, is that the resistance of the air or wind to the ball, as the speed of the ball is increased, is in much greater than simple proportion to that speed. What is meant is that if, say, the ball is travelling at the rate of 100 feet a second, the wind resistance may be 10 miles an hour, but if the ball were going at the rate of 200 feet a second the resistance would be equal to, say, 40 miles an hour. This is a simple scientific fact which we have to, and may very well, take for granted. Then it is clear that the resistance is immensely greater at the beginning of the flight of the ball than it is towards the end, and it is all the more necessary that the ball should be kept as low as possible at the beginning when it is going so fast and making such enormous resistance for itself, than towards the finish when its speed is almost spent. By keeping it low, less wind, which is so expensive to flight, is encountered; and now we see another advantage of driving in the perfect way or nearly, with no initial elevation, because as the ball skims the turf while it is going at its greatest speed it is getting off with comparatively little wind resistance. Sooner or later, when it has covered a large part of its journey, it has to rise, but then it is going very much more slowly, and therefore when it gets the full force of the wind upon it that force is con-siderably discounted. The definite fact to remember is that the resistance offered to the ball by the air or wind is proportional to the *square* of the speed of the ball, that is to say, that a ball that is travelling twice as fast as another has not twice as much resistance offered to it, but four times as much.

It will be perceived that in the case of one of the trajectories shown in the last diagram, that in which the drive is the shortest, there is what is called a kink at the top, that is to say, the ball turns over, as it were, and doubles back. This would be the simple result of driving a high ball—with much underspin—against a very strong wind, when it might be seen to reverse its course and come back a little way towards the striker. Players may remember that in the case of a very bad slice they sometimes see the ball go round at right angles and then actually begin to follow a course more back towards them than in any other direction, and this is just the same thing. It is the curl sideways instead of upwards, and if there were not the friction caused by the run on the turf interfering, and bringing that run to an early conclusion, one would see, according to the deductions that have been made, some very curious evolutions performed by these sliced balls.

A final thing to remember in connection with this question of the rotation of the ball is, that when the ball is what we call topped, the stroke is applied in such a way that a motion exactly the reverse of underspin is applied to it, that is to say, the front part of the ball is made to move in a downward direction. On the principle already explained, there is then an extra air pressure upon that ball from the top, pressing it down, so that even if the ball that is topped is somehow got up into the air from the tee, as happens, it cannot stay there long, but comes down very suddenly—"ducks," as it is called. However, a ball that ducks for this reason, nevertheless gets some benefit from this overspin when it does come down, for the spin acts in just the same way as "top" does in the case of a billiard stroke, that is to say, it makes the ball run more. If there were no rough grass and no bunkers between the tee and the hole this overspin might be an exceedingly useful thing, and the principles upon which the game of golf is played might be entirely different from what they are; but as there is rough in front of the tee, and generally a bunker at no great distance from it, topping and overspin are more frequently fatal than not, the ball coming to grief either in the rough or the bunker.

If a careful consideration of these remarks and explanations upon overspin does nothing else, it will serve to change the golfer's view of the qualities and conditions of a good drive, and will convince him of what he is often told, with much regretful doubt on his part, that strength is not everything in driving, and

that even comparatively weak men can so cultivate
their style as to enable them to drive a fairly long
ball.   Some people may say that such scientific
aspects of the game as these are best left unconsidered
by beginners, who have quite enough to think about
in getting over their early troubles.   On the contrary,
one is more inclined to believe that it will be best for
young players to give attention to these things, so
that they may know exactly what it is that they are
trying to do, and how it is done.   It may be of
interest to mention that Professor Tait found that
a well-driven ball turns once in every two and a half
feet at the beginning of its journey.

    We have so far only been considering the effect of
the spinning of the ball in the case of long shots
with wooden clubs.   As a matter of fact, and as suggested at the outset, it has also very great influence
on the play in the case of the shorter shots with iron
clubs, as may be understood after a very little consideration of the circumstances.   It is the excessive
underspin that is given to the ball by the angle at
which the face of the club is laid back, and the
peculiar way in which the stroke is played, that
make the ball rise so quickly and so high in the
case of a short pitched approach, and then make it
stop comparatively dead when it comes to the ground
again.   However much a club were laid back it
would be impossible to play these shots properly if no
underspin were given to the ball, and it seems to be
a great advantage of having the faces of iron clubs
grooved or dotted that it helps the club to grasp the
ball thoroughly while this underspin is being imparted
to it, so that the full amount is given to it, and none
is wasted through the ball slipping on the face.

It is a comparatively small advantage of the spin
of the ball, and one which does not matter at all to the
golfer at present, that it steadies its flight, particularly
if the ball is not well centred.   A ball hit through the
air without any spin would have a tendency to wobble,
and this tendency would cut its flight shorter than
usual.   Balls are now generally very well made, so
that their centre of gravity is exactly at their centre of
measurement, or very nearly.   But very slight differences in this matter have great consequences in the
flight, and it is because some balls are not properly
centred that they do not fly well.   However much
care may be given to the centring of a ball, it is
impossible for manufacturers always to get them
perfect in this respect, and that is why a bad-flying
ball may sometimes be found in a box made by a first-
class firm, all the others of which are as perfect as
could be desired.   The inaccurate centring affects
the flight by interfering with the rotation of the ball,
and the less rotation there is the more will the flight
be affected by the bad centring.   It will be remembered that a rifle bullet is made to twist in the
air for this very reason, that the rotation steadies its
flight.

One or two other calculations that were made by
Professor Tait may be briefly mentioned at the close
of this chapter, each of them seeming to convey an
idea to the golfer.   The first is, that owing to the
speed at which the ball leaves the club, the total
length of time during which ball and club are in con-
tact with each other is between $\frac{1}{5000}$th and $\frac{1}{10,000}$th of a
second, and the total length of that part of the swing
when the two are together—the length of impact—is
half an inch.   It has been pointed out that it by no

means follows from this that because the time and
space of impact are so short that follow through is of
no real account, after all, in the making of the drive.
When the follow through is properly performed it
shows that the work was properly done during that
half an inch of the swing that was all-important. If
the follow through were short and wrong it would
indicate that the work during the impact was wrong
too. What it comes to is this, that it is impossible for
any man to swing his club round with so much force
and regulate exactly what he will do, and be conscious
of the fact that he is doing it as he regulated, during
such a short space of time as from $\frac{1}{5000}$th to $\frac{1}{10,000}$th of a
second. That is quite clear. What the golfer has to
do, then, is to make sure that his swing is right at the
beginning, that is in the back-swing and the down-
swing, and also in the follow through. He knows
from instruction and experience that if all these things
are properly done the ball will go off well; and what it
amounts to is that the beginning being right and the
end being right, control being exercised over each, the
middle is right also, though in this case there is no
control over it.

Professor Tait also made some investigations into
the kind of atmosphere in which the golf ball flies best,
and he stated that, " Other circumstances being the
same, the only direct effect is on the co-efficient of
resistance. If this be taken as proportional (roughly)
to the density of the air, it may vary, in this climate,
to somewhere about ten per cent. of its greatest value,
and the drive is accordingly shortest on a dry, cold
winter day with an exceptionally high barometer.
The longest drive will, of course, be when the air is
as warm and moist as possible, and the barometer

16

very low." This theory probably accounts for the long carries that golfers notice they get on many days of the late autumn, and it may also account for some of their disappointments in the matter of their tee shots in the summer time. Of course, the statement just quoted concerns carry only, and has got nothing to do with the run of the ball, which is so much greater in the summer time, when courses are hard, than it is at any other, the result being that, even if carries are a little shorter, as they are said to be, the total lengths of drives are longer.

CHAPTER XVI

THE PLANNING OF COURSES

W HEN a golf course is being laid out largely
on sandhills at the seaside there is generally
less scope for the arrangement of the holes
according to set theories of golf architecture than
there is when the ground at disposal is situated
inland and consists of more level and less broken
country, perhaps largely of heath or moorland, or,
as is very frequently the case in these days, of
meadow land. The flatter the land and the more
sameness there is about it, then the more artificial
has the course to be, and it follows from this that
those who plan it can make and arrange it very much
according to their own tastes. But when high
sandhills, large open sandpits, and all the other
peculiarities of the sandy wastes at some seaside
places have to be dealt with, the case is different.
The opportunities for laying out courses on such land
are comparatively few ; but such courses, it goes without
saying, generally provide the best and most interesting golf, while at the same time it is both necessary
and desirable that the holes should be laid out and
arranged in such lengths as are suggested by the
lie of the land, every natural obstacle being taken
advantage of. In such a case the object will, of
course, be to approach as near as possible to the set
theories of the designers of the course.

I consider that in every case a good course should possess the following general features :—

(1) There should be a complete variety of holes, not only as regards length, but in their character— the way in which they are bunkered, the kind of tee shot that is required at them, the kind of approach, and so forth.

(2) In every case the putting greens should be well guarded.

(3) The shorter the hole the smaller should be the putting green, and the more closely should it be guarded ; so that on this principle when in good play a long shot can reach the green, that green should be fairly large and open in order to give the player the encouragement to which he is entitled.

(4) There should be alternative tees, in order that the course may be easily adapted to varying winds and dry weather, when there is more run on the ball. Unless this is done a medium has to be struck in the arrangement of the holes, which seldom makes a really good test in all conditions ; or, on the other hand, the holes have to be planned to suit the prevailing wind, and are much reduced in quality and testing power when it comes from the opposite quarter.

(5) The bunkering and general planning of the holes should be carried out with the specific object of making it necessary not only to get a certain length, but, more particularly, to gain a desired position, and the player who does not gain this position should have his next shot made more difficult for him, or should be obliged to take an extra stroke.

(6) There should be as frequently as possible two

alternative methods of playing a hole, an easy one and a difficult one, and there should be a chance of gaining a stroke when the latter is chosen and the attempt is successful.

A course that conforms to these general principles cannot possibly be a bad one. Now, from such a general statement as this, I go on to a more particular one as to the lengths of the various holes and their arrangement. I think that on every good course there should be—

(1) Four short holes, all of a different type. One of these four should be a very short one (about 120 yards); a second should be a little longer, so as usually to make the difference between a mashie and an iron; a third should generally call for a long cleek shot, or just a little more than that; and the fourth should represent a good full drive.

(2) There should be two very long holes, of fully 500 yards each or over, 550 yards being regarded as the maximum.

(3) The remaining holes should vary in length between about 320 and 420 yards, those between 360 and 420 yards, representing always good two-shot holes, predominating.

(4) There should be two stiff carries to be made from the tee in the course of the round—about 150 yards each. The predominating carry should be about 130 yards; but in some cases it may be reduced to as little as 100 yards, special difficulties in the way of placing the tee shot being presented at such holes.

(5) As a general rule, simple cross bunkers right across the course in front of the tee should be avoided. A few of them are necessary and desirable;

but preference should generally be given to the system of side bunkering.

(6) Except in a very limited number of cases, bunkers straight across the course in front of the putting greens should be avoided, and preference should be awarded to the "bottle neck" system of guarding the greens, by which a very narrow opening is offered to each, the traps in front, behind, and at the sides being numerous.

(7) The first nine holes and the second nine should as nearly as possible match each other in total length, in golfing quality, and in general character, although it is not desirable that the order of length and character should be the same.

(8) There should be either two or three—three for choice—holes of good but not extreme length at the beginning of the round, in order to get the players well away without a block on busy days. These should be followed by one of the short holes.

(9) The last two holes, or three, should all be of a good length, in order to induce a good finish to a well-contested match, and particular care should be taken to see that the seventeenth and eighteenth holes are a thorough test. A short hole for the last one is to be avoided when possible. (If it cannot be avoided it must be made extremely difficult.) The hole should generally be of full two-shot length, and the green should be thoroughly well guarded.

(10) The total length of the course should be between 6000 and 6400 yards.

I will set forth the lengths of the holes, the order of their arrangement, and the chief point, quality, or character of each, on what we may regard as an ideal course of eighteen holes :—

HOLE.	LENGTH.	POINT.
First . . .	360 yards .	Fairly long; not too difficult. To get the players away quickly.
Second . .	390 „ .	Same object; but slightly more difficult. Two good shots.
Third . .	380 „ .	To complete the object of getting the players well away. This hole should be difficult and the green well guarded.
Fourth . .	190 „ .	Meant to be a full shot for a good player. Length may be increased up to 210 or 220 yards.
Fifth . . .	320 „ .	Iron play. Very difficult near the green.
Sixth . .	500 „ .	Test of wooden club play.
Seventh . .	120 „ .	Test of delicacy and accuracy.
Eighth . .	400 „ .	Two good two-shot holes to finish the outward half. Length to the turn—
Ninth . .	420 „ .	3080 yards.
Tenth . .	340 „ .	Within two shots. To be a difficult hole, with a trying second shot.
Eleventh .	410 „ .	Two fine shots. Three needed to get on in case of slightest mistake or moderate player.
Twelfth . .	130 „ .	Difficult mashie or iron.
Thirteenth .	370 „ .	Two good shots.
Fourteenth.	520 „ .	Long hole in. Counterpart of sixth. Difficult near the green.
Fifteenth .	180 „ .	A severely testing one-shot hole.
Sixteenth .	390 „ .	Hard finish. Seconds to be difficult.
Seventeenth	420 „ .	Total length in—3160 yards.
Eighteenth .	400 „ .	

6240 yards.

There should be short tees in order to reduce the length of the course somewhat in the winter time.

This table very nearly explains everything, and, as in the following chapter I shall have some general remarks on making teeing grounds and bunkers, I will only state here what I consider to be desirable features of particular holes arranged on such a definite system as this.

The first hole should be as open as possible from the tee. There should be no difficult bunker or other hazard in the way to discourage the player at the beginning of his round, and very often spoil it for him, as the result of a bad shot which is frequently made under exceptionally trying circumstances —a long wait at the tee, a crowd on it, and the player not always at his best right at the beginning. To ensure a fairly easy start there should be two or three alternative tees, some distance apart from each other, for use according to the wind that may be blowing. Also the wear and tear of the first tee is usually greater than of any other. You may give the man a carry to make at the second hole, but it should not be too difficult; and both here and at the third it must be remembered that holes of this length demand alternative tees, or they may be completely spoiled by a change of wind. At the long holes, the sixth and thirteenth, the bunkering until the green is reached should not be too severe. Side bunkering chiefly and plenty of pots near the green will be sufficient, so long as traps are laid to catch a topped and long-running ball. The governing consideration in the case of these long holes is that the player must get length, and if he misses a shot or goes very far off the line he has very small chance of getting up to the green in the number of strokes that he would otherwise expect to do. It should also be made that his next shot is always more difficult if he deviates to the least extent from the straight.

There should be the greatest variety in the short holes. If possible, none of them should be blind, though a blind hole may still be a good one sometimes. The best kind of short hole is the opposite to a blind one—one where the tee is on higher ground than the putting green, and the player is able to look down on the latter with a full view of all the difficulties that surround it. In the case of the shortest of the four holes, I would have no cross-bunker, or, indeed, any bunker in front of the middle of the green, but I would put pot bunkers all round it, and have them right up to the edge of the green, which would also be a very small one. Thus the opening to the green would be very narrow, demanding a most accurately placed pitch, and the player would need to exercise complete control over the run of his ball after it had pitched. It is a good thing to make a green like this pear-shaped, with, of course, the narrow end nearer the tee. To insist that a pitch shot shall be played, and that the player shall have no chance of getting off with a possibly fluky half-topped pitch and run, I would have the fairway very rough up to within ten yards of the putting green. The other short hole, which is only a little longer than this one, may be constructed on the same general principles, and should be nearly but not quite so closely guarded, and there might be a cross-bunker—sunk, not raised —some fifteen yards in front of the green. The 180-yards' hole will be generally regarded as a cleek shot, calling for one that is perfectly straight and well judged. Side bunkering and a narrow opening to

the green will be best in this case, and there may be
something to carry at 150 yards from the tee.   In the
case of the longest of the short holes, I would have
a slightly raised cross-bunker, and I would place it
diagonally to the straight line of play, giving an easy
carry to the moderate player, but demanding from
him that if he takes that line he must play wide,
and then make a short approach to the green, whereas
the man who goes straight will have a long carry, but
will get there if he does it.   I shall explain this
system of making use of the diagonal bunker in the
next chapter.

Although the concluding holes must be difficult,
I would not give a long carry from the tee at the
last one, but would bunker it so that the player would
be punished for the least deviation from the straight
line.

I might say a word about the par and bogey
calculation of such a round as that I have been
speaking of.   The difference between par and bogey
is, of course, that the former represents perfect play
and the other stands for good play, with a little
margin here and there.   Although it is said that
"bogey never makes a mistake," it is evident that
it does give a chance now and then, which par
does not.

In order that the real value of the holes may be
properly defined, I think that it is well to reckon
that value in par figures.   There is generally no
doubt about the difference between 3's and 4's,
but the question is as to how you shall separate the
4's and 5's.   There should not be such a thing as a
par 6.   In a general way I would make holes of 390
yards and over, 5's, and under that distance 4's, that

is when they are over 3's. The longest of the short
holes must, of course, still be a 3, though it may be a
bogey 4. In distinguishing the 4's and 5's, however,
it is well to remember that length is not everything,
and that a hole of 385 or 390 yards may be easier to
get a 4 at than another hole of 360 yards. Questions
of uphill and downhill, and the bunkering about the
green, need to be considered, and some judgment
exercised in fixing the values. I would place the
par values of the holes on the course I have been
writing about as follows : 4,5,4,3,4,5,3,5,5—out, 38 ;
4,5,3,4,5,3,5,5,5—in, 39 ; total, 77. A par score
of this kind, however, is only for players' own
knowledge and satisfaction, and is too severe for
bogey competitions. One fixed and unalterable
bogey score is not generally a good thing, because
in certain winds quite a large proportion of the holes
may have wrong values attached to them—that is to
say, with the wind they may all be too easy, and
against it all too difficult. It is then a simple thing
and a very satisfactory one to have two bogeys for a
course for the purpose of competitions, and to decide
which of them shall be in force on the morning of the
competition. One bogey would be set out for one
wind and another for another. For example, if the
wind was against the player at the first hole (360
yards), and with him on his return journey at the
thirteenth (same length), you would make the former
a bogey 5 and the latter a bogey 4, and reverse the
figures if the wind were in the opposite direction.
For bogey I would give 5's for every hole between
370 and 450 yards, and after that 6 might be allowed.
The general bogey (with variations according to
wind, as I have suggested) of the course we have

been considering might be placed as follows : 5,5,5,
3,4,6,3,5,5—out, 41 ; 4,5,3,5,6,3,5,5,5—in, 41 ; total,
82. It is well, for reasons already suggested, to
make the bogey of the first hole easy ; but there is
no reason why it should be easy at the end.

However carefully the bogey score of a course is
arranged, and even when two bogeys are made, it is
seldom that there is complete satisfaction with the
figures given to every hole. A 5 is often too much
where a 4 is too little—that is to say, such a hole is an
easy 5 but a difficult 4, and it will often fail to dis-
tinguish between good play and bad. What seems
to be wanted is a reckoning in half strokes, and
though you cannot play such halves, a stroke being
a whole stroke or none at all, there does not seem to
be any reason why bogey should not be considerably
improved by letting him have half-strokes. To take
a case, in normal conditions of wind and weather you
might make the longest of those four short holes a
3½, and holes of about 360 to 380 yards might be
set at 4½. This would mean in the former case that
the man who got his 3—and it would be a good 3—
would win the hole, while the man who took 4 would
lose it, because almost anybody could play such a
hole in 4. Even this, however, leaves a little to be
desired, because at these holes it removes the chance
of halves being made, when halves would often
represent just the value of the play. This difficulty
can be got over by allowing halves in the handicap,
and seeing that they are given at the right holes.
For example, at the 3½ hole we have just been speaking of, we might allow the very moderate player half
a stroke instead of either none at all or a full one.
The result would be that if he played this hole out in

4 strokes, which would generally be the best he could do, he would halve it with bogey. This system of halves is much simpler than it may appear at the first glance, as anybody may find out after a few minutes' consideration, and it certainly seems to offer a chance of making bogey a much more satisfactory and exact sort of thing than it generally is.

CHAPTER XVII

THE CHARACTER AND PLACING OF TEEING GROUNDS, BUNKERS, AND PUTTING GREENS

LESS attention is given to the matter of the preparation of suitable teeing grounds when making a golf course than its importance requires. There are seldom enough alternatives, and such as there are do not always get placed in the right positions. Often they are too small. There is nothing so good as a big tee, not only for the opportunities that it affords of making slight variations in the drive, as suggested by the weather conditions, but also, by moving the box and plate, preventing too much wear and tear in one place. Small tees necessitate more alternatives, or else they are quickly worn away. In making a tee, a point to be remembered is, that while it should generally be level, or the lie of it should correspond to the general lie of the ground all the way to the hole when that lie is uphill, there should also be a part of it on a slight slope upwards, so that if the player needs a stance of that kind for the playing of the shot that he wants to make, he can have it.

If space and cost are not the chief considerations, every hole of any length should be supplied with not fewer than three teeing grounds. The arrangement of these may vary, but the most useful system is to place them in triangular form, with the base of the triangle nearest the hole, and at right angles to it. Of course, the distance that these tees are separated from each other will depend a little, perhaps, on the length of the hole, but more particularly on the length of the carry that has to be made with the drive ; while it may, of course, also be regulated by the extent of ground there is available. These are matters upon which no rule can be laid down ; but if the arrangement decided upon is a wise one, these tees should afford the best play under every variety of wind conditions. It is particularly necessary that there should be at least one alternative tee in the case of the longest of the short holes, such a hole as in normal conditions represents a good full shot, because it would be completely spoiled by an adverse wind if there were only the regular tee to play from. What is absolutely essential in a case of this kind, is that there should be one tee much farther forward than the general one, and in the straight line to the hole, so that the player may always be given his chance of getting up in one shot. If he cannot do this, then he has not the advantage over a short driver that he ought to have. Teeing grounds to the left and right are not so necessary in the case of holes of this kind, as the player may very well be left to deal with the difficulties that may be caused by strong winds from either side. It will be obvious, also, that an extra forward tee is quite necessary at those holes where the carry in normal circumstances is a severe one, such, for example, as the two holes mentioned in the course described in the last chapter, where the carry was made as stiff as possible. Evidently, with a strong wind against him, it would be impossible for the player to clear the hazard, and he would be reduced to playing short, which is an extremely unsatisfactory thing to do, besides which the hole would generally be spoiled.

In this chapter I am not concerned with the choice of seeds and turf, but it might just be mentioned that it is bad to have a too fine turf for a teeing ground, as it is so soon worn away. A rough, strong grass should always be selected; and in the case of wet soil, when possible the teeing ground should be raised up, and be supplied with a bed of cinders, or some other loose stuff, to assist the drainage in rainy seasons.

Now a word as to putting greens. On a course there should be all kinds, that is to say, they should be of various sizes and of different characters of undulation. It has already been pointed out that the greens should be large when they are expected to be reached in good play by a long shot, and correspondingly small when it is generally an iron club that will be used to get to them. It will be noted that the size of the green is not at all dependent on the length of the hole—that is to say, if there is a hole of, say, 300 yards' length, it is clear that the approach should generally be a very short one, and the green should therefore be small. So, too, in the case of a hole that is getting on for 500 yards in length, which cannot be reached in two shots, but ought never to need more than a short third, except in the case of an adverse wind. Long bunkers right in front of a green are not a good form of hazard; but when they are made, the green should be of a fairly good size, to give the

player a chance of staying on in the case of a
following wind.

This raises the point as to the general shape of
the green, which should be governed by the kind
of approach shot that will usually have to be made
to it. Many greens are made very much the same
length from side to side as they are from front to
back, so that they are nearly square or round ;
but there are evident reasons why this is not always
the best shape. For example, in the case we have
just been thinking of, where the player needs room
to stay on, he may be given it in length of the
green forward and backwards, without the width
being increased also. Such a green would be
rectangular in shape, the long way being with the
proper line of play.

Then there is the question of surface conforma-
tion. There are flat greens, greens with many and
pronounced undulations, greens on plateaus, and
saucer greens. Generally speaking, the former are
not good, as they do not make sufficient test of the
putting abilities of a player ; but one or two of them
on a course are to be recommended. You might
have such a flat green, being also a large one, at
the very long holes, when the player has already
been severely tested before he has to begin his
putting, and in order also to give him a more than
usually good chance of holing in one putt and effecting a fine finish to very satisfying play through the
green. For the same reason, at such long holes as
these you might have a saucer green, that tends to
draw the ball a little towards the hole, so that the
player may reap the fullest advantage from a long
and straight shot up. At such times he deserves

17

to be treated with more than usual kindness in matters of this kind. Reverting to the flat green, one is not out of place at the eighteenth, so that the finish of a match that goes to the home green may depend as little upon luck as possible, for, no matter how skilful the player may be, putting on a very wavy green, particularly if it is in a fast state, is necessarily attended by more luck than on a flat one. Therefore any undulations that there are on the home green should not be very pronounced, and the bigger this green is the better.

As to the undulations, they may be of all kinds, and a pronounced knob, not in the very centre of the green but a few yards to one side, is generally an excellent thing; but the hole should never be cut either on the knob or very close behind it, because that would make it next to impossible to hole out from the other side. The purpose of the knob is to make the player avoid it or to play his approach to the side on which the hole is; and if he fails to do that and gets the knob in between his ball and the hole, he will have an unusually difficult putting problem to think out. But you do not need a knob of this kind on every green, and it ought never to be of a much exaggerated size.

There is the plateau green still to consider, and it is one that generally makes the approach difficult. Such a green should be of good size, and it should not generally be just beyond a bunker in the straight line of play. By this I suggest that the approach to the hole should be of such a kind as to encourage the running-up shot, which is usually the best one for this kind of green.

Having dealt with the tees and putting greens,

the beginning and ends of the holes, let us now consider the bunkers and the placing of them, but first of all their formation.

Bunkers are not placed on a course haphazard, but they are made at particular places to catch particular kinds of defective shots. Therefore they should be made in such a way as to give their own shots the least chance of escape. To assist them, the fairway round about such bunkers should be hollowed slightly, so as to draw a ball that comes in that direction towards them. A ball that is running a little distance from such a bunker may escape ; but one that gets very near will be drawn in. This not only penalises a shot that ought to be penalised, but reduces the likelihood of luck helping the player by letting him just skim the edge of the bunker with a ball running slowly. Of course, one cannot supply every bunker on the links with this drawing power, and very often there will be no occasion to help them in this way ; but it is very advisable at times, particularly in the case of small pots. Next, so that the bunker may have the best chance of catching its shot, it should be set out so that its longest side faces the direction in which the ball will be coming. Thus if a bunker is put on the left side of the course, in order to catch a pulled ball, it should not generally be placed exactly at right angles to the straight line of play from the tee, but turned round somewhat so that the right-hand end is nearer the fairway, and the general line of the bunker is at right angles to the line in which a pulled ball would travel towards it. There is less chance of the ball slipping past the ends of such a bunker than there would be if it were placed quite straight ; and to still further help the bunker the front—or in this case the right hand—end of it should be curled in

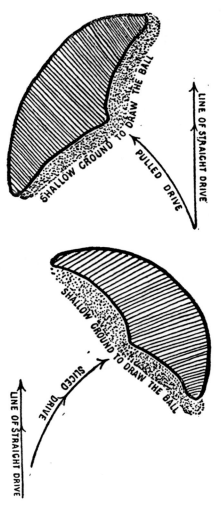

a little, the shape of the bunker being somewhat after the style of a double crescent as shown in the sketches. The bunkers on the other side of the fairway, set there to catch sliced balls, will be made on just the same principle ; but, of course, laid in the opposite direction, so that they also will be at right angles to the line that is taken by the balls which they are designed to trap. Pot bunkers nearer the middle of the fairway, put there simply to be avoided and to demand placing of the shot, may be oval or round, preferably oval.

While every assistance should be given to the bunker to enable it to catch its own kind of shot, it must be remembered that it is not part of the game that the ball should be kept there for long, and the player being punished by having to play out, generally with a niblick, should be given, at all events, a fair chance of playing forward. Therefore it is not generally a good thing, particularly if the bunker is a small one, and the ball that finds it naturally gets to its far or face side, that this face should be either very steep or very high. The top part of the face may be just fairly steep. Again, there should be no sudden drop into the bunker on the near side where the ball will enter it, because in such a case, if the ball simply trickled in, it would be left with a bank just behind it, and that bank would effectually prevent the player from getting his club to it. Therefore the entrance to the bunker should be, if possible, on a level with the turf, from which point it may sink down gradually.

These points chiefly concern pot bunkers at the sides of the course, and it has only to be added that there should be such a bunker on each side to catch nearly every pulled and sliced ball that is of full length, allowing for the pull and slice ; that is to say, there should be one on each side to deal with erratic tee shots, and then there should be others farther on to catch pulled and sliced seconds after good tee shots had been made. As a pulled ball generally travels farther than a sliced one, it will be borne in mind that the bunkers on the left should be a little farther up the course than those on the right.

There is very little that need be said concerning the shape and placing of long cross-bunkers in the middle of the fairway, their object being chiefly to insist upon the player making a certain length of carry. A point, however, is that they should not generally go right across the whole width of the fairway, but should be short at the ends, so as to give short drivers a chance of getting round the ends of them. Those who take this course will always run the risk of getting into the rough—in fact, they will generally find it difficult to avoid it; while even if they escape this danger they will lose considerable length. To make their task even more dangerous and difficult, the ground round about the ends should draw towards the bunkers. Even if they escape being bunkered, then they will still have a more difficult shot to play than if they were out on the open fairway. Another point of importance concerns the means of passage for the player himself either over, through, or across the bunkers, since he will not wish to walk the whole way round them. Steps over bank bunkers are not a good arrangement, for they sometimes lead to unexpected difficulties in the playing of a shot that may have got on to or near them. A narrow open passage should be cut through such bunkers, and in order to prevent the possibility of a ball having the luck to run through it, it should be cut in an

S-shaped pattern, so that this cannot possibly happen. In the same way, instead of a straight plank or path being laid across a sunk bunker extending across the fairway, it also should be shaped like an S, so that the ball that gets on to it at the beginning will fall in immediately afterwards.

Let me now say a few words about a form of bunker that is too seldom used as an alternative to the usual straight bunker, either of the raised bank or sunk pattern, going straight across the course and intended to be carried with the tee or second shot. This latter bunker has the disadvantage that a ball that may be off the line may be short of it, while one of the same length that is straight may find it, which is not proper justice. Besides this, it offers no temptation to a short player who feels that he cannot carry it. The alternative bunker that I recommend catches the short and crooked ball, and gives the better chance of being let off to the ball that is short but straight, while at the same time it offers distinct temptation to the short drivers. It is a bunker constructed on either a single or double diagonal pattern. Everybody knows what are the distinguishing and excellent qualities of a good dog-legged hole. The player has a carry to make from the tee over a hazard that runs at an angle to the straight line to the hole, and he can choose his own length of carry. If he can drive far and will take risks, he goes over the farthest point— straightest for the hole ; and if he makes a good shot he is much nearer to the hole than he would have been if he had taken the short carry, and ought then to be given a good or even easy chance of getting on to the green in comfort with his next stroke. On the other hand, the short driver may take an easy carry, but he will then probably be out of range of the green. The good qualities of this type of hazard are apparent, and they may easily be applied to made bunkers at straight holes. The bunker that has to be carried is simply placed diagonally across the course instead of straight, and it makes no difference whether it is a sunk bunker, a line of pots, or a bank. In the case of the single diagonal you place one bunker—or line of pots—at an angle of about forty-five degrees across the course, the end nearer to the tee reaching the edge of the fairway, while the other end extends just a little beyond the middle of the course. Therefore the player who can drive well and wants to take the short cut to the hole goes for the long carry over the middle, while another man, who is a short driver or is afraid, can play over to the right or left as the case may be. (I think it would generally be best to let the near end of the bunker be on the right, as shown in the diagram I have drawn (p. 269), so the player would be induced to make his shot in that direction. This would give him less chance of escape if he sliced—slicing being more frequent than pulling— than he would have if the far end of the bunker were on the right.) But note that the man who does thus take the short carry is losing extra distance by departing so much from the straight line, and also that he stands a very fair chance of going into the rough if he is not careful, while the bunkers in the neighbour-hood of the green will be so arranged that his next shot will be considerably more difficult than it would have been if he had kept straight. Thus, while the short driver is quite as well accommodated as he has any right to expect, the bunker is distinctly one that encourages him and makes him try to improve his length. This is the single diagonal, and as the far end of it will be, as stated, very little beyond the middle of the course (it would clearly be no use continuing it to the other side, giving an impossible carry on that side, or, on the other hand, leaving a free space for the short driver there), the course must be protected at that end by a good-sized pot bunker to prevent the ball that runs in that direction from getting round it, or otherwise going free. The diagram on p. 269 illustrating a method of bunkering a short hole, chiefly with a diagonal, shows the situation exactly. The double diagonal is simply the substitution of another bunker corresponding to the first one for the pot bunker at the end, making one big bunker of it in the shape of a wide inverted V, the point being nearest to the hole. In this case the player who wants his short carry can go either to the right or to the left, while the other man who hits a long ball goes straight down the middle as before. A very little consideration will convince anybody of the sound advantages of this system of cross-bunkering.

When the run-up approach shot is encouraged, instead of the player being asked to pitch nearly everything, an effort should be made to make the ground for some little distance in front of the green slightly undulating, so that more things than the mere strength of the stroke will need to be taken into consideration by the man who is playing the shot. This makes the most fascinating kind of play.

We may now consider briefly the possible good placing of the bunkers at holes of different lengths. First of all take the very shortest hole, such a one as that of 120 yards which was mentioned in the last chapter. By far the best way of making this hole as good and difficult as it ought to be, is by placing a small green in the centre of a nest of pot bunkers completely surrounding it. What I would do, therefore, would be to keep or make the ground as rough as possible for about a hundred yards from the tee, or let the grass grow for that distance if that is the best

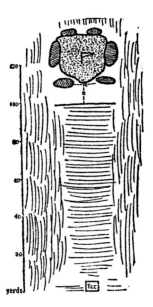

that can be done. Then for ten yards up to the nearest point of the putting green the fairway should be smooth, so that a ball may be pitched upon it—as it may have to be if there is a following wind—and run on quite nicely. But the passage of admission to the green should be very narrow, and should be flanked on either side by bunkers that would be certain to catch the ball that was not quite straight. An opening of twelve yards' width is quite sufficient.

The green should preferably be pear-shaped, and
should be of a width of not more than twenty-five
yards.   On either side of it there should be large pot
bunkers touching its very edge, and beyond it there
should be a series of smaller pots reaching almost
the whole way round.   A glance at the plan on the
opposite page will show the design of the hole.   It is

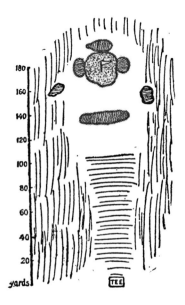

obviously a difficult hole.   One of this length that
was also easy in the matter of bunkers would be no
good whatever as a test.   For a really short hole I do
not think there is any good alternative to this system
of bunkering, and therefore, on this occasion, need not
trouble to seek one.

For longer short holes, those representing a full
shot or nearly with a cleek or a driver, something to
be carried must generally be put in, and there are

alternatives, one of which is the use of the diagonal. This latter had best be reserved for the longest of the short holes, that which needs a really good full shot to get up. Taking a shorter hole into consideration first, a straight bunker might be placed at right angles across the course at a distance of about 140 yards from the tee, but the ends of it may be left open to give the short drivers a chance of going round if they feel disposed to try. They cannot reach the green in one if they do so; and having to play their second shot at an angle, they will need to be very careful not to run into one of the bunkers that will be placed on each side of the green and touching it as before. This green may be of a width of about twenty-five yards. The diagram shows the idea of the whole thing.

The alternative, or the system of bunkering at another hole that may be rather longer, in which the diagonal is used, is clearly explained by the plan. Here the carry over the middle of the bunker may be a stiff one of about 150 yards, while the carry over the short point at the right-hand corner would be less than 130 yards. But the player who takes this short carry has to be severely dealt with if there is the least thing wrong with his run-up to the green. As before, we must have pot bunkers at each side of it, but instead of their being round and covering practically only the middle section of the green, let them be made more oblong in shape and brought a little more towards the tee. That on the right should be so far down that if the man who has taken the short cut has still got a fairly long ball, he will have this bunker to pitch over before he can get to the green, while this bunker and the one on the other side combine to still

further increase his difficulties.   It will be necessary for
him to hug the bunker on the right very closely if he is
to get near the pin, unless the latter is far away on the
left-hand side of the green ; while if he is afraid of
this bunker and goes too much to the left, and is
the least bit strong, he will find the other one.

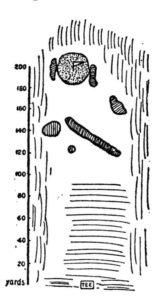

If the green slopes towards the left in this case, so
much the better.

On many occasions it will be found possible to
adapt these ideas exactly to the planning of short holes ;
but they are intended merely as ideas and suggestions
upon which the constructors of a course may act as
closely as they may be disposed.   What they do
indicate are principles, and these same principles are
properly applied to the laying out of long holes as
well as short ones, and therefore it is not necessary

to describe at the same length the different ways in which those long holes and medium long ones may be made as difficult as they generally ought to be. After all, it has to be remembered that a long hole is merely a short one with a wooden club shot, or more than that, tacked on to it, and what extra is necessary in its case is that these wooden club shots have to be attended to, while at the same time the green is generally not quite so closely guarded, consideration being paid to the fact that before the player comes to approach it he has already had to pass various tests. Thus it would hardly do to set him an approach like that laid out in the case of the first of the short holes described; another reason for not doing so, being that the distance from which he would be approaching would seldom be the right one for such bunkering. Therefore while much the same principles may be employed in guarding the greens, they should be applied more leniently, and here and there a bunker entirely omitted.

Holes of medium length, such as those between one and two full shots, present no difficulty in the matter of bunkering, and afford plenty of scope for variety. It has already been stated that there should be traps at the sides of the fairway for the pulled and sliced balls. This should be the general rule, and the distance from the tee to the centre of the bunker that is set for the slice may be put at about from 140 to 160 yards, the pull bunker being from 10 to 20 yards farther. A hole that is intended to be a first-class two-shot hole, the length of it being from 360 to 420 yards, should not generally be very closely guarded, and the carry for the second shot ought not to be too severe, because unless the second shot is a good

one it cannot reach the green. Where a carry is set
for the second shot—a diagonal bunker would be a
good one—a little allowance should be made for the
drive having been a trifle below the best. Thus it
would not generally be wise to put the bunker for the
second shot more than 300 yards from the tee. The
man who drove 180 yards, representing a fair but not
really long drive, would have an easy carry for his
second, while the man who was short with his tee shot
would still have a chance of getting over if he hit
his very best. Besides, wind has to be considered.

Finally, we will consider alternative ways of
bunkering a really long hole, one of, say, 500 yards, and
two plans for doing it are presented on the next page
and will explain themselves. In the case of the first,
no carry at all has to be made from the tee, but the
player has to hit a really first-class drive of about 200
yards to have any chance of carrying the bunker with
his second. Even with his 200-yard tee shot he will
have a carry of 160 yards to make with his second.
This will necessitate his hitting for all he is worth,
which is just what we must make him do at these
very long holes. He may perhaps be left un-
penalised for pulling, but a trap should be set for
a sliced tee shot, and another bunker may be cut
a little to the right of the middle of the fairway,
and some way short of the one in the middle,
which may be crossed by a man who has sliced or
who has been otherwise short with his drive. This
is simply a case of the diagonal bunker being cut in
two halves, and, if it is desired, the simple diagonal
may be put in instead. Then put a bunker at the
other side of the bottom end of the diagonal, or short
bunker, in order to catch the ball that goes over the

latter too easily and is sliced. After this, one bunker at each side of the green, for its general protection and to threaten the approaches of the men who went out to the right, will be quite sufficient.

In the alternative, we make the carries easier, giving comparatively simple ones for both first and second shots; but at the same time we insist on

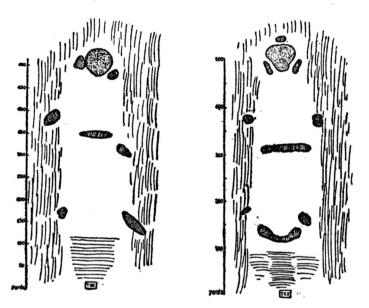

straightness, and bring into the fairway formidable bunkers to catch both pulls and slices, also making the passage to the green much narrower by the means of bunkers on the right and left, closing up about half of it. With another bunker behind, this hole should be quite a good one and very interesting, and if there are two long holes on the course, these alternative systems of planning them might both be employed with interesting results.

It is not always easy to make good dog-leg holes, so much depends on the natural formation of the ground ; but they are excellent when they are well done. When, to get the best results, the drive should be sliced and the second shot pulled, or *vice versâ*, a splendid test is afforded. Practically, these holes amount to a good arrangement of diagonal hazards.

I think that if the principles I have described are applied to the planning of a course, so far as it is possible to apply them, and with any such modifications as may be necessary or desirable, the constructors of the course cannot go very far wrong. When an inland course is being laid out, and one on which there are certain natural hazards, such as trees, streams, and so forth, the general aim will be to make the best use of them as hazards, and to get them in the right places, since they cannot generally be avoided altogether, even if it were desired to do so. There will not generally be such a desire, for the more natural hazards there are on a course, whatever their character, the more interesting that course ought to be, and generally is.

18

CHAPTER XVIII

ON PLAYING THE CHAMPIONSHIP COURSES

THE following are a few notes on the way of playing the different holes on the six championship courses—St. Andrews, Prestwick, Muirfield, Hoylake, Sandwich, and Deal—when it happens that one way of playing them may be better and safer than another. Of course, it must necessarily happen that in some cases there may be differences of opinion as to which is the best way, and what I offer is merely my own, and that which is suited to my game under normal conditions.

Beginning with St. Andrews, the first hole calls for no special suggestion ; good, straight play is what is needed. Going to the second hole, it is better to drive to the left when the green can be reached in two good shots ; but if the player cannot get there in two on account of adverse wind or for any other reason he had much better take the longer line to the right, which will leave him with a much easier approach shot. At the third hole, keep to the right. Play at the fourth hole must be regulated according to the exact place in which the hole has been cut. There is a big knoll standing up in the middle of the fairway right in front of the green, and it is generally a considerable factor in settling the kind of approach shot that has to be played. It is very difficult to get at the hole with

a long approach when the flag is right behind this
knoll, and the player has gone straight down the
middle of the course with his drive. It should
therefore be his object, when the hole is so placed,
to drive to one side of the fairway, and of the two
sides the left is much the better for this purpose.
Therefore, when the pin is behind the knoll, place the
tee shot to the left ; but when the hole is on either
side of the green, go straight down the middle. Going
to the long fifth hole, drive slightly to the left ; to the
sixth, drive straight ; and to the seventh, either take
a straight line with the tee shot or one that is just
a little to the left. Difficult as they are at all times,
the other holes up to the twelfth do not call for
or permit of any special suggestions being made on
the way of playing them. The player must use his
own judgment, and consider the circumstances, which
are rarely the same twice running. At the twelfth,
where there is a dangerous bunker in the straight line
for the hole, and just at the distance of a good tee
shot, I think it is the best thing to go out well to
the left, although many players prefer making for the
right-hand side. By playing well to the left in going
to the thirteenth hole it is made much easier to get at
it. The second shot at the fourteenth should be
placed to the left of the " Hell " bunker. The
fifteenth need not be remarked upon. My advice
at the sixteenth, a hole which I have good cause
to remember, is to play to the left of the Principal's
Nose. The seventeenth is a most trying hole in
every respect—for the judgment as well as for the
skill. If you feel certain of clearing the corner of the
Dyke make the attempt, but if you are not certain
keep to the left of the bunker with your tee shot, and

then play the second in to the right again, so as to make the approach as easy as possible. It is extremely difficult if the second shot has been pulled to the left. In approaching, bear in mind the dangers of attempting to pitch. It is a case of straightness at the eighteenth.

Now, Prestwick. I think it generally pays to take a club at the first tee that will not give you full length, as the farther you drive at this hole the narrower is the space left you to drive along. The short second hole is there for everybody to see and consider for themselves. Going to the third, play short of the famous Cardinal bunker, and then try to reach the green with a long second. At the fourth, it generally pays to keep to the left with the tee shot. The fifth, where the Himalayas have to be crossed, calls for no special remark ; but approaching the sixth, it is best to play just short of the green with a pitch-and-run shot. Any other kind of approach is dangerous. Passing over the seventh and eighth, one may recommend driving to the left at both the ninth and tenth ; and, skipping the next hole, there is a long second wanted if the wall is to be cleared at the twelfth. I need say nothing about the thirteenth and fourteenth, but the fifteenth will often need much thinking over. It is a long shot over the bunker, and if you are doubtful about being able to do it, it is best to play short on to the plateau and a shade to the right. Keep to the left again at the sixteenth; and going to the seventeenth, where there are the famous Alps in front of the green, remember that it takes a good second to clear them and the bunker and to get home safely. The last hole is plain sailing.

Muirfield can be considered next, and I am writing of it in its altered state as brought about in 1907. Of the first five holes, the only one that I feel I should make any remark upon is the third, where it is best to play short of the rough wet ground from the tee. At the sixth, it is wise to play to the left, if you are doubtful of being able to carry the bunker. Keep to the left again at the seventh, with the object of being clear of the pond when playing the second shot. The eighth, ninth, and tenth holes have been reconstructed. In the case of the eighth, some length has been added, and the stone wall has been demolished. The game is now to play quite straight, instead of to the left as used to be the case. There is nothing to say about the new hole at the ninth, except that the bunkers are now in place, and that the green is more to the left than it used to be. The tenth is now a good two-shot hole, the drive just reaching the place where the old ninth green was, or going a little past it. In going to the eleventh, drive a shade to the right, the bunker being farther away on that line ; while if a direction to the left is kept with the tee shot at the twelfth, the approach is then made easier than it would otherwise be. Again, at the thirteenth the approach shot is easier if it has to be made from the left. Of the remaining five holes, the only things to be said are that it is best to keep to the left for safety at the fifteenth, and at the seventeenth the approach is made easier by again going a trifle to the left with the tee shot.

Coming south into England, there is, first of all, Hoylake. The first hole is never an easy one, and changes of wind make a great difference to it. Generally the game is to drive wide of the corner, and the second shot should be played as low as possible, in order to get run and to reduce the chance of going out of bounds. Try to place the drive at the second hole so that you can make your approach from the right, which is the easiest way, but be careful to avoid the bunker that may sometimes catch such a drive. Straightness is essential at the third hole. Going to the sixth, the Briars, play for a long carry to the left, as you get a much better lie that way. The seventh hole is a difficult short one, and it is more than usually difficult if the player attempts to go straight for it. It is much easier for the ball to run up to the pin from the right-hand side of the green, and I think the proper game is to play wide to the right with a little hook. Drive to the right at the ninth, to avoid a nest of little bunkers, if the wind is behind; otherwise go straight. At the tenth, keep the second shot a shade to the left. Play a little to the left with the tee shot at the fourteenth, and do the same at the fifteenth, unless you are sure of carrying the ditch. So, too, at the sixteenth; while at this hole you must go off to the left again with your second shot if the carry that is before you is too much.

It is difficult to say much that is very definite about the course of the Royal St. George's Club at Sandwich, since it is generally understood that many alterations are pending. However, taking it as we have known it for so long, I suggest that it is best to make for the left-hand side of the course with the tee shot at the first hole, in order to get a better lie than would probably be found on the other side. If you are certain of being able to carry the bunker, go to the left again at the second hole, as the approach from that side is much the easiest. At the third hole

keep to the right for safety. A direction a little to
the right at the fourth hole is useful, as it makes the
second shot so much easier. It is the safe game to
play to the left over the big bunker at the fifth, but a
good driver may often reach the green if he goes
straight for it. The sixth is the Maiden, who may
be passed in silence. Drive a little to the left at
the seventh in order to escape the bunker. At the
eighth—the short "Hades"—make certain of the
position of the hole on this large green. You get
better ground if you drive to the left at the ninth, and
for the same reason it is policy to play to the right
at the next hole. Leaving the eleventh, you should
drive to the left at the twelfth in order to get over
the hill, which gives an easier second to be played
than would be the case otherwise, and the hole is in
full view. If you are able to reach the green in two
shots, go to the left again from the tee at the
thirteenth ; but if not able to reach the green in
two, it will be better to place the tee shot to the
right. There is a very difficult approach to be made
at the fourteenth, which will need all the player's
powers of calculation and skill in playing. The great
question at the fifteenth hole is whether you are able
to carry the bunker guarding the green with your
second shot. If so, well and good ; but if not, you had
better go as near to the bunker on the right with
your second as you dare. Drive a little to the right
at the seventeenth.

Finally, there is the course of the Cinque Ports
Club at Deal, which was added to the list of
championship courses in 1907. The first hole needs
no comment. It is best to drive down the right-hand
side of the fairway in going to the second, for there is

a smooth passage for the ball along that side, whereas the ground is very bumpy on the other. Go straight for the third hole, but keep a shade to the left with your second shot if you are unable to get up in two. The fourth is the Sandy Parlour—a blind short hole. Going to the fifth, drive to the left, and then play straight at the hole, not forgetting the bunker on the left a little way in front of the green. The way in which the sixth hole should be played depends largely on the direction in which the wind is blowing ; the only thing to be said is that the safe line is to the left. Play the tee shot at the seventh hole straight down the course, but mind the bunker on the right when playing the second shot, steering a little to the left if anything. If you cannot reach the eighth green in two shots, it may pay to place the second just a trifle to the right in order to make the approach easier. Drive as far as possible at the ninth ; and the tenth also simply wants a straight drive and then a careful approach, which may be either very long or very short according to the wind. The carry from the tee at the eleventh may be difficult if the wind is adverse, and this is a matter that the player will do well to remember. The twelfth is an easy short hole. Extra bunkers in the vicinity of the green have made the thirteenth hole more difficult than it used to be ; but it is not a hole that needs much comment. The fourteenth is another short hole. The four last holes are well known, and none of them is ever easy. Playing the fifteenth, keep to the right with the tee shot, as thereby you get a better line for your second. Remember that the green slopes downwards steeply from the left. There are different tees very wide of each other at the sixteenth.

If the play is from the one on the right-hand side it
is best to hug the rough fairly closely with the tee
shot—that is, if you expect to get up in two. Playing
from the left-hand tee you go straight at the hole,
and have plenty of room.   Going to the seventeenth,
keep a little to the right, but be careful of the rough.
The approach shot here needs very careful play.   At
the last hole take the line to the left over the corner
if you can drive far enough to clear it.   This will
leave an easy second ; otherwise, go just a shade to
the right with the tee shot.

CHAPTER XIX

SOME PERSONAL MATTERS

IT was not my intention originally to press any account of my own golfing career upon the readers of these pages ; but while the book was in course of preparation it was represented to me very strongly by many amateur friends, and particularly some of those in Scotland, that there would be something wanting in the volume if I did not offer one ; and that a fuller narrative than I have hitherto made of the outstanding recollections that I have of the early and the recent events of my experience, as well as of my own personal impressions of the championship meetings in which I have taken part, would be much appreciated by those kind and indulgent people, to hundreds of whom I owe gratitude for the favour they have shown me in one way and another.

Well, then, beginning in the proper place, I was born at Earlsferry in Fifeshire, on 6th February 1870, and it was probably not at all an unlucky day to be born on, since it happened to be a Sunday. As everybody knows, there is, as one might say, very little but golf anywhere on the coast in these parts, and Earlsferry and Elie make a great centre of the game, where it was—and is—practised with great enthusiasm by the local people of all ages and of all classes. Only a few miles north of Elie—the distance being very much shorter across country than along the coast—is the great Mecca of the game, St. Andrews, which was looked upon by the youth of our little place —and not merely the youth only, but a large proportion of the old people as well—as being the centre of all things. A shorter distance along the coast, in a westerly direction, are the famous links of Leven. At the time that I was there at Earlsferry—and I have no doubt it is much the same to this day—unless a man played golf, or there was no very plain reason why he did not, he was generally taken to be something of a crank. It has often been said, and with a great deal of truth, that the Earlsferry children show an interest in the game, and it is certain that as soon as they can walk their first efforts in the way of doing anything with their limbs are directed towards hitting a ball with a stick, which is golf in its simplest form, the ball being hit from where it may lie in the street.

They say that I was just like the average Earls-ferry boy, but that I was a little more precocious than some of the others in golfing matters. My first dim recollections of anything at all in this world were of some vague happenings about the time when I was five or six years of age, and they are of my always being about with a miniature golf club in my hand, and running about outside my parents' house knocking a ball with it at every chance that presented itself. The tendency towards golf, therefore, seemed strong, and the natural result of it, seeing what were my parents' circumstances in life, was that I should be a caddie—during school holidays only. I went to school in the usual way, and filled up my spare time in carrying clubs for the visitors; but when there were no visitors I spent the odd hours in practising all manner of shots; and thus when I was a very small boy I had already begun to take the game seriously and was starting on the right lines, since I was watching a good deal and then practising with just an odd club—which very likely was all that I possessed at the time, so there was not much self-sacrifice really in this kind of practice. My driver generally consisted of an old wooden head that I had picked up somewhere after it had been discarded as worthless, and to this was attached a shaft that had been found somewhere else in the same way. People nowadays talk about the modern system of socketing the shafts of wooden clubs on to the heads, as if it were a recent invention, whereas the caddies of my generation certainly socketed the shafts of the clubs that they made for themselves in this way, the method being the simplest possible, namely, boring a hole through the head and fastening the shaft in it as tightly as possible. As for iron clubs, we had never more than one, and that one was usually a cleek with a long and well-lofted head. We had no such things as putters and niblicks in those days. The cleek had to do all the work, and, with the practice we had with it, we made it do it very well. Reflecting on the practice got in this way by boys who have no money to spend on clubs, one cannot but think, however hard their lot may have appeared to them at the time, that it was exceedingly valuable, very likely more so than it would have been if a set of clubs had been available.

I never had any lessons; I simply watched and copied. The Earlsferry course was not quite the same then as it is now. At that time it was made up of nine good holes, and besides these there were three others in Melon Park, which were taken in whenever it was thought desirable to do so. By the time I was seven or eight years of age I began to show pretty good form for a boy such as I was, and I was apparently a little better than the other youngsters of my age. The visitors to the place gave prizes every year for a competition among the caddies, and some of the boys who took part in these contests achieved considerable distinction afterwards. Among them were the Simpsons, who were, of course, much older than I was. I was only eight years old when I first entered in one of these competitions, and they put me to play in the junior section that time, and the test was score play over nine holes, these nine being the three in Melon Park played over three times. I won with twenty strokes to spare, and thus came out a winner in the first competition that I ever played in, which was encouraging. My score on that occasion was 54, which, all things considered, was not at all bad. I found in those early days that I could reach the green in three shots at the long holes, and nobody could get there in less than two. In the next competition that I took part in, Archie Simpson, who was four years older than I was, had to give me eight strokes start, and he beat me by two for first place; but in the two following competitions, in which I had to play from scratch, I won the first prize each time, so that I won three times out of four, and I should add that in the last three competitions I played with the senior caddies over the full nine-holes course. This brought me to about the end of my schooldays, and the beginning of another important period in my life.

I was naturally very keen on golf at this time,

and was full of dreams and ambitions as to what I might do in the future. Jamie Anderson, the famous champion of a generation that has passed, had something to do with the stimulation of this ambition, and I shall never forget the encouragement that he gave to me on one occasion when I was only a little boy of about nine years of age. What he said was in its way rather remarkable—to my mind, at least—in view of the things that have happened since then. He was taking part in a match between amateurs and professionals at Earlsferry, and, being Open Champion at the time, his play naturally attracted a great deal of attention. As for us boys, we were, of course, inclined to look upon him as not much less than an idol, and he fascinated me in particular to such an extent that I followed him round the links in a very doglike way, thought it a great thing to touch his clubs, and listened intently to the most trivial remarks that he made, so that I could repeat them to the other boys. Then I hit a shot or two myself to show him what I could do, and he took particular notice of the way that I played them, and asked me to do one or two over again, so that he might make another examination of my style, if such it was to be called. He seemed really to mean what he said, when at last he patted me on the shoulder and told me to go in for as much golf as I could, and practise as thoroughly as possible, and that if I did that I should be Open Champion myself one day. Another incident of these caddie days that I remember very well, was a challenge that was sent by the caddies at Earlsferry to play the caddies at Leven. There was great rivalry between the boys of the two places as to which could put the strongest team on the links, and one day a couple came along from Leven in a boastful manner and declared that if we played them we should not see the way they went. We felt offended, and after consultation among ourselves we sent a formal challenge to the Leven caddies, which, alas! they did not see their way to accept.

Having left school at the age of thirteen, the usual question arose as to what was to be made of me. For my own part I was, as might be imagined, very anxious to keep to the links in some capacity or other ; but my parents had a very strong prejudice against the game. No doubt they were right in their reasons, for golf then in many respects was not what it is now, but their attitude upset me very much. However, they would not hear of my having any more to do with the game except as a recreation in my spare time, and to settle the matter finally I was apprenticed to a joiner in a little village three miles from Earlsferry. Having to walk forwards and backwards between my home and the village every morning and night, and, having a long working day in the joiner's shop, I had very little time left for play, except in the summer time, when I usually managed to get in an evening round, and on Saturday afternoons. I joined the local Thistle Golf Club when I was fifteen years of age and won several prizes in its competitions, and generally did fairly well when representing it in the team matches that were played against the St. Andrews Club. By the time I was sixteen I was playing a very useful game, for I was not only down to scratch, but I won a scratch medal and broke the record of the course, which now consisted of eleven holes. This record stood to my credit for two or three years. I might mention that at this time I was playing with heavy clubs, which were also rather longer in the shaft than usual— longer, in fact, than those with which I play now. My style, I suppose, was pretty well what it is now, except that my swing was certainly much shorter, in fact it was a very short swing, and this was a matter that worried me rather, because I felt that I should never do much good in the long game until I let the swing out more. I tried to lengthen it gradually, and, while it was at its shortest when I was about fourteen, I managed to improve it considerably during the next two years. However, it made no material difference to the length of my drive, and it was an unpleasant fact for me at the time that though strong physically, and tall, I was an unusually short driver. I could get no length at all, and almost everybody who could golf respectably could get a longer ball than I could. I tried every known alternative to my system, but to no purpose, and I felt I must resign myself to being a short driver. My driving had, however, the merit of being both steady and straight, and this helped me a good deal. Besides this, my game suffered seriously in another respect, for, as is generally known, I was quite a bad putter until recent years, and during all the years when I was coming on at the game my putting was at its very worst. For my short driving I could make up a great deal in the rest of the play through the green, for I was good with my irons ; but I could not save my matches when I was putting in the shocking fashion that I so generally did, and whenever I lost it was nearly all due to this weakness—with the short putts. I was always fairly good at the long ones. It was not until many years afterwards that I overcame this weakness, and did so as the result of hours and days and years of hard practice.

How I came to be cured of my weakness in driving I really do not know, but the cure in this department came long before the other, in fact I was still in my teens when I got to driving a long ball nearly every time. I am not conscious that I made any difference whatever in my style or methods. I was simply going on in the same old way when suddenly I found myself driving farther and farther, and the complete conversion from short to long was effected within a week. As I have often said, it was just the same as if I went to bed a short driver one night and got up a long driver in the morning. It was then, and is still, the greatest golfing mystery that I have ever come across ; but the happy result of it was that, while at one time certain rivals were getting twenty yards past me almost every time, at the end of that week I was getting that much past them, and, except for brief lapses, I have never been a very short driver since those days, the long balls not going away again in the same mysterious manner that they came, as so often happens in this tantalising game.

When I was nineteen I left home for the first time and went to work as a joiner at St. Andrews, and as by that time I was playing a very good game, it naturally happened that I got many good matches with the best players there, which served to pull me out and to improve my own game considerably. Thus I had many fine games with Andrew Kirkaldy, and also with his brother Hugh, now dead. I found that I could hold my own in these matches in almost every department of the game except on the putting greens. Even now, when time was getting on, I had no idea

19

of ever adopting golf as a career, and very soon after
my arrival at St. Andrews there came an interruption
in my game, for my employers sent me to work in
different parts of the country, and during that time I
had very little play, and did not get the opportunity
to keep myself in any sort of form. This lasted for
two or three years ; but in 1891 I left St. Andrews and
went to Edinburgh, and there, with the fine course on
the Braid Hills available for everybody, I soon got
very keen again, and joined the Edinburgh Thistle
Club without delay. My best form came back to me
immediately, and I won the scratch medal of the club
for two years in succession, besides which I gained a
few prizes in the club tournaments. Of course, all
this time I was an amateur. I had a handicap of
plus 2 or 3, and was generally chosen to represent
the Thistle Club in the competition for the *Dispatch*
and *Glasgow Evening Times* trophies. As most
people who are acquainted with general golfing
matters know, these are important competitions in
Scotland, and arouse great interest in the Edinburgh
and Glasgow districts. Both are by foursome, two
pairs representing each club in the one case and one
in the other. The first year that I played for the
Thistle we were knocked out in the final for the
Dispatch trophy, while we were beaten in the semi-final
for the other by the club that eventually secured the
trophy. The most important success that I achieved
so far came my way in 1892, when I won the Braid
Hills Tournament, open to members of the Edinburgh
and Leith clubs. The competition was very keen,
for there were a hundred and forty players entered.
One round, by strokes, had to be played, and I started
from scratch, broke the record of the course, and

won the first prize. This was my top achievement as an amateur. I look back on a very pleasant time spent in Edinburgh.

Soon afterwards the great change in my place and status as a player were brought about. I had remained a joiner all this time, but now an old friend of mine, Charles Smith, who was employed at the Army and Navy Stores in London as foreman club-maker, wrote to me to ask if I would like a job as a clubmaker there, as there happened to be a vacancy at the time, and he thought I could get it if I desired to put in for it. It needed very little thought to bring me to a firm and welcome decision when temptation was put before me in this way. A few years earlier the prejudices and objections of my parents would have carried weight; but I was completely detached from home now, and, besides, there were already indications that golf was making great strides, and that it was going to be held in much higher appreciation by the public generally. I had a fairly good job as a joiner, and had a comfortable living assured to me; but my heart was in the game of golf after all, and now I felt doubtful as to whether I should ever be satisfied if I did not have a lot more to do with it than I was having. So I wrote back to Smith to say that I would accept. From one point of view this was a rather bold thing to do, because I was going to the Stores as clubmaker, and up to then I had never made a club in my life! However, my experience as a player had taught me what a good club ought to be, and then it was rather lucky that I was a joiner, and was quite at home when working with wood and tools. The result was that the first club I went to work on was quite a success, and I was never in any difficulty.

It was late in 1893 when I took up this post in
London, and I remained at the same work until 1896.

Because of my being a clubmaker, I was now, of
course, a professional, and apart from the fact that
there were no public courses in London, I was too
busy to get much golf. I practised chiefly on
Saturday afternoons at Chiswick on the old twelve-
holes course that has now been done away with, and
I also got some golf at Sudbrook Park and on the
course of the Mid-Surrey Club at Richmond. I played
in public for the first time as a professional on the
occasion of a competition that was held at Stanmore.
A special prize was offered for the best single round,
and five men tied for it, four being Hugh Kirkaldy,
Alexander Herd, J. H. Taylor, and J. Cuthbert, and the
fifth was myself. The chief prize was for two rounds
of medal play, and in this competition I managed to
get into fourth place, which was not by any means a
bad beginning, considering the class of players who
had entered.

I had made up my mind now to go in for the
life of the professional golfer very thoroughly, and
entered for the Open Championship in the same year,
1894, when it was played for at Sandwich. As, however, I devote the next and last chapter in this book to
a few recollections of the championship meetings in
which I took part, I will say nothing more about them
here. The first time I played in a public match as a
professional was at West Drayton, towards the end
of 1895. My opponent on this occasion was J. H.
Taylor, and the play was over thirty-six holes. The
match was halved, and this was an achievement of
which I had considerable reason to be proud at the
time, for Taylor was then the Open Champion, and

had been for two years in succession. He did two rounds of 73 each, while I did a 73 and a 71. Taylor was dormy two, but at neither of the last two holes did he get up to the hole with his tee shot— both holes being on the short side—whereas I did, and managed to win both, so that it required a big effort to save the match. I remember the play during that day as vividly as I remember anything in the whole of my golfing life. I was driving an exceedingly long ball, and was getting my long putts very dead, while on some occasions I had the good fortune to hole my short run-up approaches from short of the green, just off the edge of it. On the other hand, Taylor was not doing so well with his long putts, but his holing out was quite wonderful. He was missing nothing at two yards or thereabouts. My holing out was weak, and so on the whole things balanced pretty well, and a halved match was a fair result. There is nothing that happened in those early days of my professional career that I remember so well as an incident that occurred when I was making my last putt in that match, a putt on which everything depended, and which was in its way the most important putt that I had ever had to make in my life so far. I addressed myself to the ball twice, and each time was just on the point of making the stroke when I was disturbed by a spectator immediately behind me striking a match. However, after two attempts he either got his pipe alight or decided to wait until the game was over, and at my third attempt to putt I got the ball away without interruption. One is not generally blessed with any luck after waits like this, and I was more than usually pleased to find that the ball went in.

CHAPTER XX

CHAMPIONSHIP EXPERIENCES

THE first time that I ever played in the Open Championship Tournament, this being at Sandwich in 1894, I did fairly well to tie for ninth place, and the man who was bracketed with me was poor Mr. F. G. Tait, that fine gentleman and magnificent player who was killed in the South African war. In 1895 an injured hand kept me away from the championship meeting; but I attended again in the following year, when it was held at Muirfield. By this time I had left the Army and Navy Stores, and was very comfortably situated as professional to the Romford Club. On the way to Muirfield, I, along with most of the other professionals, took part in a professional tournament at Musselburgh, and was beaten by my old rival as a boy, Archie Simpson, who eventually won the tournament, which was played by matches after a qualifying competition at the beginning. I did nothing much worth recording in the championship—finished fifth, I think. In 1897, however, I made a distinct step forward, being second to Mr. Hilton at Hoylake, and having a putt on the last green to tie with him. Mr. Hilton finished very soon after I started on my last round, and at the eleventh hole I was made aware of the fact that if his score remained the best,

as it was up to then, I had a round of 77 for the
championship, and one of 78 to tie with him.   It
must be remembered that those were the days of
the gutta ball, when 77's and 78's were not quite so
easy to do as they are now, despite the fact that
courses were rather shorter.   I took 40 strokes to
go out, which was not bad, particularly as I made
a poor start, and I played the tenth and eleventh
in 4 and 3, when it really began to look as though
I had quite a respectable chance of winning.   I
wanted just a little bit of luck with my long putts
to make my chance a rosy one, for I was playing
very steady golf, and did not look likely to come
to any serious disaster.   However, that luck would
not come my way, though it had two or three opportunities of doing so, and eventually it happened that
I had to do a 3 at the last hole to tie with Mr.
Hilton.   This meant that if my drive and cleek shot
were all right, I should have to get a more or less
long putt down, for the hole is a par 4, and one
with which no liberties can be taken.   I was about
ten yards past the pin with my second, and took
great pains with the putt.   Mr. Hilton, who was
watching, has said that it was an extremely difficult
one, owing to the situation in which the hole was
placed, that he felt quite confident I should never
hole it, and that I missed it by my ball going to
one side of the hole.   Little discrepancies in recollections of this kind are easily made, and though
Mr. Hilton is a very close and accurate observer,
I feel obliged to say that I did not consider the putt
by any means a difficult one, having due regard to
its length, and that I have the clearest impression
that the ball went not to the side of the hole, but

right over the very middle of it. The putt was
good enough, and it did not go down, and therefore
I failed to tie for the championship simply because
I did my duty in the circumstances by giving the
hole a chance—just a little too much of a chance,
as it turned out. It would have been more madden-
ing to have been short, and I was just a wee bit too
strong, though the same putt would probably have
gone down sometimes. However, it was satisfactory
to be second, as it proved to me that I had now
got well among the leaders, and might reasonably
hope to achieve one of the big honours of the game
some day.

All through 1898 I was not feeling very well, and
I could get no nearer than seventh in the championship which was played at Prestwick. Next year it
was played at Sandwich, when I got into fifth place,
Harry Vardon being the winner that year. At the
end of the first day Vardon led with a score of 152,
Taylor was next, a stroke behind, and Willie Park
and I were together in the third place with 156. It
was a very windy and difficult day for play on the
second day, and I made a rather bad third round
of 85, my final score being 322. The year 1900
was that in which Harry Vardon came over from
America, where he had been touring, in order to
compete at St. Andrews. Taylor, however, was in
great form at that meeting, and won rather easily,
and I finished third to those two. That championship occasioned me more after-regrets than possibly
any other in which I have taken part, for though
at the end I was thirteen strokes behind Taylor, I
consider that I have rarely had a better chance of
winning, or nearly, than I had that time, if I could

only have putted in the least degree creditably. I was at the very top of my form, and I think that I was then driving better than I had ever driven before or have done since, and not only my driving, but the rest of my game, except the putting, was as good as it has ever been. But my weakness on the greens was at its very worst at that meeting, and I was taking three putts over and over again, and no man can win a championship if he does that.

At last, when the championship was played at Muirfield in 1901, I came out at the head of the list. I was in good form again that year, and on the way to Muirfield I beat all records for thirty-six holes at Musselburgh, in the course of the customary tournament before the championship, obtaining an aggregate of 140 strokes, made up of 36, 34, 35, and 35. I finished the last round with three 3's. The Royal Musselburgh Club very kindly made a special present to me of a clock, in recognition of my breaking the record. This was in the qualifying competition, and in the ensuing match-play tournament I came out victorious, defeating Herd in the final by three and two. Going on to Muirfield, Harry Vardon and I led the field by five clear strokes at the end of the first day's play in the championship, we being 155, while the next man to us was Taylor, who was 162. I was very steady in the third round, and at the end of it I held a great advantage, for my aggregate then was 228, and the nearest man to me was Vardon with 234, Taylor being next to him with 236, and Mr. Hilton fourth with 244. I had only to keep something like steady to make practically certain of winning ; but as the last round went on I began to get a little anxious, for I was slipping a putt here and there when I ought not to have done so. I was rather too timid on the greens, and this was, I think, to some extent caused by too much kindness on the part of my friends, who were patting me on the back and telling me that I was sure to win, and so forth. This encouragement had rather the opposite effect to that intended, for when playing the last round in a championship in circumstances of this kind, particularly when it is to be the first championship won, one needs to think as little of the result as possible, but to keep one's mind steadily fixed on the shot that has next to be played, without any regard to the after-consequences. The situation seemed to be getting desperate at one time, but I steadied myself towards the finish, and eventually won the championship with a score of 309, Vardon having picked up three strokes on me in that last round, and being second with 312.

My experience in the following year at Hoylake was rather curious. It will be remembered that this was the year when the Haskell ball first came in, and Sandy Herd was the only professional of note who was playing with it. These balls were very scarce at that time, and nobody knew much about them or had any great belief in their future. For my own part I stuck to the gutta. Vardon led at the end of the first day, and I was fourth, five strokes behind him, with a score of 154. I was third, eight strokes to the bad, at the end of the third round, and by this time Herd had taken the lead, and was three better than Vardon. My chance at this stage seemed a rather poor one, and it was made no better at the opening holes of the last round, when I kept on dropping strokes in the most aggravating manner. Herd had finished before

I got to the turn, and I knew then that I was eight
strokes to the bad and had only nine holes to play, so
that my prospects seemed absolutely hopeless.   When
a man is in this position there is only one sort of game
to play.   He must go all out for everything, and
trust a good deal to his luck.   If everything comes
off he may have a slight chance after all; if it does
not, he cannot be any worse off than he would otherwise have been.   An ordinary sort of game, however
good it may be, is useless; to gain strokes to this
extent something very exceptional has to take place.
As it happened everything came off, and I began to
pick up those strokes in the most wonderful manner.
It turned out I had a 3 and a 4 at the two last holes
to tie with Herd for first place.   They are both par
4's, and the 3 all but came off at the seventeenth,
where my putt jumped over the top of the hole.
For the second time in my life I was then left to get
a 3 at that last hole at Hoylake to tie for the
championship, and, as before, all depended on my last
putt.   But I had a lot to do, and failed, making a tie
with Harry Vardon for second place with an aggregate
score of 308.   Mr. Maxwell came next to us, only one
stroke behind.   Both he and I did 74's in our last
rounds, whereas Herd took 81.   But Herd had got
the opening hole in 4 and we took 6 each, which made
all the difference.

Prestwick was the scene of the championship
tournament in 1903, and it does not appear to be a
course that is very kindly disposed towards me, or it
may be that such small peculiarities of play as I have
are not very kindly disposed towards Prestwick.   I must
not be understood to be grumbling about the course,
which is one of the very finest to be found anywhere.

I have great admiration for it, but there is just the coincidence that on the two occasions that I have played in the championship there I have been at very nearly my worst. I was much too timid with my putts until the last round, and that last round, when I did a 75, was the only one of the four in which I played really well. I was six strokes behind the leader at the end of the first day, and I never looked like picking them up. I finished in the fifth place; the winner being Harry Vardon. My failure was all the more marked, as I had played really well in the international match with which the meeting was opened, and gained an easy victory over Vardon in the singles by five up and four to play.

The meeting at Sandwich in the following year will never be forgotten by anybody who took part in it, or who witnessed the play. The course was very fast, and being on the short side in the outward half now that the use of the rubber-cored ball had become general, records were being made all the time, so to speak, from the first day until the finish. The then existing record went by the board in the first round, but the new figures had not a long life, and Taylor's great round of 68 was a wonderful thing. In my third round I did a 69, and it was chiefly remarkable for the 3's that I got at both the seventh and fourteenth holes—pretty hard 4's at the best of times. I was playing very steadily in the fourth round, and knew that I was bound to be somewhere near the top at the finish. At the fifteenth hole a spectator told me that he had heard that Jack White had finished in 70. White was the man I had most to fear then, and on reckoning up the situation, taking the information given me as accurate, I found that I had to get three

4's and a 3 to tie. As luck would have it, the 3 came
right away at the fifteenth hole, and thus, according
to my reckoning, I had three 4's left to tie—not by
any means a difficult task, though one which left no
margin for error or missed putts. In the circumstances I was naturally inclined to play the cautious
game ; and thus at the sixteenth, instead of giving the
putt a chance, and very likely coming back to the hole
off the hill behind, I was short by two yards, and then
missed the next one for a 3. Still two 4's to tie, and
the seventeenth was duly played in 4. I was still
acting on the information about White's 70, and at
the home hole I was on the green with my second
some yards past the hole. Playing as cautiously as
possible for a 4, I laid my ball dead, but short, and
then holed out. I thought I had tied, and not until
then was I made aware, to my great disappointment,
that White had finished his last round, not in 70, but
in 69, and that therefore I had lost the championship
by one stroke. Of course, it might have made no
difference in the result if I had known the proper
figures all the time, but it would certainly have made
a difference in my play both at the sixteenth and
eighteenth holes, and at one of them, the sixteenth for
choice, I might have got the 3 that was necessary to
me in the position that I then really was. However,
the play was altogether of the very highest order, and
White thoroughly deserved to win.

This made the third time that I had had a putt to
tie for the championship when on the last green, and
each time the ball stayed out of the hole. There
may be no particularly bad luck in this, as one cannot
expect to hole long putts for championships on the
last green ; but at all events I have never won one by

doing so. However, to win a championship, one ought not generally to be pushed so close as this, and it is a significant circumstance that as each year comes round there is generally supposed to be next to no difference between the quality of two or three different players, and that over four rounds they, or some others instead of one or two of them, are certain to average almost exactly the same score, the much overdue tie being talked about at the beginning of every last round; yet it is found that after all the winner wins pretty easily almost every year, and that despite the fact that at the end of the second and third rounds there is often very little to choose between two or three of the candidates. Massy won quite easily in 1907, and after he got well going in the last round there was rarely much doubt about the result. In 1906 I beat Taylor by four strokes, and the year before I was five in front of him. In the Sandwich year that we have just been talking about, it is true that the issue was desperately close, just as it was at Hoylake in 1902, but in neither case did the men who, as it were, made it close—those who came along with a big effort after the ultimate winner had finished—succeed. In 1903, Vardon won with six strokes to spare, and in various other years there were great gaps between the men who finished first and second on the list. The man who wins must be able to play with comfort and confidence, and feel like winning, and in this mood things go well with him and he is never in difficulties. The man who is feeling an enormous strain upon him, due to his not being able to afford the loss of a single stroke, or to knowing that it is absolutely necessary that he must gain some when to gain them is enormously difficult, has too big a handicap, and rarely achieves his object. In this matter I quite agree with what Taylor once said, that when he is going to win a championship he feels himself to be winning easily and to have a lot in hand, and that it is difficult to win a championship unless you do win it easily. It may be rather different in the case of a man's first championship, when he feels the strain of winning, no matter how easily he may be doing so, very much more than he ever does afterwards. This time he is being broken in, and after that he always seems to know when he is winning and when he is not. Of all the four rounds that have to be played, I think that in a general way the third one is the most critical, and, assuming that things have gone pretty well in the first two, I would rather do well in the third than in the fourth, because it makes all the difference between feeling confident and otherwise. Let me make a good start in the third round, and I feel that I have done the best possible thing towards achieving the honours of the competition.

As a last word upon that 1904 event at Sandwich, I might be permitted to mention that my 69 and 71 in the two last rounds, a total of 140, constitute the lowest aggregate for two rounds in one day at any championship meeting. Taylor also had a putt to tie with White, and his ball hit the hole.

It was my luck to win a championship for the second time at St. Andrews in 1905, and here, according to the principle I have just laid down, I was winning easily all the time on the last day, although some rather exciting incidents towards the close of the last round seemed to put my success in danger for a few minutes. After playing the first nine of the third round, which I did in a good score, I felt that if I kept steady I should have a good chance of winning. I finished in 78, and had then a very useful lead over the next man. I was very steady going out in the fourth round and gained another stroke, while I was helped a little by the news that reached me that my most formidable rival had had a bad hole somewhere. I made no mistake of any kind until I had played the first five in. Then came the railway, and I am not likely to forget my experiences on it. Going to the fifteenth, I sliced my second shot on to it. Playing off it I hit a man, and the ball rebounded from him and went to a nasty place, where it was tucked up against a bush. The hole cost me six strokes, and though this was the loss of a couple, I was still, according to my reckoning, in a very comfortable position. But at the next hole the case began to look rather serious, and it was very fortunate that I had made my position so strong early in the round, or that hole would very probably have been fatal to my prospects. From the tee I drove right over the Principal's Nose and pitched into the bunker beyond. I was lying rather well, with the result that I became too venturesome and attempted to put the ball on to the green instead of being satisfied with a 5, which would have been quite good enough for my purpose. Instead of putting it on to the green I got it on to the railway, and when I went up to it I found it lying in a horrible place, being tucked up against one of the iron chairs in which the rails rest. It was on the left-hand side of the right-hand rail, playing towards the hole, and the only crumb of comfort was that it was not on the other side of either of the rails. I took my niblick and tried to hook it out, but did not succeed, the ball moving only a few yards, and being in much the same position against the rail. With my fourth, however, I got it back on to the course, but in a very difficult position. It went some thirty yards past the hole, near to the bunker on the left of the second green. As the ground was, I had only about a yard to come and go on with a run-up shot, which was plainly the proper stroke to play in the circumstances, if I wanted to get close to the hole, as I must do if I was to get a 6. It was a bold and very risky shot to play ; but I played it and it came off, the ball running dead, so that I got my 6. In all the four rounds of that championship I think that that was the best shot that I played, because it was a good shot and it was played at a time when I was excusably very anxious, and knew that almost everything depended upon it, for it had to be remembered that there was the dreaded seventeenth hole waiting after that one. The fact that this little run-up came off as I so much wished, and that I got my 6 after all that trouble, put new heart into me, and I tackled the seventeenth without any fear. Besides, I had then two 6's to win. Seeing how I was situated when I got on to the railway at the sixteenth, I think that perhaps I was injudicious not to have lifted from the place, and lost two strokes. I could have afforded them, and that hole might very easily have cost me one or two more than it did ; in fact, I was extremely well out of it in 6. There was no further incident, and I won with five strokes to spare.

Fortune favoured me again when the championship was played for at Muirfield in 1906. On account of the large number of entries, it was found necessary

20

this time to play only one round a day at the beginning, and to allow the meeting to extend over three
days, two rounds being played on the third day by all
those competitors who had survived the eliminating
process. Even as it was, with some men starting
first thing in the morning and others not finishing
until the last thing in the evening, there was sure to
be considerable disparity in the conditions under which
the various competitors played, and it would not
generally be regarded as in a man's favour that he
was drawn to play as one of the last couples going
out. I got such a bad place in the draw as this, and
made the mistake on the first day of going down to
the course too early, and waiting about far longer
than was good for the game of anyone. Hanging
about the first tee at a time like this, when, however little
nervous one may be, one has naturally some anxiety
concerning the immediate future, the nerve tension
is often greater than it is when actually playing, and
this waiting is the very worst thing possible, and can
hardly fail to have a bad effect on one's game when
at last it comes to be played. On that first day I did
a 77, which was far from being brilliant. Mr.
Graham broke the record of the course the same
morning with a 71. On the second day I took care
to keep away from the course until it was nearly time
to start, and occupied myself pleasantly by playing a
quiet round in a foursome on another course near by,
just to keep my hand and eye in, and my mind
engaged. However, the result was I did another 77
in the championship, although I was undoubtedly
playing better than the day before, and felt that I was
doing so. But I could not get my putts to drop in.
I was constantly laying them on the lip of the hole,

but they would not go down. Nevertheless I felt that the state of affairs was tolerably satisfactory, because if I kept up that form on the greens the putts would be sure to go in sooner or later, and, as it happened, they began to do so in the third and fourth rounds on the last day, when they were most useful.

I was a few strokes behind at the beginning of the proceedings on that last day, but I started playing very steadily—quite well, in fact. At the end of the third round the championship was a very open thing. Taylor led the field with a score of 224, and Rowland Jones was only one stroke behind, while Harry Vardon and I were 227. Jones dropped out in the last round, and eventually the issue lay between Vardon, Taylor, and myself. I was much later in starting than either of the other two, and when I went away from the first tee I knew that my most dangerous opponent would finish in 81 if he took the par score at the last two holes which he had still to play, and that Vardon, who had about four holes to play, could scarcely do better. Thus it appeared to me that if I could keep up my steadiness there was still a chance left for me. Taylor got the last hole in 3, one under par, and finished in 80, and this left me to do a 76 to win the championship—not by any means an easy thing to do, but still one that was quite possible. I had a little luck at the first hole, where I pulled my drive on to the second tee, but still got a 3. Things went pretty well up to the turn, where my fate was still hanging in the balance. I wanted just a nice piece of luck on the putting greens to make my chance a rosy one. And I got it. Two good putts went to the bottom at the eleventh and twelfth, and after getting safely past the thirteenth (I am always glad to get past that hole) I felt that I was in a winning position. I had fifteen strokes left for the last three holes to win, and was fortunate enough to get a twenty-yards putt down for a 3 at the seventeenth. So I had 7 left for the last hole, but only required the regulation 4. My winning score was 300. Taylor was second with 304, and Harry Vardon was one stroke behind him. I should like to add, that as a preliminary to the championship meeting a professional tournament was held on the Braid Hills, Edinburgh, and it gave me a very special pleasure to win it, for the reason that it was on this course that I won my first tournament of any description, and many of my pleasantest memories are connected with it.

The championship of 1907, the event taking place at Hoylake, marked an epoch, for it was the first time in the history of golf that the honour of being Open Champion of the year was achieved by any but a British golfer. The distinction was well and worthily won by Arnaud Massy, the French golfer, who entered from La Boulie, Versailles, where he is the resident professional, and the only satisfaction that British golfers could derive from the result was that after all Massy learned his golf from British players and finished his game at North Berwick. Certainly he deserved to win, and I might here say that just before the competition began I was asked by some parties, who were very anxious to obtain a thoroughly candid opinion, who I thought stood a first-rate chance of being champion—not an ordinary chance, but one that was to all intents and purposes as good as that of anybody else and considerably better than that of most. I answered that

I thought that Taylor, Harry Vardon, and myself would need a good deal of shaking off, but that there were three other men I considered to be extremely dangerous, these three being Massy, Tom Vardon, and George Pulford. I said that I felt that so little would turn the balance in favour of any one of these six, and that it was really so much a question of a little luck and being on top of one's game, that it was next to impossible to make any distinction between them. It proved to be not at all a bad guess. Massy won, but both Tom Vardon and Pulford were in the running when the last round was entered upon. Massy was playing with Pulford, and he began well, and things went his way at the opening holes, while they did the reverse for Pulford, or the latter might have been very dangerous indeed. Taylor looked quite a likely winner until he began to meet with trouble at the third hole in the last round. As for myself, I thought at the beginning of the week that I had a good chance. I was playing very well, and there was absolutely nothing in the idea that was suggested by some people after my failure that I had played too much and was stale. The fact was that I was not feeling very fit, and this was accentuated by the perfectly shocking weather that prevailed. To play one's best golf under very severe weather conditions one must be as fit as possible. A man who is feeling below par may bring out a good game when the sun is shining and it is warm and dry, with no wind to fight against; but bad weather will generally find him out. That was just how it stood with me. If the weather had not been so boisterous I should probably have made a much better show. As it was, I began driving unsteadily, and got a bad 8 at the sixth hole, where several other players did the same : this hole, which goes by the name of the Briars, being a very trying piece of golf in weather such as then prevailed. To cut the story short, I was in a very bad position, that is, so far as prospects of winning were concerned, at the end of the second round, and by the time the third round was completed it was clear that I should have to do something very exceptional in the fourth to have any chance whatever, having regard to the way in which Massy and Taylor were playing. On that last day I was playing quite well, and was putting all right, but could not get the ball down. As in the case of another championship that I have mentioned, I had to go for everything in my last round, and everything had to go my way, particularly the long putts. I played well up to the thirteenth, but kept shaving the hole with my putts, while at the Rushes I missed quite an easy putt for a 2. There was then just one small chance left; but at the next hole I drove into a ditch and then got into a bunker, taking 6 for a possible 4, and then it was absolutely all over. Massy showed wonderful form at the meeting, and, as I have said, thoroughly deserved to win. I should say that for three or four years before that I had considered him a very dangerous man at the championships. What the future has in store for all of us at the championships we must wait and see.

It may be expected that I should say something about the annual tournaments that are held under the auspices of the Professional Golfers' Association, for prizes amounting to £240, kindly given by Mr. George A. Riddell and the other proprietors of the *News of the World*, since these tournaments are practically professional championships, and the test is a very severe one, both stroke and match play being included, the one in the qualifying stage and the other at the final meeting. The first prize each time is a gold medal and a cheque for £100, and I have had the good fortune to win it three times out of five.

I had some rather interesting experiences the first time the tournament was played, that being at Sunningdale in 1903. In one round I had A. H. Toogood to play, and, being two or three up on him a hole or two after the turn, it looked as if I had the match well in hand. Then, however, he started holing putts all over the green. I have rarely seen such putting as he accomplished on that occasion, and the result of it was that the match was halved and we had to go on to the nineteenth hole. Whether it was that the strain of the effort that he had made had told on him, or that his fine putting had made him too confident, it is certain that at that nineteenth hole he was not the same man, for after being about two feet off the hole with his run-up, he failed to hole the next one for the half. How very often does it happen that the man who has had to struggle so hard to get square at the eighteenth hole and to save the match at that stage, seems to fall completely away at the nineteenth hole. It is the strain that has told on him, and while the man who has been having his lead taken away from him towards the close of the full round, usually feels "the shakes," and is liable to play a very ragged sort of game, he often comes right on to it again when he goes to the nineteenth hole, and it is a case of then or never. In the final of that tournament I had to play Edward Ray of Ganton, a very powerful player, whose game has always to be treated with respect. I happened to be just a little up on him at the turn in the second round, but not so much that I could afford to give anything away. The loss of a single hole at that stage would have been a serious matter, and the case was not at all promising when my tee shot from the tenth landed the ball in the bunker on the left of the course. Nine times out of ten one would have been quite satisfied to get clear of the bunker in one shot with a niblick, but that would have left me a very poor chance of winning or halving the hole that time. It was a time for desperate measures, and it was clear to me that the only chance I had of saving the hole was by getting the ball on the green, and the only club that could possibly get it there was an iron. There was just a possibility of success, and I had no hesitation in making the attempt, with the result that I did get the ball on to the green, quite close to the pin, and then I holed the putt for a very curious 3, winning the hole from Ray, who took 4. It was extremely rough luck on my opponent, who deserved all the sympathy that anybody extended to him, for he played three perfect shots and was dead for a 4, besides which he laid me so much of a stymie that I touched and shook his ball in holing my putt. The bunker shot that I played on this occasion was the most remarkable one I ever remember playing, and it is quite conceivable that that shot alone was worth the first prize to me ; at all events, without it I should certainly have had to play desperately hard for that prize.

In 1904, when the tournament was played on the

course of the Mid-Surrey Club at Richmond, and Taylor was a popular victor on his own green, weak putting in my match against Herd disposed of my chance. Herd and I ran up against each other in the following year at Walton Heath, this time in the first round. It was a great match. I had just a trifle the best of it all the time, and had putts of four feet to win both the seventeenth and eighteenth holes, but failed at each. The match had to go on to the nineteenth, where I had a putt of about three yards for a 3 and to win the match, and managed to get it down after it had hung on the lip of the hole for quite a long time. After that match there was nothing very remarkable until I got into the final, when Tom Vardon was my opponent. He put up a very strong game, and he was soon two up on me. The playing of the fourth hole (a long one) in the first round was a strange business. Vardon pulled his second about fifty yards wide of the green, whereas with my second I placed the ball only about three yards from the hole. It seemed as certain as anything can be in golf that it was going to be my hole, but my opponent played his third beautifully and got just inside me, and then in some extraordinary fashion I managed to take three putts and lost the hole in 5 to 4. At the end of the round I was two up, and after the sixth hole in the second round I got the upper hand, and finished the match at the fifteenth, where I hit the flag with my mashie shot.

At Hollinwell, in 1906, one of the features of the week was the remarkable form displayed by George Duncan, and I was one of his victims. Some of his recoveries and his putting were very fine. In 1907 the tournament was again played at Sunningdale, and though the weather was anything but good, the meeting was remarkable for the high standard of play that was shown all round. I doubt very much whether at any big meeting of any kind whatsoever the play generally has reached anything like the same high standard as it did at this meeting. I had the good fortune to win the first prize for the third time, and I can say this for the golf that I had to play to win, that after the first nine holes in the first round it was somewhere near an average of 4's all the way to the finish of the final, and you must be playing pretty well—and luckily—to keep that up for five successive rounds on a first-class course like Sunningdale.

As a last word, let me give a general answer to a question that is often put to me, as to what is the longest drive that I have ever made. So far as I can recollect it was in 1905, when playing a round at Walton Heath with Mr. Riddell. The course was frostbound, and the wind was at our backs when we were playing the fifteenth hole, and I hit my tee shot a distance of 395 yards, carefully calculated afterwards. Of course, you can drive a ball wonderful distances when the turf is frozen, and such a feat as this is no test of one's general capacity ; but, on the other hand, it was so cold that I could scarcely grip my club, and I feel sure that if I could have held it properly I should that day have driven very much farther. At the eighteenth hole in the same round I drove to the bunker guarding the green, which was another drive of nearly the same length. As to what distances I have driven under normal conditions, I really do not know. Once, when I was playing a match against Harry Vardon at Hythe, I made a carry which was generally remarked upon at the time as being something very much out of the ordinary, but I do not remember what was the exact length of it.

It would be ungraceful and wrong if I were to conclude this brief account of my experiences and impressions without making some expression of the great pleasure of my association as professional with the Walton Heath Club. It is a considerable advantage to have the opportunity of playing constantly on such a course as that at Walton Heath, anything superior to which, of its kind, it would be difficult to imagine. And to the members of this club I am deeply grateful for the kind feeling which they have always extended to me, which received a very tangible expression after I won the championship at St. Andrews in 1905.

INDEX

Printed by
MORRISON & GIBB LIMITED
Edinburgh

Printed in the United States
95583LV00003BA/13/A